Call Center Operation

Call Center Operation

Design, Operation, and Maintenance

Duane E. Sharp

Digital Press
An imprint of Elsevier Science
Amsterdam• Boston • London • New York • Oxford • Paris • San Diego
San Francisco • Singapore • Sydney • Tokyo

Library of Congress Cataloging-in-Publication Data

Sharp, Duane E.
    Call Center handbook / Duane E. Sharp.
        p. cm.
    Includes bibliographical references and index.
    ISBN 1-55558-277-X
    1. Call centers—Management. I. Title.
HE8788, S53 2003
658.8'12—dc21   2003043821

British Library Cataloguing-in-Publication Data

A catalogue record for this book is available from the British Library.

This book is dedicated to my wife Myrna; my children Heidi, Brett, and Dana; and my grandchildren Tara, Adam, and Mathew

and

to the many thousands of employees who work in call/contact centers around the world.

Contents

Preface

Over the last several years, corporate cultures around the world have changed to place increasing emphasis on customer relations and to establish policies and procedures to enhance these relationships. Where there are hundreds of thousands or even millions of customers, as is the case in the financial, communications, automotive, travel, and insurance sectors, for example, the task of establishing a one-to-one relationship with each customer is extremely challenging. Success in achieving the highest level of customer relationships requires a number of components to be integrated into the changed corporate culture, including human resources and technology, and the effective management of these resources.

The need to establish and manage highly productive relationships with large numbers of customers has led to the development of technologies specifically designed or adapted to assist organizations to manage, analyze, and respond to the challenges posed by large customer databases and the need to communicate effectively and productively with each customer. Many organizations have established a central department that uses these technologies to manage customer relationships. These departments respond to inbound customer communication of all types and are proactive in communicating with customers as well. This facility or department, generally referred to as a *call center, customer interaction center*, or *contact center*, has gained considerable prominence over the last several years. The total number of call centers of all sizes, internal and external, in North America alone is estimated to be well over 100,000. Today, in many organizations, the call center is a central focus of all customer-oriented activity—the eyes and ears of the organization.

The call center, the term that will be used most often in this book, may be internal to a corporation or it may be an external, outsourced function.

Those organizations that have outsourced their call center operations, for lack of financial or human resources, have been able to take advantage of the experience offered by large, often multinational call center operations. These firms specialize in providing customer-related communications services using sophisticated software and communications technology and skilled customer service representatives.

The foundation for automation in call centers has been the integration of computers and telephony (CTI). CTI is not a new concept—it was first implemented in the mid-1980s in large corporate call centers. Since that time, advances in public telephone network technology and computing make CTI a powerful tool for businesses of any size, and reduced hardware costs make the combined technologies affordable for smaller organizations.

Effective management, use, and distribution of information have become increasingly important business considerations in today's fast-paced business environment. In particular, the adoption of appropriate technologies to accomplish these objectives can provide and sustain competitive advantage. Technology by itself cannot attain business goals—how people use the technology makes the difference in effecting improvements in communications and operational processes. CTI, the integration of computer and telephone technologies, has the capability to liberate human and system resources and to maximize the benefits of both technologies for the user community.

This book describes the evolution of the call center, analyzes the technologies that have contributed to its growth, and describes the technology tools available. It also provides guidelines for the development and implementation of a call center as well as the management of the facility, and it strongly emphasizes the human factors that can make a call center a successful operation. This book also describes how call centers benefit businesses, how closely these facilities are related to the corporation's overall CRM strategy, and how technology and changing business trends are reshaping the workplace. These trends have resulted in more horizontal organizations, high-performance workgroups, empowered employees, and, in general, the ability of staff members to do more with less.

Many sources have been consulted and used in preparing this book, and I am indebted to those authors whose works have contributed to the text; these are referenced in Appendix C.   I am particularly indebted to Janet Sutherland, senior consultant with Bell Canada Contact Centre Solutions, for contributions to Chapter 4, "Selecting and Training Call Center Staff," for reviewing the manuscript; and for providing valuable knowledge and insight on call center operations in general.

Duane E. Sharp, P. Eng.
Mississauga, Ontario
Canada

Introduction to Call Centers

During the past decade in particular, the influence of technology on the relationships between organizations in both the public and private sectors has increased dramatically. Today, companies depend heavily on technology of various types to conduct their businesses and to deal with their customers, whether through a business-to-business (B2B) or a company–customer relationship. The call center industry especially is changing the face of business throughout the world and is having a significant impact on economies and the way companies do business.

1.1   Overview

Call centers require the integration of several different technologies to maximize the use of information and to streamline the activities of call center operators. Advances in technology and the adaptation and integration of synergistic technologies have resulted in the development of numerous feature that have enhanced the growth of call centers throughout the world.

The computer and the telephone are two of the major and most familiar tools of technology that have converged to make call centers more efficient and productive. When used properly along with software technology that assists operators to assimilate and analyze customer data to respond knowledgeably to customer inquiries, the benefits to both the customer and the organization are substantial, as this book will demonstrate.

The impact of CTI

Over the past few years, there has been much discussion of the pros and cons of a new set of technologies involving the integration of the computer and the telephone, referred to as *CTI* (for computer telephony integration, frequently shortened to *computer telephony*). Computer telephony was developed specifically to integrate these two technologies to enable more effective and productive communication between companies and their customers. CTI is best viewed as a loose but complicated amalgamation of interlocking technologies—not one piece of hardware or software, but a method of combining the two streams of information—voice and data—through open, standards-based systems.

As the combined technologies matured, CTI found many applications in the business world; however, one of its most significant contributions is to call center operation. When well implemented, it can dramatically improve the way a company interacts with its customers, the fundamental purpose for implementing a call center. Computer telephony overcomes the traditional limitations of either of the component technologies and brings them together in a way that improves them both, by bringing more information to both parties in a communication environment.

Software tools

Software is a driving force behind call center development. Although call centers have traditionally been telecom entities, the growth and maturation of CTI have led to computing-based centers and applications. Software is one of the best and most widely used tools for translating business parameters into technological terms. Call center software can fulfill a number of functions, including the following key applications:

- Retrieving customer information
- Managing queues
- Providing sales scripts and product information
- Acting as an interconnection to back-office applications

In the past, call center managers have had to juggle business objectives with flexibility, because frequent changes in marketing campaigns affect call center operation. A call center can't stand still—it is important to build the change dynamic into the system at the beginning. Today, software vendors are combining functional capabilities in single products, some of which are ready-made products and others which are sets of tools for greater customization. This evolution in product design virtually eliminates the need for organizations to develop their own systems from scratch. The range of choice in specialized software means that writing an entire call center system in a standard software environment is no longer required.

A well-planned call center implementation involving the integration of computer and telephone technologies and human resources will provide several specific benefits to organizations, including

- Increasing timely access to information

- Enabling the sharing of current and new information

- More effectively communicating and presenting that information to customers

- Allowing more timely response to information requests from customers

Chapter 2 provides a detailed description of the technologies required to operate an effective, responsive call center, as well as guidelines to assist in the evaluation and implementation of these technologies. There is also a brief review of the evolution of the computing environment, describing the basic functions of a computer and leading up to the prevalent "model" of computing—*client/server architecture*—as well as background on the evolution of CTI from the two founding technologies. An overview of telephony and the basics of public networks and business telephone systems illustrates how computer and communication technologies are integrated to maximize the benefits of both. Detailed descriptions of the various elements of call management are also provided.

Inside the call center

The advanced call center operation of the 21st century consists of many elements and is not simply a collection of phones, computers, and operators. The first call centers were often large rooms with a PBX (private branch exchange) phone switch and desks of service representatives taking calls over the phone. Customers in many cases endured long response times and had to repeat information such as account numbers or descriptions of their problems. In these earlier call centers, little, if any, customer information was available to customer service representatives (CSRs). This kind of service regularly resulted in frustrated customers and customer representatives. There may be vestiges of these days in some call center operations that have not kept up with changing technology, staff training processes, and corporate culture changes in managing customer relationships, but these antiquated facilities will not last long.

In today's Internet-paced world, with e-commerce flourishing and many more opportunities for customer contact with companies, customers will not tolerate a long, tedious response process, and it is no longer sufficient for customer representatives to depend solely on reference books when troubleshooting or assisting customers. They need to have customer information available immediately and presented on their computer screens, as well as the capability to modify this information during a communication session with a customer. CSRs become the focus of customer interaction with a company in a well-planned, well-managed call center operation.

Call center/contact center

Call centers provide a single contact for customers who may try to reach a company via multiple channels: e-mail, Web chat, fax, phone, or VoIP (voice over Internet protocol). Call centers, often called *contact centers* to reflect the multiple points of access, provide staff with consistent information throughout an integrated system. (In this book, the term *call center* is used interchangeably with *contact center*). These centers capture data from across the enterprise and consolidate customer-related information into a central database. This integration improves the customer's interaction and satisfaction and enhances the efficiency of the business operation.

Businesses have several issues to consider in their daily relationships with customers:

- Keeping customers satisfied before and after sales
- Managing customer data scattered all over the enterprise
- Planning and budgeting resources to invest in customer retention

Call centers are an essential part of any business that deals frequently with customer queries. Integrated call centers decrease customer waiting time, improve customer access, and improve call routing. The end result is that companies benefit from satisfied customers who come back for more business. In spite of the high costs of a call center, most organizations, large or small, that value customer service and strong customer relationships need to have one.

A call center's services can be essential for the smooth running of a business. Once a call center is in place, it integrates technology from customer databases, order-entry systems, fulfillment, and knowledge databases, enabling call center CSRs to respond with current information when communicating with customers. Technology provides many features to assist in the communication process, including providing quick access to customer information for the CSR and call management (transfer, voice response, messaging, etc.)

1.2   Analyzing call center requirements

There are many aspects to designing and developing a call center operation, including selecting the location, telephone equipment, networking equipment, and software. This combination of technologies and the complexity of integrating all elements effectively and economically present a challenge to the call center development team.

Building a call center internally may be feasible only for very large enterprises—smaller companies should consider outsourcing their call centers to organizations that specialize in providing these services and already have the latest technologies installed and operating, with trained staff. These organizations can often provide excellent customer-oriented services, relieving smaller organizations of the financial, managerial, and human resources issues involved in an internal, corporate call center. Calculating the overall budget for the project will determine whether to build and manage a call center internally or to outsource some or all of the operations to keep costs down and focus on customer retention. Building a call center can run to several million dollars in capital equipment alone, not to mention the cost of hiring staff and managing the day-to-day operations.

With the Internet and potentially rapid response opportunities, new ways for customers to reach companies—e-mail, Web chat, and voice over Internet Protocol (VoIP)—have been added to the traditional forms of communication. To prepare for these multiple communications media and to efficiently serve customers, companies need to capture information from across the enterprise and consolidate customer-related data into a central database. In most cases, customer data resides in many systems, such as order history, fulfillment, shipping, and billing. The number of sources of data can reduce the ability of CSRs to handle requests and can also contribute to errors and duplication. For corporations to handle these multiple customer contact channels effectively, integrating the varied systems is essential. Its call center facility requires carefully selected technology tools.

A complete analysis of the technology and human relations components of a call center reveals a number of planning and selection challenges for the project team charged with development, management, and maintenance of the call center operation. It also highlights the major issues to be addressed for the start-up and on-going management of the center. This analysis will involve the following major activities:

- Location and size

- Technologies

- Staffing and training

- Communication channels

- Monitoring and measuring performance

- Call management and handling

- Integrated call centers

Location and size

A first step in implementing a call center is to decide on the location of the facility. Whether it is a small department in a local facility or a large, enterprisewide center, this step is important to corporate growth and the bottom line, so it must be planned carefully. The high cost of real estate in populous areas is driving many call center operations to locate in rural areas. This is especially true throughout North America, where call centers are concentrated in several regions of the United States, as well as in Canada. With the communication and computer technology available today, it is very easy to locate call centers in any area where high-speed, high-quality communication resources are available, and many organizations have made this choice.

The size of the call center refers not only to square footage but also to the number of CSRs required, telephony and LAN equipment, client desktops, and other switching and computer hardware. Because call centers usually grow in size, it is a sound planning practice to choose a site with room for expansion.

Technologies

As noted previously in this chapter, there is a wide range of technologies available to the call center development team, as well as many sources of excellent advice—consultants, vendors, and users with experience in call center implementation. The core technologies of a call center involve many underlying components, including the following:

- Computer telephony integration (CTI)
- Networking hardware
- Automated call distribution (ACD) facilities
- PBX phone switch
- Software

Integrating all the components of the enterprise is time-consuming and expensive. It is important to determine which systems and applications need to be integrated with the call center operation, including

- Legacy systems
- Disparate relational databases
- Internet technologies

For ease of integration, it is important to select specific tools that will enable the interconnection of telephony equipment and software components.

Staffing and training

Hiring skilled staff is more important than ever in a call center operation, where the impact of effective, responsive customer communication can be critical to a company's customer relationship management (CRM) strategy. Modern call centers are much more complex than earlier facilities and require well-trained personnel. Customers are more demanding; they expect immediate response and intelligent help.

It is important to train CSRs, often for specific roles, and to give them call center responsibilities that reflect their areas of expertise. For instance, some are better on the phone and others are better at handling e-mail. To streamline the distribution of contacts and the effective use of trained staff, choose tools with workflow process support and skills-based routing. The latter feature enables the system to take a call regarding a specific product or application and then automatically route it to a representative with the appropriate skills to handle the request.

Once CSRs have been hired and properly trained, retaining them is just as important as retaining customers. Customer service representatives need to be kept up to speed on support methods, products, and processes. Keep knowledge bases up-to-date so that agents can satisfy customers in the best manner.

Advanced training, recognition, and competitive salaries are essential in retaining an effective, productive, call center workforce.

Communication channels

The variety of different customer channels available for contacting a call center means that incoming calls need to be answered in a timely manner. Response processes and call management features that enable the appropriate agent to assist the caller require a definition of workflow processes and SLAs (service-level agreements) with customers. Call centers that have automated workflow and skills-based routing can effectively route the incoming calls and ensure that the calls are being responded to appropriately by trained CSRs. Integrating with the Internet is critical, because this capability provides more avenues for assisting customers with chat, self-help, and live agents.

Monitoring and measuring performance

Monitoring tools and reporting features are essential for measuring response times and the number of calls received; these data help ensure that corporate goals are being met and can also be used to increase productivity. The process of keeping a call center running smoothly is an ongoing task that needs to be reviewed and revised from time to time to address problem areas and to help improve customer relations.

Call management and handling: websites

Corporate Websites are an important adjunct to call centers. More and better information on Websites assists customers; they benefit from on-line knowledge bases and FAQs and can often resolve issues without contacting a call center, thereby easing the load on the call center. However, when Internet-savvy customers need to interact with the call center, they may prefer to use e-mail, and they tend to ask more complex questions, which require call center representatives to be better skilled.

Integrated call centers

Call centers are changing as a result of the influence of the Internet and its integration into the call center. Integrated call centers decrease customer waiting time, offer alternate access to an organization, improve customer access, and improve call routing. Numerous studies and surveys have demonstrated that companies benefit from satisfied customers, who come back for more business. In spite of the high costs of a call center, most organizations with either a large number of customers or a frequent requirement to communicate with even a small number of customers need this facility to successfully compete in the 21st-century business environment.

1.3   Vendor solutions

A number of vendors have proven success in assisting organizations to develop, implement, and integrate call centers into their corporate customer management structures. Appendix A provides a selected list of these vendors with contact and product or service information. The technology tools offered by these vendors range in price from very expensive licensed solutions, in the range of $200,000 to $300,000, to relatively inexpensive hosted models, averaging $600 to $1,000 per call center position (seat).

Selection

Among these tools, it is important to select those that fit the organization's needs and integrate well with existing telephony equipment and current applications. The tools should be compatible with PBX equipment and dispersed data sources from data warehouses, shipping, and customer accounts. Also, the tools selected need to have the capability to handle multiple customer-access channels, such as telephone, Web self-help, e-mail, fax, and Internet chat.

Integration

Integrating all these components is time-consuming and expensive; however, it is necessary to the development of an effective call center that is fully responsive to customer interactions. The list of systems and applications that need to be integrated might include the following items:

- Data warehousing systems
- Legacy systems
- Disparate relational databases
- Internet technologies

It is important to select vendor tools that are capable of integrating telephony equipment and software components with all of these systems and applications.

1.4   A 10-point call center development process

The following 10 guidelines provide a logical, step-by-step process for developing and managing a call center operation.

Select a location for the call center where there is an educated workforce

Determine the size of the facility and the number of service representatives. Real estate and labor are two key cost factors in any call center operation.

Select the underlying technology components

These will include: PBX, voice mail, automated call distribution, computer telephony integration, and network equipment, such as routers, servers, and desktop PCs.

Decide which channels to support in the call center

Channels will include e-mail, chat, phone, Web forms, text chat, VoIP.

Select software solutions that meet requirements and will integrate with existing systems

Typically, these systems will be those that contain customer information—data warehousing systems, accounting systems, and contact information.

Integrate systems when feasible

Call centers must be able to handle multiple customer channels. Integrated systems help customer representatives answer questions more quickly by having more customer information available to them. Integrating with the Internet is critical, as it provides more avenues for assisting customers with chat, self-help, and live agents.

Determine SLAs and business processes

Implement best practices—workflow and e-mail routing—for skills-based routing capability. Establish hours of operation and standard procedures for handling calls.

Hire and retain staff

Establish a hiring and training budget. Hire skilled individuals and provide training, retraining, motivation, and rewards. Identify required skills and set appropriate goals to keep representatives trained.

Finalize the budget

Make presentations to management regarding budgets and benefits. Factor in all costs, including training, hiring, hardware costs, deployment, and integration.

Establish measurement and performance processes

Software for monitoring service levels and performance is the key to measuring call center results. Survey customers to ensure satisfaction. Evaluate response times. Utilize reporting tools and continue to improve service.

Establish on-going policies for training and updating CSRs

The CSR is the lifeblood of the call center and it is important that these employees be kept up-to-date on the tools used in the center and that their job functions be kept interesting and challenging.

1.5   How to use this book

This book contains practical information on setting up and running a call center based on the 10-point development process just described, including guidelines for hiring and retaining staff along with a series of case studies that demonstrate how successful call centers operate. It will be a useful reference and guide to information systems personnel, customer service

supervisors and CSRs, call center managers, sales and marketing personnel, as well as members of senior management in any organization who
wish to understand the significance of a well-organized, well-managed call
center operation.

Summary of topics covered

Chapter 2 provides background and a detailed analysis of the technologies
required for an effective call center operation, how to evaluate and select
the right technologies, and how to implement them. Chapter 3 offers
guidelines for the organization and management of a typical call center,
based on the experience of established, successful call center operations.
Chapter 4 provides an analysis of the equally important human factors,
including staff selection and training, that are so important in meeting call
center operating and service-level objectives.

Chapter 5 is an important chapter for learning and understanding how
successful call center operations have been implemented using a range of
vendor resources and management techniques. In this chapter, a number of
case studies are presented in a format that will enable the reader to assess
the environment in which each call center was established, the challenges
encountered by the development team, and how these challenges were successfully overcome to arrive at a successful, productive call center operation.

In Chapter 6, the significance of the call center in enhancing an organization's corporate CRM (customer relationship management) strategy is
described in detail with examples of how the call center can become a major
"hub" in this strategy.

Appendix A contains a selection of call center vendor resources, with
brief descriptions of products and services as well as contact information.
Appendix B is an extensive and comprehensive glossary of call center and
CRM terms and definitions. Appendix C provides the reader with a selection of references used in the preparation of this book, as well as a bibliog-
raphy of other texts relating to call centers and CRM.

2

Call Center Technology

Chapter 1 described the essential components of a call center and the importance of technology, particularly the integration of several technologies, in the implementation and operation of the call center and in providing the range of services required to manage customer communications effectively. This chapter describes the evolution of call center technologies and provides a detailed analysis of these technologies and how they function as well as how they can be applied to meet call center requirements.

Advances and changes in technology have made many new features available to call center operations, providing increased efficiency and better opportunities for serving customers and empowering CSRs with the capability of better managing customer interactions. Most call centers use several systems and applications with specialized functions. In parallel with these advances in technologies that are internal to the call center, more "intelligent" network services offered by carriers make possible the routing of calls based on a wide range of criteria—area code or prefix, dialed number identification service (DNIS), time of day, day of week, and other parameters that are under the control of call center management. Call allocation facilities are also available that can program the network to send defined percentages of calls to selected sites.

Other significant changes that have occurred in the call center because of the availability of enabling technologies include the following:

- Accessing of applications using icon-based GUI windows, allowing for simultaneous task execution

- Scanning and retrieval of on-screen documents, a process that increases the speed of document handling

- Prerecorded CSR introductory greetings, with digital clarity

- Enhanced fax-handling capabilities, including presorting and generating faxes automatically from the CSR terminal during talk time, automated fax-back, and fax on demand

- Capability to monitor and blend calls, switching CSRs automatically from inbound to outbound calls when traffic permits

- Call selection techniques using a PC control window that enables CSRs to point to a call to answer from a list of calls in a queue

The technologies that are required to support an effective, high-productivity call center operation can be classified under the following major headings:

- Computer telephony integration (CTI)

- Call distribution technology (ACD)

- Database software.

As pointed out in Chapter 1, effective management, use, and distribution of information are important elements in today's fast-paced business environment. Technologies play an important role in the accomplishment of these objectives and provide and sustain competitive advantage. Technology by itself cannot attain business goals, it is how people use the technology that will ultimately lead to improvements in communications and operational processes. CTI, the integration of computer and telephone technologies, is one of the applications of technology that has the capability of maximizing the benefits of both technologies for the user community. CTI is an approach to merging two fundamental modern-day technologies, bringing together the disparate and advanced technologies of computing and telephony in a manner that focuses on providing user organizations with choice and flexibility in the implementation of call center operations.

2.1 Computer telephony integration (CTI)

The significance of the integration of the computer and the telephone (CTI), is reflected in the growth of the communications market, around which CTI has been developed. Telephone call volumes are growing exponentially: In 1980, Americans made about 200 million international phone calls, and by 1998, that number had risen to 4.5 billion. The global fiber-optic networking market is expected to reach $52 billion in 2003, $25 billion higher than in 1999. The rapid growth of networked systems, and the increasing demand for more bandwidth have enhanced the importance of

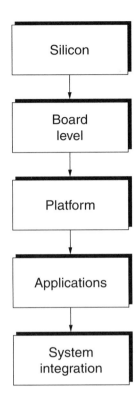

Figure 2.1
CTI—An open architecture.

CTI as well, as illustrated by the sophistication of enterprise systems such as call centers. The impact of open systems, new technologies such as the Internet, VoIP, and wireless computing are altering fundamental business models. (see Figure 2.1)

The evolution of CTI

One of the overall design objectives of CTI was to enable better contact between companies and their customers through the seamless and intelligent integration of both technologies. It has been defined as a "loose but complicated amalgamation of interlocking technologies," a way of combining the two streams of information—voice and data—through open, standards-based systems. It has uses in many areas of today's technology-based business, but certainly one of its most significant applications is in the call center. In this facility, it provides opportunities to improve the way a company interacts with its customers, the key focus of any call center operation.

A brief review of the evolution of both the computing and telephony environments is provided in this chapter to give some background on the technological advances that define CTI and to the current prevalent "model" of computing—*client/server architecture*. An overview of telephony, the second of the two technologies that make up CTI, is also provided, describing the basic functioning of public networks and business telephone systems. Finally, the two technologies are brought together with the integration of computerization into the communication environment, illustrating how they maximize the benefits of both in the call center environment.

The computer environment

The distributed computing architectures that have become commonplace in today's business world began with the mainframe, a massive structure of processing and data storage elements. The mainframe environment provided centralized "host" facilities to run applications—users outside of the computing department used "dumb" terminals and cumbersome commands to access applications and request actions.

Mainframe computing

Mainframe computing platforms are still an integral element of many IS environments and are often referred to as *legacy systems* in reference to the legacies of information they still retain, the considerable investment they represent, and the role they play in today's computing architecture. That role is usually focused on the handling of record-intensive functions such as employee or customer financial databases (health care records, automobile licensing, inventory, etc.). (see Figure 2.2)

Rapid advances in processing technology and the demanding desktop/workgroup requirements of the marketplace stimulated the evolution of the minicomputer in the late 1970s and personal computing—the ubiquitous PC—in the early 1980s. This widespread availability of relatively inexpensive computing power allowed new architectures to evolve. (see Figure 2.3) The architecture of choice in today's computing environment is *client/server* computing. In this model, an intelligent terminal (PC) is connected to various applications and services by a local area network (LAN), and in large enterprises users are usually connected to remote locations via a wide area

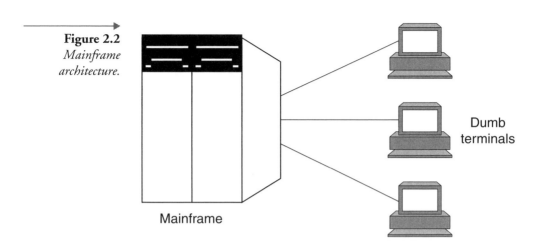

Figure 2.2
Mainframe architecture.

Mainframe

Dumb terminals

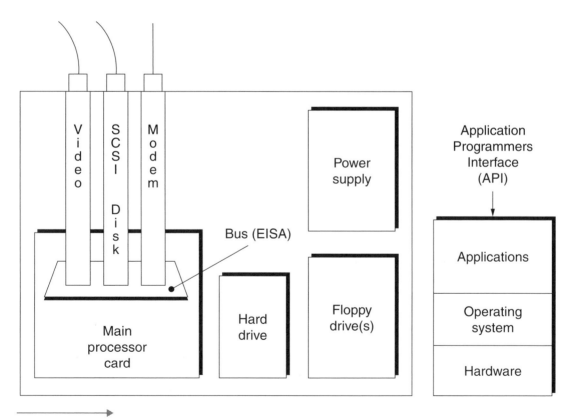

Figure 2.3 *PC architecture.*

Figure 2.4
Client/server
architecture.

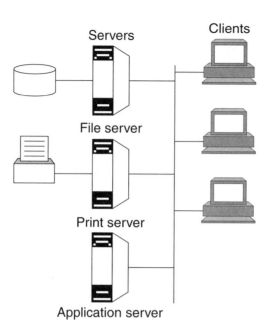

network (WAN). These networks of computing power are commonplace in the business world of the 21st century.

Client/Server computing

Today's typical office environment includes a variety of input and output devices—PCs, scanners, printers, and so on—all connected by a LAN. The client/server model extends "sharing" to files, databases, and more importantly additional applications by putting the shared elements into a shared PC (the server). By doing so, each desktop PC (the client) accesses the server to extract or input information. When users update a record, the server database is updated, so that everyone in the workgroup is sharing up-to-date information. Client/server applications allow users to configure their screens to meet specific needs and preferences, yet have the benefits of shared information. (see Figure 2.4)

The capability of mixing and matching machines from different vendors in an open system environment is another feature of client/server computing. The user can select the server best suited to the task but choose PCs from a different vendor, based on a preferred graphical user interface (GUI) or other application parameters.

The communications environment

Most call center applications require a dedicated piece of hardware for pure telephony switching; however, all the add-on functions of value—the call center specific applications—can reside on a "telephone server" connected to the phone switch. One product that is commonly used in this application is a Windows NT box.

In addition to interoperability standards, there are other links in any data/voice application. "Voice," for example, could refer to different kinds of calls—traditional phone calls are one example, recorded calls in the form of messages, fax traffic, and even the digits callers enter when they pass through a voice response system are other examples of voice traffic. Data traffic originates with the host information in databases and includes the subset of host data that moves to the desktop and back, as well as MIS data that passes through the corporate LAN, through intranets, over the Internet (including company Web traffic), and e-mails.

Prior to the advances in network technology, it was relatively easy to isolate voice-form data streams; however, now a corporation's system might also be dealing with varying combinations of new technologies that include elements of both voice and data: voice over the Internet (VoIP), fax over the Internet, speech recognition, browser-based transaction processing, and "call me" buttons that appear on Web pages.

Standards for CTI

The switch technology resulting from the partnering of computers and telephony has resulted in the design and production of switches that contain CTI hooks built in and a suite of applications from vendors and their partners built to meet joint industry standards that take advantage of the interconnections between the computer and the telephone. When PBX vendors decided to make their switch technology freely available, a more solutions-based set of technologies resulted, largely due to the widespread adoption of technical standards for interoperability between vendors and applications industries. These standards included specifications for the operation of component hardware at the board level, as well as specifications from individual vendors that enabled applications to function correctly on particular board sets.

The computer software industry also created standards for the applications that work with operating systems. The key standards, TAPI and TSAPI, were set up by Microsoft and Novell, respectively, as a way to push the switch vendors into compatibility so that developers could use these operating system platforms as the basis for CTI applications.

Call control

Some of the new applications focused on *call control*—the movement and tracking of calls in a phone network. Many others were applications that took advantage of the growing LAN/phone system connections to bring data to the desktop at the same time as the phone call arrived. Wherever voice and data networks come together, standards are required to ensure that the integration goes smoothly.

The Internet has required the implementation of additional standards. Building applications combining call control and data manipulation became a lot easier with the adoption of Java and TCP/IP (transmission control protocol/Internet protocol), as standards for data communication. The development of standards to manage these combinations of "information traffic" makes it easier to move data and voice together. It has become irrelevant what form the information takes. What is more important is how that information is used and who has access to it.

CTI has become more precisely defined as "*any technology that combines some form of real-time, person-to-person company communication with a background of data that adds value to that communication.*" CTI was first implemented in the mid-1980s in large corporate call centers. Since then, advances in public telephone network technology and computing have made CTI a powerful tool for businesses of any size. Along with technological advances have come reductions in the cost of implementation, making CTI available and affordable to a much broader range of organizations.

Computer telephony can trace part of its origins to the fact that adding to a typical office PBX required purchasing the add-on to the equipment from the original vendor through a third-party company that wrote to the PBX vendor proprietary specification. For most of the 1990s, this was the method use to install CTI systems—customization, with detailed on-site upgrading and continual fixing of both major and minor glitches to keep the system working. Current CTI systems have benefited from these early experiences and are now much easier to implement. They can now meet the requirements of both large and small companies, in relatively standard versions that require little, if any, customization.

The adaptation of CTI was further hindered in the early days of the technology by the fact that software companies were reluctant to develop add-ons because the cost of developing them for multiple switch vendors was prohibitively high. However, the more perceptive members of both the PBX and computer industries realized that their technologies were more alike than different. Switches were really high-performance communications servers, and if the specifications could be opened up and standards developed, both sides would benefit from the many application requirements that would be met by the combined technologies.

Switch-to-host integration

As noted previously in this chapter, advances in technology have brought sophisticated capabilities within the price range of even the smallest call centers, and *switch-to-host integration* has contributed most significantly to this change. Switch-to-host integration represents a total transformation of the capabilities of a call center. Small companies can now avail themselves of technology that takes advantage of a range of network-provided services to provide more options with each customer communication.

Voice response

Voice response systems deliver recorded information to incoming calls and are an important element in any call center operation. Interactive voice response, IVR, is two-way: It responds with information when a caller enters digits on the touch-tone phone. The response information is generated from a database, and this application is one of the key functions of CTI. In the typical voice response application, this feature is available on a 24/7 basis, and customers can make a variety of inquiries regarding their accounts or order status. The IVR engine queries a database in the background and reads the information to the caller. This is a dynamic function and represents a much better form of customer communication than a canned, prerecorded response. When converted to an Internet-based operation, the utility to customers is expanded dramatically. Any visual or text image, from catalogs to product schematics, can be displayed on a customer (or CSR) desktop. Customers can help themselves when problems arise. From both the company and customer viewpoints, this feature has several benefits:

- Customers learn about products before they buy.

- They are better prepared to talk to CSRs.

- Calls are shorter, more effective, more profitable.

- Shoppers do their shopping without consuming valuable resources.

- The buyer gets full attention.

CTI applications

Some of the specific applications for CTI in inbound call centers include

- Synchronized voice and data delivery
- Simultaneous voice and data transfer
- Voice and data conferencing
- Automatic retrieval from callers
- Segmentation and prioritizing callers
- Caller-specific messaging and routing
- Enhanced performance reporting
- On-line training tools
- Enhanced marketing research
- Automated switching between inbound and outbound (call blending)
- Desktop-based productivity tools

Computer telephony surpasses the traditional limitations of both component technologies (phones and computers) and combines their best features to bring more information to the person on the phone and to make data more accessible and more useful to CSRs. Computer telephony adds computer intelligence to a phone call. Everything from simple screen presentations to predictive dialing is a CTI application. The capability of integrating the computer and telecom system brings customer phone calls along with data files right to the CSR's desktop as the call comes in. This translates to massive savings in 800 line charges and agent labor. In practice, implementing CTI has been a tricky proposition. In its early configurations, it was usually custom-made for a particular application. Companies used a systems integrator to pull together the necessary links, proprietary interfaces, and special connections to applications.

Integration of CTI

There are several issues related to the integration of CTI with other corporate systems. These issues include the following:

- Linkages to multiple disparate data sources
- Limitations imposed by vendor-specific protocols

- Upgrades to attached systems that may cause changes in other systems or disable some functions

- Combining standard and custom applications

The benefits of CTI

CTI in the call center brings many benefits as well as changes to businesses, by changing business trends, reshaping the workplace, and providing opportunities for increased productivity, increased revenue, and ultimately, increased profit. The resulting changes in the corporate world are reflected in more horizontal organizations, high-performance workgroups, and empowered employees. CTI also changes the roles of call center personnel and requires skilled CSRs who can identify and resolve customer problems. Call center managers are required to coordinate and manage a broad range of activities and technologies.

The main focus of any organization should be its customers: fielding their calls, delivering service, ensuring orders are filled, and making sales. Customer databases are significant in the application of CTI, as the traditional computer and telephone are replaced by a single unit combining both communications devices. The easier it is for customers to communicate with companies, the better the relationship will be. Establishing and maintaining good customer relationships is one of the ultimate objectives of call center operations and a prevailing focus of this book. Companies that do the best job of opening the door to customers, making it as easy as possible for customers to find out what they need to know, are the ones that have the best track records in the long term. Small and medium-sized companies that have adopted customer-focused attitudes eventually become "giants" in their industry sectors.

Among the benefits that CTI brings to both businesses and their customers are the following:

- Shorter calls

- Significant reduction in hold time

- Fast transfer of information to the CSR's desktop, then to the caller

- Reduction in telecom usage costs (the second biggest expense in a call center)

- Happier customers

- Most problems solved faster, on the first call

- More sales opportunities

- Capability to cross sell or upsell while building loyalty

- Better use of staff

- Enabling Internet or company intranet connections, offering a range of multimedia sales and service tools

A call center that uses computer telephony knows who its customers are and why they are calling. It knows what they like, what they dislike, and how much they are worth to the company. CTI lets a company respond faster to changing market conditions, but it must be implemented correctly with clear and ongoing support from upper management and a clear-eyed view of the company's goals for the technology.

Call center applications

Applications run on top of operating systems and are designed to perform specific functions (e.g., create spreadsheets, perform word processing functions, manage e-mail, provide contact management data, etc.). In single-tasking environments, such as DOS and Windows, only one program runs at a time; other programs are suspended until the user restarts them. In a multitasking environment—Windows, UNIX, or OS/2—multiple programs can be running with the user switching (or linking) between programs as required. One of the key elements of modern application development and design is the concept of an *application programming interface* (API). The API provides the defined interface between various devices or software layers in the computing model so that software developers can focus on the application. A printer API is a good example of this type of software. APIs are relevant to both desktop PC applications as well as server applications and are also an important element in CTI.

CTI and call center productivity

CTI is an information delivery tool that will assist CSRs to communicate intelligently and knowledgeably with customers by providing them with information they need to address customer needs. In addition to the information-handling features offered by CTI, this combined technology also provides the capability to perform *quality control measurements* in a call center, enabling calls to be monitored, recorded, and archived so that the CSR and the supervisor can review them and assess performance. The analysis process is made much more productive when it is augmented by the data that passes through the agent's screen during the call. A company record of every transaction can be kept indefinitely, providing an audit trail and a training aid.

Call center productivity improvements resulting from CTI include the following:

- Reduces operating costs through staff reductions—more calls can be handled by fewer staff

- Enables smaller companies to look like big ones—without sacrificing the personal touch

- Enables companies to present an image of greater capability than they may possess—providing automated 24/7 response

A more detailed analysis of performance measurement techniques is provided later in this chapter in Section 2.3 under "Call Monitoring."

2.2   **Network structures and CTI servers**

A network structure is made up of several components—client computers and servers consisting of transport mechanisms—forming a physical interface and network architecture. Some examples of network architectures are Ethernet, 10BASE-T, Token Ring, and ATM (asynchronous transfer mode). A communications protocol (TCP/IP or SPX/IPX (sequenced packet-eXchange/internetwork packeteXchange)) is also required to link the elements of a network. Each PC on the network has a LAN card to provide an interface to the network.

The server is a device that empowers the network and the attached users. There are several types of servers in LAN environments: file and print servers, departmental database servers, and legacy hosts acting as database servers. CTI introduces a new class of servers to the LAN infrastructure— *telephony servers.* (see Figure 2.5) Server platforms generally consist of the same basic hardware as the desktop PC but have some differences in operating characteristics. Generally, they are faster, more powerful, and have much more memory and disk space. They come in a variety of configurations and levels of robustness, depending on their intended use and the importance of maintaining data integrity or network connections. *Telecom servers* are a special class of telephony servers that deliver high bandwidth and require higher-capacity buses. These devices are described in more detail later in this chapter. (see Figure 2.6)

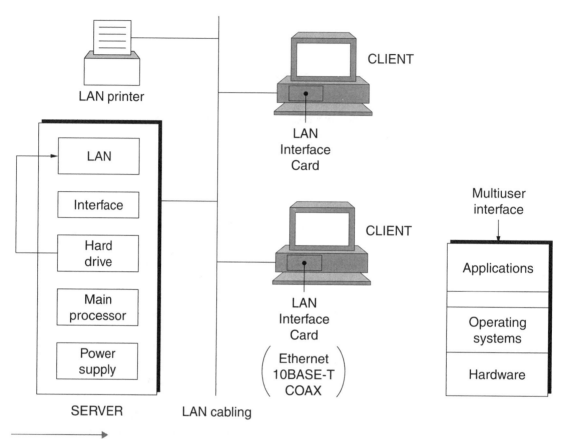

Figure 2.5 *LAN server architecture.*

As the LAN industry matured, developers started designing network-based applications that could be used in a network environment by many clients simultaneously. These applications are tolerant of delays imposed by multiuser access and led to the development of network operating systems: Novell NetWare, IBM LAN Manager, and Microsoft MS Windows NT.

Communications in the call center

There are a number of different telephone operating models, all of which may have a role in call center operations. The communications environment chosen for a call center will be related to the call volumes anticipated, number of seats in the center, and the geographical extent and coverage of

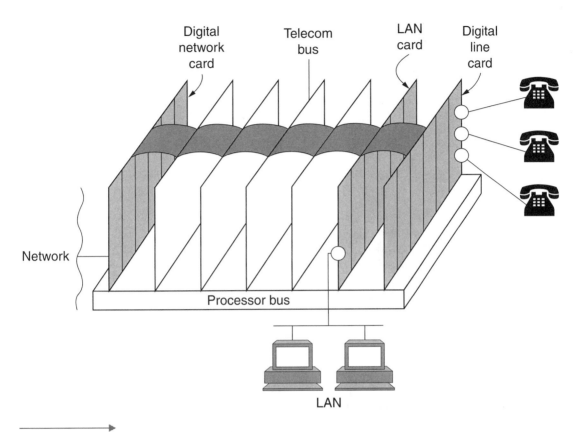

Figure 2.6   *Telecom server architecture.*

the call center. Two of the most popular communication models are described in this section:

- Public network

- Customer premise

Public network model

The most important telephony elements related to CTI are services provided by public telephone networks and the capabilities of *call processing* and *call control*. The world's public telephone networks are complex, with millions of endpoints hard-wired and connected through thousands of central connecting points called central offices (COs). The public network has evolved over the years from its POTS (plain old telephone service) analog beginnings to the broad range of advanced, sophisticated services provided by today's digital technology. (see Figure 2.7)

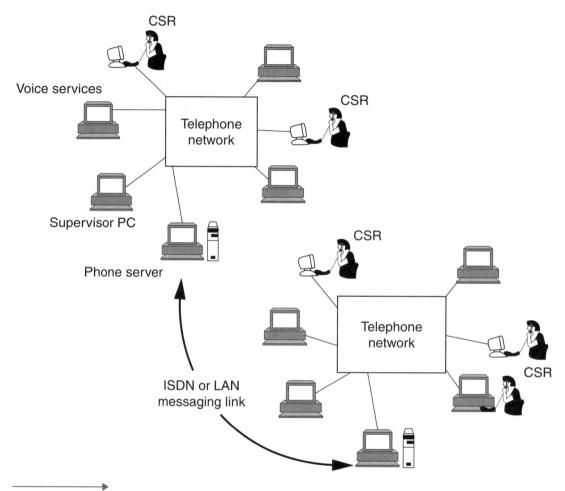

Figure 2.7   *Routing calls in the network.*

The public network model has relatively simple communications architecture. Users with a "terminal device," such as a telephone, are connected
by the network to a service provider—actually, a server. Once connected,
the user can ask for any of the wide range of services generally available—
from dialing a number to directory assistance or voice messaging. In general,
the network operator or service provider can change or enhance capabilities
without disrupting existing services. This model is present in many telecommunications environments. As a terminal device, a telephone handset has
many variations. It may be analog or digital, with buttons and displays, and

it can also be wireless. Terminal devices also include fax machines, modems, video phones, alarm systems, WAN equipment, and multimedia boards for PCs. Broadly defined, a terminal device is "any piece of hardware attached to the network, and capable of accessing the service provider."

The basic network infrastructure resembles a giant spider web, consisting as it does of a set of switches (the central offices referred to previously) interconnected by a variety of transmission media—fiber-optic cable, satellites, radio, underwater cables, and so on. In the public network circuit-switched service, a call is connected across the network and travels a number of different paths to get to its destination. The most basic service is the telephone call. The sequence of events is as follows:

- The user picks up the phone (goes off-hook), which gets the attention of the network.

- The user then dials a string of digits (which the network recognizes as an address).

Hidden from the user is all the logic for routing the call through the network, handling exceptions (such as routing invalid numbers to a recording), or invoking special features. This logic is delivered by a service provider attached somewhere within the network—again invisible to the user, other than through prerecorded messages.

In the public network, along with basic call-handling services there are a range of supplementary services available, the most popular being ANI and DNIS. ANI (automatic number identification) is the ability of the network to identify the calling number. With ANI, the user knows who is calling before answering. DNIS (dialed number information service) is the ability of the network to identify the number that was dialed to reach a user. These two features are important in call center operations.

Customer premise model

As the telephone became a must-have business and management tool, the logistics and costs associated with adding a new telephone line for every new employee or every new phone became overwhelming. *Customer premise equipment* (*CPE*) was developed to overcome these problems; it falls into two categories:

- Access points to network services

- Extensions of the network itself

The following two examples illustrate the differences:

Key systems (access products)

For small businesses requiring several telephone lines, the *key system* provides the user with direct access to the network line corresponding to that key. Other users are provided with a small light or "busy lamp" to indicate when a line is busy.

Private branch exchange (PBX)

In large businesses, smaller versions of central office switches, called *private branches* or PBX systems, enable hundreds or thousands of employees to handle the volume of internal calls. As well, they can share access lines to the network and provide operator services.

For very large corporations with multiple buildings or sites, complete private networks may be installed to carry internal traffic as well as to interconnect to the public network at strategic points to get the best geographic coverage for the lowest cost.

Telecom switching systems

The following elements are found in all telecom switching systems:

- *Operating system software* that controls the hardware
- *Call processing software* that makes connections, provides features, and delivers services
- *Line side* interfaces connecting the switch to the end-user telephone set
- *Trunk side* interfaces connecting the customer's switch to the network
- *A switching fabric* linking the various interfaces

Operating system software

In the telecommunications environment as in the world of computing, hardware is controlled by operating system software. The telecom environment has special needs for multiuser, real-time, fault-tolerant operating systems. The complexities of the features available have resulted in switch products that use proprietary operating systems, a parallel to the proprietary legacy systems of the computing environment.

Call processing applications

The heart of a modern switching system is a set of software applications known collectively as *call processing*. This software provides all the functionality seen by the user—from the basic call setup to delivering caller ID. This software also provides user features (such as call forwarding), enhanced network services (such as least-cost routing), and specialized call handling for call centers. Call processing is the basis for powerful CTI applications that can make a call center highly effective and productive.

Interfacing hardware

Modern telecom systems operate by converting analog voice signals into a digital format known as *pulse code modulation* (PCM). The digital format is far superior for clear transmission, storage, compression, and even encryption. This process is accomplished by a silicon chip, a CODEC (for code and decode) designed into the line interface. The CODEC samples the voice signal 8000 times per second and transforms it into the digital signal, ready for transmission. At the other end, another CODEC chip transforms the digital signal into a recognizable voice signal.

The switching device performs the function of connecting the digital signal from the line interface to the destination, which might be another line interface (*intercom call*), a trunk interface (*network call*), or a common resource (such as a *conference bridge*). Once established, the connection stays up for the duration of the call. The trunk interface is a shared pipe into the public network. There are various types of trunk interfaces, defined by their bandwidth capacities—T1, T2, T3. For example, a single T1 trunk provides 24 circuit paths for digitized voice as well as the signaling to access the network services. Typically, these 24 circuits can provide service to about 150 users.

2.3   Basic CTI services

The starting point for all CTI development is a set of basic services, which include *call control, call monitoring*, and *feature activation*. There are two recognized industry standards (CSTA (computer supported telecommunication applications) and SCAI (switch to computer applications interface)) for performing these functions as well as several dozen proprietary designs.

Call control

Switching software is the core technology enabling CTI to provide an outside application with some form of control over switch functions. The outside application is offered or can access a set of commands; for example, make call, answer call, and transfer call. When a command is issued, the switch tries to complete its assigned task and reports back to the application with a result. That result might mean complete success (the call went through), progress has been made (the other end is now ringing), or failure (the dialed number is busy or goes unanswered). This information has to be provided on a real time basis as events occur. The application design must allow for communications situations that occur in real life in call centers, such as peak times when all the lines are busy or power users who switch back and forth between several calls on hold. Users have come to expect almost instantaneous response times from their telephone systems; the CTI application designer must now deliver on that expectation. In this simple model, call control expects the application to act as if it were a telephone set (anything that a telephone could do, the application can now do). By extending that model to include the features of a modern business telephone (multiline, speed call, displays, etc.), the power of this basic service becomes apparent.

There are two approaches to call control:

- First-party call control

- Third-party call control

First-party call control

The basic premise of first-party call control is that the CTI application is acting on behalf of one user. In this model, the application is running on the user's desktop PC, and there is an actual physical connection between the application, the user's PC, and the user's telephone line. Through an application, the user can control the telephone call. Examples of these applications include the following:

- Personal directory

- Personal organizer

- Personal answering machine

- Personal call accounting

Third-party call control

The basic premise of third-party call control is that the CTI application acts on behalf of any of the clients in a workgroup or department. In this model, the application is running on a shared server and there is no direct physical connection between the user's PC and the telephone line. Instead, there is a "logical" connection: The user's PC application communicates with the server, which in turn controls the switch. The server provides a coordination point for all calls being handled in the workgroup. This makes possible a much more powerful (or useful) level of call control. The central server-based application can handle the distribution of all calls to the members of the workgroup, including activities like call screening or back-up answering. This has been a key element in the application of CTI—*the potential for breakthrough productivity gains when used in high-performance workgroups.*

Call monitoring

Both of the call control models described previously expect the application to act like a telephone. This is helpful in explaining call control, but it clearly ignores the range of capabilities of a PC. Recognizing this, the designers of CTI built in services, such as call monitors, that capitalize on the strengths of the PC.

The application can set a *call monitor* in the PBX (private business exchange) to collect information on almost any activity. For example, by setting a monitor on a single user's telephone set, the application can watch every button pushed, every digit dialed, every picking up or replacing of the handset. Similarly, by monitoring any trunk, the application can see each incoming call, collect ANI or DNIS data, watch where the call was directed, and know when and where it was answered. By selectively monitoring telephones, groups of telephones, or trunks, the application can get as detailed a picture of the PBX activities as required to make the application work. This is especially valuable in generating management reporting and performance measurement statistics.

Feature activation

The last of the basic CTI services described in this section is *feature activation*. Modern PBX systems provide over 200 features to improve call handling, although the majority of users never use more than 4 of them. The use of PC-based applications (which can be set to the user's preferences) unlocks the power already built into the telephone system by allowing simple computer screen-based control of features, such as arranging a conference call by clicking on the names of the parties involved.

In this application, commands are provided that activate, suspend, or turn off features within the switch. For example, the *personal organizer* application could set up call forwarding for a user who is away from the office and turn off the same call forwarding when the user returns. Similarly, a CTI application could modify call screening by a secretary on behalf of a workgroup. It would be turned off at the end of the business day and the calls would be automatically redirected to an answering service.

2.4   CTI in the call center

Earlier in this chapter, CTI was described from the perspective of a PBX environment, because the technology originated in the PBX community. In a call center application, the PBX switch is capable of relaying information that the PC can interpret and that operators can use to respond to a caller rapidly. CTI is the technology that enables a range of multifaceted call management features to be implemented in a call center. Advances in telephone and computer technology, as well as in other technologies, such as data warehousing and database management systems, have resulted in the increasing sophistication of modern call centers.

Open systems and standards

As described previously, CTI is made possible by the integration of many different components, subsystems, applications, and technologies and is based on an "open system" concept. Open systems and common standards allow a telephony server to be added to an existing LAN, thereby making possible the sharing of applications across an enterprise. In this environment, legacy systems also play a major role by providing customer data and employing other long-standing internal corporate standards. CTI applications can share LANs with different servers because telephony APIs have been developed by leading network specialists and customer premise equipment (CPE) manufacturers. Although CTI came from "closed proprietary" roots, its evolution has motivated the telecommunications community to adopt an open system/multivendor environment, a process referred to previously in this chapter.

The integration of computing and telephony, with its myriad of components and standards, is a natural environment for this approach in which numerous players can contribute knowledge and expertise at the right point in the process. On the computer side of the CTI house, major computer vendors are active in client/server architecture and CTI solutions. At the same time, switch vendors have endorsed two of the more prevalent APIs—TSAPI and TAPI (see the Glossary in Appendix B). The significant advantage of open system architectures is that they provide developers the opportunity to focus on designing the application, rather than getting involved in the various components or peripherals it may try to control. Application development in CTI is facilitated using APIs provided by operating system designers and manufacturers of peripheral equipment, while CTI developers are free to concentrate on their own application requirements.

The fully automated call center

Previous descriptions of CTI in this chapter have stressed the high level of automation this hybrid technology brings to call center operations. To accomplish the goals of an organization planning to implement a fully automated call center, the following must be considered and evaluated:

- Integrating the new CTI architecture with currently installed systems and incorporating the capability for future growth

- Minimizing requirements for new hardware and software on existing PCs and in the PBX

- Incorporating industry-standard hardware and software

- Building in the capability to track and report on call center operations, including operator productivity and the effectiveness of the CTI implementation

An effective call center operation will keep pace with the communications preferences of customers, while maximizing network resources and customer service, by integrating a wide range of communication tools with the organization's human resources and databases.

Switch links and PBX

Early CTI implementations that used switch links had a number of designations for the link or interface between the computer and the PBX, but what they had in common was architecture rooted in computer-to-mainframe PBX. This complex, high-end system was the result of technology alliances between big switch manufacturers and big computer manufacturers, which yielded an enterprisewide solution. In a typical large call center operation, the application ran on a minicomputer/mainframe and controlled a PBX using an intelligent link. The user's screen was controlled by the same application so that the application could coordinate the call arriving at the desk with the proper and timely presentation of information. If the operator needed to transfer the call to a supervisor, the application made sure the information screen traveled with the call.

Telecom servers

The new approach uses a *telecom server*, which is installed as another node on a workgroup LAN and equipped with the hardware and software elements necessary to deliver CTI solutions to that workgroup. The telecom server connects directly to the public network to handle all calls coming into the group and connects directly to the desktop client to deliver those calls. This approach allows all the "priority" customer contacts to bypass the enterprise PBX. As a result, the enterprise PBX no longer needs to be upgraded. The telecom server has a few simple connections back to the legacy PBX to allow internal calls between the workgroup and the rest of the organization, a feature that is one of the major technological advances in a CTI implementation.

Telecom servers contain a basic computing component, which is enhanced for CTI applications by adding four card types:

- *A digital trunk card* to connect to advanced network services

- *A digital line card* to transfer voice or video connections to the desktop

- *An analog trunk card* to connect internal voice calls to the legacy PBX

- *A special-purpose resource card* with a range of available technologies configured to match the services required

The traditional PC bus is not designed to handle the large bandwidth required to transport real-time voice and video information, for example, from the digital trunk card across the digital line card or to the voice processing card. To solve this problem, a secondary telecom bus is added to the server architecture.

Enhanced CTI services

Telecom servers extend the range of services available to the CTI application developer. Basic call control can now be integrated with DSP (digital signal processor) cards to deliver the broad range of services described next.

Voice processing—voice mail/automated attendant

Voice response systems were discussed briefly as one of the call-handling features enabled by CTI. This feature involves a single-card voice mail system that is designed by programming a DSP resource card to compress the caller's voice so that it can be stored on a mass storage device such as a hard disk. The voice is already in digital format when it arrives from the digital trunk or digital line card. The application software in a voice mail server is basically a simple file-and-retrieval system available from several vendors that uses a desktop PC application to control the system.

IVR (interactive voice response)

IVR systems use essentially the same technology as voice mail and can be designed with a single DSP card. IVR applications allow users to create structured scripts that guide the caller through a series of menu options to obtain a final response. The IVR will play digitally stored messages and solicit a response from the caller at each step, generally using a Touch-Tone telephone pad. The response will then cause the next set of messages to be played, according to the script.

Speech recognition

Speech recognition is another DSP-based technology that can be delivered to the server as a resource card. It gives the computer the capability to analyze digitized voice signals, compare them with other voice patterns, and recognize the words being spoken. This technology can be used to supplement IVR systems in situations where the user can't use the Touch-Tone keypad or to reduce the number of menus that the caller has to navigate.

Text-to-speech technology

Text-to-speech or speech synthesis technologies are another resource card option, enabling the computer to produce speech from written or spoken information. This capability is useful for e-mail or free-form messages when a terminal is unavailable (e.g., at the airport, on a cellular phone, etc.)

Fax processing

The DSP card can be programmed to function as a fax modem, which provides a shared fax server resource. The fax image can be downloaded over the LAN and converted by the fax card, then transmitted over the digital trunk to the network. In reverse fashion, an incoming fax from the network will be converted to file format and sent to the desktop PC.

Media conversion

Media conversion, along with other technologies, has the potential to improve access to information from anywhere, a useful feature for mobile workforces.

Optical character recognition (OCR)

OCR is another DSP-based technology that converts a scanned image into text. When used with fax images, it can convert an incoming fax to a document that can be edited or pass it to a text-to-speech application to be read aloud.

2.5   CTI implementation guidelines

The implementation of a CTI solution begins with the selection of an overall system architecture. One of two options may be selected:

- Traditional mainframe level (enterprise)

- Workgroup (client/server) level external to existing telecommunications switches and infrastructure

These options represent two philosophically different approaches to CTI. The advantages and disadvantages of each are described next.

Implementation at enterprise or PBX level

The enterprise or PBX level requires additional intelligence in the PBX. Considerable time and expense will be required to upgrade the software and hardware, however, possibly requiring complete replacement of the PBX. In addition, the existing proprietary software used for call control and call processing, as well as the complex interactions between call processing and the features and functions accessible through desktop telephones, may not be capable of upgrading, thus requiring a complete system upgrade.

Implementation at client/server or LAN level

At the client/server or LAN level, integration is accomplished by the addition of an applications or telephony server to the existing LAN architecture. As a result, the legacy PBX investment is maintained and CTI functionality is delivered by another server on the LAN. The server takes control of telephone calls and serves as the interface between telephony protocols, server software, and the clients using the applications.

Once the implementation alternative has been selected, a key business parameter related to the implementation of CTI, and more importantly, to the objectives and goals of a call center operation, must be addressed. This is the *overall enterprise objective for customer interaction*, or in more current terminology, the corporation's *customer relationship management* (*CRM*) strategy. (see Chapter 6). Assessing the impact of CTI on this strategy means evaluating every possible contingency and every possible combination of customer communication, including e-mail, telephone, Website hits, fax, and even regular (snail) mail. The correct CTI process or product is the appropriate mix of applications and core technologies that add value to a company's existing operations and allow it to do more to enhance its CRM strategy.

A number of specific CTI applications may be considered at the evaluation stage for their contribution to meeting call center objectives:

- Voice mail

- Unified messaging

- Advanced call routing

- Fax redirection

- Internet telephony

- Call center applications

- Customer service software

- Salesforce automation

Once the CTI implementation option has been selected, there are several logical, practical approaches to meeting the specified requirements. The 12-step, chronological CTI Project Checklist described next is a process that has been tested in the development of successful call centers. It is flexible in that it can be modified to meet specific requirements and is applicable to either of the implementation options.

The 12-step CTI project checklist

The following activities will take the CTI project from inception to complete activation and should be addressed in chronological order:

1. Convene an initial meeting of all stakeholders, users, and departmental representatives involved in the call center operation.

2. Identify workgroup/project for pilot program.

3. Identify key objectives for CTI implementation—internal and external benefits, ROI (return on investment), individuals and processes affected.

4.   Develop detailed vendor/supplier briefing or RFP (request for proposal), including objectives.

5.   Visit vendor sites and hold briefing sessions.

6.   Issue call for proposals.

7.   Evaluate proposals relative to expectations/objectives and ROI targets.

8.   Select vendors and other contractors.

9.   Install pilot site and train staff.

10. Introduce CTI components on a phased basis beginning with call control, and moving into call processing.

11. Introduce full CTI feature set and application functionality.

12. Review progress and adjust as necessary.

In the PBX approach, primary vendor contact will be with PBX legacy system representatives. If the client/server approach is selected, primary contact will be with a supplier having LAN, computer, and telecommunications experience. Expert advice is also available to the CTI project team from a number of other sources. Component vendors can be consulted in the early stages and often point the way to application partners whose products works with the core elements. Other organizations that are operating call centers may be willing to share their experiences. Telephone companies and other large service providers can also help integrate the components of CTI to meet performance specifications.

To ensure success, companies implementing a call center need upper management to buy in, to direct the goals of the project, and to establish a clear, consistent view of the relationship between the company and its customers. This last issue must always be in the forefront of the call center development team's planning process and needs to be stressed in initial project meetings and management presentations.

Selection and integration of CTI components

Putting the pieces of a CTI system together involves a high degree of coordination between products and vendors at several levels. Once the 12-step project checklist has been completed, the project team can move into the actual implementation stage, in which equipment is assembled, tested, and proven and the pilot site is brought to an operational state. The fundamental hardware and the integration elements are the foundation, including

- Boards that process voice and data channels, servers, and networks that meet specifications for high reliability and reflect mission criticality

- Middleware—the standards and open protocols that interconnect equipment from different vendors

The other major components are

- Hardware elements

- Dual networking infrastructures—phone switch and data network

- Application layer

The phone switches are usually PBXs or dedicated high-volume call-routing switches called *automatic call distributors* (ACDs). These devices are described in detail later in this chapter.

Telephone service is obviously a core component of any call center, and as carrier networks upgrade their services to deliver advanced call-processing features through the network, acquiring premise-based equipment to provide these functions is no longer required. For smaller businesses, this means that if messaging or call-routing applications are available from the network, there is a significant cost savings.

Middleware

Between the phone and data networking areas lies the middleware layer. Originally, many middleware products focused on interconnecting a single vendor switch and a single host format. Older and more widespread databases involve more complex middleware, which gave rise to many problems in implementing CTI. These problems occurred because companies with old legacy systems and extremely customized databases had to endure a difficult period of customization of switch-to-database interfaces before they could achieve the benefits of CTI. The incorporation of middleware connectivity in the switch is eliminating this technological hurdle and making call center development easier.

Application layer

The next level of product in the CTI hierarchy is the *application layer*, the software that actually makes people more productive, providing features such as messaging or speech recognition, automating salesforces, or taking orders over the Web. When considering a transition to CTI, it is important to start with a concrete idea of what the system should accomplish by identifying the applications that suit the business and then to build up and down to integrate those applications with the existing infrastructure.

Consulting services and systems integration

There are consulting services and systems integration knowledge and expertise available that can assist an organization to integrate all of the elements of CTI. Generally speaking, CTI is not an off-the-shelf system. It requires the interconnection of different technical realms that are usually managed by different departments and personnel having different mindsets and priorities. Because of the inevitable and often unforeseen problems associated with integrating the two core technologies, making CTI work can be a challenge, despite the best efforts of standards committees and vendors to make the process easier. As well, there are many things that can't be anticipated by outsiders, which is another key reason to have an internally directed plan rather than hand everything over to a consultant or a systems integrator.

Many companies need help defining the scope of what CTI should do in a business context (not just from a technical point of view). Consultants or systems integrators familiar with the business environment may be able to coordinate the entire implementation plan, help select the products from the various layers, and, if necessary, create any custom linkages or applications to suit the situation. As noted previously, vendor assistance may also be available, a resource that is becoming more viable as the vendor community develops better knowledge of CTI and its components in order to provide end-to-end coverage of the entire CTI process, from the component layer through the applications service. Vendors often set up umbrella systems through application partners from which a customer can choose a variety of applications that are precertified by the vendor to work with selected hardware.

Before deciding on implementing any computer telephony technology in the call center, the internal environment must be defined. One rule of thumb that may be applied is that *areas with high volume are going to have the highest payback when implementing open applications*.

Guidelines for the 12-point CTI project checklist

As additional support for the 12-point checklist, the following guidelines will assist call center development teams to assess and meet their requirements.

Size up your host solution

LANs, minis or mainframes? For smaller centers, a local area network can serve as the entire host side of the solution. Recently, application development and the experience of established call centers have shown that a LAN-based or client/server-based application provides more flexibility for importing telephone functions to the workstation. If there is already a mainframe or mini in place, use the existing hardware. These systems may be used as host servers and connected to workstations via local area networks, combining the flexibility of a LAN with the processing power of a mainframe.

Confirm savings and goals with vendors as part of the selection process

Before contacting vendors, evaluate the time and cost of handling a given call. Compare this information to the vendor's proposal, in order to calculate projected savings. Demand detailed projections and scenarios, and ask to speak to a few happy customers. Even among happy customers you may find some potential drawbacks to a particular system.

Consult colleagues about their call center experiences

In noncompetitive situations, colleagues can be valuable sources of information on open applications they may have implemented.

Start over or improve on existing applications?

If a call center is being upgraded, many applications can be integrated without difficulty into an open CTI environment. For example, an application that calls up customer profile information by having the CSR key in the customer's Social Security number can be replaced using ANI in which the open application automatically summons the field to the agent's screen by replacing the Social Security number with a home phone number. Many open applications, like predictive dialing engines, are more efficient or economical if purchased as turnkey applications. In this situation, it is more practical to keep the existing application than to attempt to adapt a new one.

Develop a test program

There are two ways to test computer telephony applications prior to full implementation. Dummy applications are available that simulate call traffic, the workforce, the planned equipment, network services, and application programs. A test region can also be made available on the host platform where pilot tests can be run while changes are being made and load analysis is being performed. Many telecom managers prefer to phase in the new regime gradually using such separate testing areas, for example, phasing in 10 or 20% of the customer base, then gradually broadening the application to include the entire base throughout the call center.

Avoid fancy features that do not really contribute to productivity

Some CTI applications can perform feats so stunning that even the most conservative telecom center manager can get carried away.

Provide appropriate training for CSRs

Plan and organize training sessions, coordinated by the applications developer, on new applications well in advance of the installation so that CSRs can master them before they are implemented. Keep in mind that the introduction of automation into any process involving human resources means fewer employees are required. Perhaps the budget will permit the diversion of CSRs to a larger support group or complaint division; otherwise, the call center workforce may have to be reduced through attrition or layoffs.

Be prepared to implement new evaluation criteria for CSRs

If an application incorporates a voice response unit, for example, the unit will handle most of the simple inquiries without any live intervention. This means that CSRs will handle only the more difficult calls, and therefore the duration of calls fielded by CSRs will increase while the number of calls handled will decrease.

Conduct reality checks

Evaluate each new application 3 months after it is in place and again in 12 months to determine if cost savings have been achieved. It is relatively easy to calculate lower toll-free usage and the savings resulting from fewer CSRs staffing phones, but other benefits are more difficult to gauge. For example, in an insurance application, it is difficult to determine how many new policies have been purchased simply because the CSR was able to transfer both the data file and the screen immediately from the life insurance division to the accident group. These reality checks may require altering long-distance contracts, CSR scheduling, and even computer capacity to accommodate a changed call processing environment to generate real cost savings. Incorporating changes of this nature will result in a faster return on investment. The experience of some call center users indicates that the payback period on investment ranges from 9 to 16 months.

Summarizing the Benefits

A properly planned and implemented integration of computer and telephone technology can provide several specific benefits to organizations, including

- Providing more timely access to information

- Enabling the sharing of current and new information

- More effectively communicating and presenting that information

- Allowing more timely response to information requests

2.6   Automatic call distribution (ACD)

Automatic call distribution is a function performed by several components—software and hardware—in a call center. ACD essentially involves taking incoming calls and moving them to the right place—the CSR's desktop computer screen. Behind this simple description of the function of an automatic call distributor are a number of underlying processes and technologies, including

- Voice mail systems

- Auto-attendant routing

- CTI

- IVR

- Public networks

- Workforce management software

(see Figure 2.8)

Managing information effectively with ACDs

As call centers have evolved, a number of changes have affected the ACD and its functions. The ACD is responsible for more than moving or routing calls; it also *manages the information associated with those calls.* The ACD function is performed by a variety of different kinds of processors.

The following ACD options are offered by vendors:

- Traditional PBX with either internal ACD software or external server-based software

- Stand-alone ACD

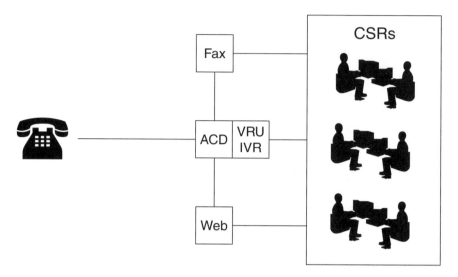

Figure 2.8
Communicating
with a call contact
center through an
ACD.

- Multifunctional contact handling system

- Hosted software ACD

- VoIP-integrated platform with ACD

At the low end is the PBX with built-in ACD that routes calls to CSRs. This function may also be performed by a software application. Calls may also be routed within carrier networks, using the intelligence built into these networks. The ACD, however, is the real engine of productivity and the single piece of technology that can make the call center effective and productive for inbound sales, order taking, and customer service. The ACD enables call volumes to escalate intelligently, in increasingly specialized complexity. It is not simply a call-routing feature, it is the *nerve center and control point* for the call center, for both inbound and outbound voice calls and data traffic. It is a call center's arbiter: setting priorities and alerting supervisors to patterns and crossed thresholds.

ACDs: all shapes and sizes

ACD functionality is available in a wide range of telephone switches that vary in size and sophistication. Earlier versions of ACDs were very specific types of telephone switches with highly specialized features and particularly robust call-processing capabilities that served at least 100 stations (or extensions). One of the primary applications was in airline reservation centers.

Among the various types of ACDs available to the modern call center are the following:

- PC-based ACDs
- Key systems with ACD functions
- Key systems integrated with a computer and software to create a full-featured ACD
- PBXs with sophisticated ACD functions
- Stand-alone ACDs that serve centers with less than 30 CSRs
- Traditional stand-alone ACDs—usually the most sophisticated
- ACDs integrated with other call center technologies
- Nationwide networks of ACDs

ACD functions and features

There is simply no technology more suited to routing a large number of inbound calls to a large number of people than an ACD. The ACD ensures that calls are answered as quickly as possible, and it can provide special services for selected customers. ACDs are capable of handling call rates and volumes far exceeding human capabilities and the capabilities of other telecom switches. They provide a high degree of call-processing horsepower and augment human resources very effectively. An ACD provides the resources to manage the many parts of the call center, from telephone trunks to CSR stations and from callers to CSRs and other staff members.

Despite the availability of all of these call-handling options in a variety of open and modular products, some organizations still prefer an expensive, stand-alone ACD in their call centers, for two reasons:

1. *Power*—a first-tier stand-alone system has a tremendous call-processing power, and no other product is so uniquely suited to meeting the needs of the larger megacenters found in the reservations or financial service sectors.

2. *Technology*—integration with other call center systems, IVR, data warehouses, and intranets is significantly easier with a powerhouse ACD. This is also true for multisite networking and skills-based routing, two of the most popular inbound features.

Smaller systems—PC-ACDs and PBX/ACD hybrids—which account for much of the industry's phenomenal growth in small centers, have their place in the range of call center solutions. However, for high-volume applications there is no substitute for the call-managing power of the stand-alone ACD.

Vendors are providing stand-alone ACDs in several different ways. Some acquire the technology envelope with their switches, while others concentrate on software development to add value to the core switch. Still others are paying more attention to integration with third-party call center technologies like the Internet and IVR. Some are adapting their switches to smaller, departmental call centers in an effort to capture some market share in this call center segment. The benefit to the user community is that there are a number of options available from vendors for installing ACD functionality.

New challenges for the ACD

The role of the ACD is changing because of two significant, current trends in call center operations. ACDs are required to channel more information, of many different kinds, in more directions. In earlier call center models, the ACD handled two kinds of information: the call itself and raw log information about the total number of calls. To analyze this data using a PC and software, call details were provided from a special port.

Call center managers need information in a form that makes it easy to understand and analyze. Vendors have added data management modules to the high-end ACD, and there are many outside programs that can connect to the ACD and transfer data in and out. These modules provide two key functions:

- Workforce management tools that forecast loads

- Software systems that convert real-time and historical data into any required format

Along with these new tools, supervisors are now able to modify the ACD while it is in operation, to accomplish such functions as creating groups "on the fly," moving calls and personnel around, and monitoring quality.

Alternative methods of call delivery

Another dynamic change concerns the kinds of calls the system has to route. Call centers have been integrating ACDs with IVR and fax communication for a long time. Systems now have to integrate Websites and the Internet with calls that come in from PCs and that terminate in databases instead of with CSRs. As a result, the call center is now being referred to by a broader, more appropriate term that better describes its enhanced scope and current role in this age of technology: *the contact center for customer communication*, which recognizes that the transaction between the customer and the company is what is important, not the communication medium and the process that carries the transaction.

Skills-based routing

Skills-based routing is another advanced feature that has changed the role of the ACD. This feature was added by switch designers because it was an interesting and available technology that could be added easily to a switch, not because call centers were clamoring for it. Unfortunately, it has taken a long time for call centers to understand and to derive benefit from this feature, because skills-based routing has some negative aspects involving the proper use of workforce management software. Nevertheless, skills-based routing is a very interesting advanced technology for distributing calls handled by an ACD. Traditional routing is based on two factors—an equitable distribution of calls among available agents and the random nature of incoming calls. Skills-based routing changes this by routing calls to the "best-qualified" CSR, using individual call center parameters to define this attribute.

The ACD routes calls in two stages, the first being to identify the needs of the caller using some front-end technology. This operation is usually accomplished through a DNIS, ANI, or an IVR system. Once the caller is identified, the information is matched against the sets of CSR skill groups. Two advances in ACD technology allow skills-based routing to operate effectively:

- Leaving a call in an initial queue while simultaneously and continuously checking other CSR groups for availability

- Allowing a CSR to be logged on to more than one skills group at a time, assigning priorities to those groups by skill type

Corporate requirements to link call centers together into multisite call center networks have caused changes in call routing to be implemented at a faster pace. This development can be viewed as an extension of skills-based routing, because in some situations, it is not enough to select the best available agent; it may be desirable to select the best available agent at the most appropriate location, based on factors such as

- Skill clusters

- Call priority

- Time of day

- Traffic at one or more sites

Requirements for small centers

Small call centers may have different needs than large ones, and they may have financial and human resource limitations. For those centers that cannot afford an expensive, stand-alone ACD, call routing is available as part of the PBX configuration, thus making the same tools available to these facilities as to larger call centers. A smaller call center within a larger customer service center, such as the 5- to 10-person collections department in a larger company, is an example of this type of application. The CSR needs are the same as those of CSRs in larger centers, and advances and refinements in call center technology, as well as economies of scale in electronics manufacturing processes, now enable these smaller centers to take advantage of state-of-the-art features at a reasonable, affordable cost that will be within their budgets.

In addition, staff members in these smaller departments are not always dedicated to call center functions and roles. They need flexible solutions that build on the systems already in place and that also provide room to grow. For these situations, the PC-based ACD, a new type of call-handling system, is available. The previously mentioned new-found openness of switch vendors has resulted in the development of these products, making possible a host of software products that add ACD features to key systems and hybrid switches.

ACD rules of thumb

It is less expensive to incorporate ACD features into an existing business phone system—there is no capital expenditure on a large piece of hardware. There are also rules of thumb for the number of agents per ACD. At the level of 6 CSRs, or even up to 30 agents, it is difficult to justify large ACDs. However, systems and products are much more flexible than they used to be, and it is now relatively easy to integrate top-notch systems like interactive voice response or voice mail, giving a small center a very professional appearance to customers.

Another feature critical to call center operations is third-party call control. Third-party call control can, for example, provide special treatment to customers based on the language they speak and call routing can be accomplished based on skill sets or on time of day for full 24-hour coverage. Using the PC, it is not difficult to set up a rules-based system for directing the right call to the right CSR. This has become a low-end solution for small call centers.

The PBX/ACD allows an organization to implement a call center in stages; however, a low-end ACD in a PBX switch will only allow a facility to grow to a certain point—here the rule of thumb is about 50 CSRs. At this point, it will be necessary to explore larger, stand-alone ACDs. Low-end systems should be evaluated for their upgrade capabilities. Vendors can now offer systems that can be upgraded smoothly in stages, a result of their efforts to capture some share of the small call center market. PC/ACDs or PBX/ACDs may handle smaller centers—typically, 10 to 15 CSRs—very well, placing them on the same technological level as bigger centers. Organizations that already have in-house PBXs can experiment with available ACD software. A commonly used technique is to convert a few users, and if this conversion works well, to expand the availability of the ACD function to other CSRs.

In addition, there are software products available (see Appendix A) that allow overflow patterns to be set among multiple small groups and that also allow these parameters to be changed quickly, with a minimum of software knowledge. These systems do not deliver the same functionality as a dedicated ACD, but in many situations that is not necessary. Departmental needs differ—for example, few need multisite routing—and department heads may need reports on sales and costs rather than call traffic.

It is interesting to note that many small "call centers" have not realized that they are call centers! Once they are recognized as call centers, these facilities, need the same kind of technologies that larger ones have been using for several years. After all, customers demand the same high service standards, no matter how big or how small the organization. The small-scale ACD solution allows small organizations to obtain a much higher level of customer relationship management at a reasonable cost.

Networking ACDs

One change in switching technology is the use of the network itself as a platform for queuing and routing even after a call has been answered. Call-routing systems that let the call center perform ACD-style call flow manipulations directly within the network are available from some vendors. This system works well with a variety of phone switches and carrier networks. It has the advantage of turning a collection of linked calls into a true, single "virtual" center. The switch data is processed by intelligent query services, which direct the carrier where to send the call before it enters the switchboard. Network-based call routing works in conjunction with routing schemes that may already be in use, such as CSR skills and time-based routing, ANI, or caller-entered information, just as if the CSRs were working with a single-site ACD. Networking also allows these techniques to be applied across varied and remote sites.

Another approach to networking ACDs is the use of software-based products with ISDN (integrated services digital network) to provide full ACD features to CSRs wherever they are required. This technology directs calls to geographically dispersed locations from within the public network and does not require dedicated T1 links or ACDs.

Carrier networks can provide many features, including off-site transaction processing and call routing. A long-term goal of carrier organizations is to replace on-premises equipment with network infrastructures that provide the same capabilities, thereby growing their business by making it possible for them to obtain additional revenue from the value added by network features.

Switching and routing systems

Suppliers of switching and routing systems for call centers are numerous. Some of the major vendor organizations are listed in Appendix A, with special emphasis on those vendors that have established reputations for supplying reliable, proven call center products and for being market leaders, as reflected by their commitment to develop new features and seek out third-party partners. These organizations have also captured significant market share.

Among the capabilities offered are those that allow customers to use a broader range of software applications, including some that appeal to the smaller department or distributed call centers. These products enable the linking of multiple integrated application modules (IAMs) from the main unit to create a chain of interconnected applications, all processing customer communication in tandem. Some of these software products also provide a construction and maintenance tool that places call-routing templates on a single drag-and-drop desktop, including such things as IVR integration and call delivery channels from multiple media.

A newer tool that has come on the market for the growing e-commerce/ Internet call center activity is a real-time, browser-based information sharing tool that can be added to a call center for about $1,000 per CSR, including CTI connectivity. These products enable the person on either side of a Web transaction to navigate though different pages and allow the CSR to guide the customer through a series of screens according to a script. In this scenario, the product works through a choice of multimedia options, including a desktop IP connection, Web-based text chat, or a traditional two-line callback using the public network.

Open system products

One of the most important aspects of some of the more recent call center products, from a user perspective, is that they are "open system" products. This means that they will work with other ACDs, interface on the network side with existing IT and telecom infrastructures, and are easy to integrate into existing systems. The advantage to "Webifying" an existing call center seat is that it allows the organization to leverage trained CSRs and equipment to sell existing products, no matter how complex, to a "Web lurker," who might not even have been an overt caller. Converting these Web lurkers into callers is the first step in turning them into customers.

Some vendor organizations are attempting to assemble an end-to-end, all-in-one call center system. The concept of the "call center in a box" has been popular for some time; however, the complexity and variety of call center technologies make it unlikely that a single vendor will be able to create and "shrink-wrap" a complete hardware and software application to meet all call center requirements. What has evolved in the marketplace is a collection of integrated applications from which to choose that are certified to meet the required specifications under the management and control of a single vendor.

Competition among switch vendors serving the call center market has created a growing portfolio of technology that is often very interesting and innovative but does not really meet real-world functional requirements and therefore has not become part of the established set of operational tools. Among the examples of this exotic technology are some that have been discussed previously, including skills-based routing and universal agent blending; "call-me" buttons on Web pages are also in this category. The more exotic technology has not found a place in call center operations because of the many operational and cultural hurdles to their implementation and application in real-life call centers.

The considerable degree of competition among vendors on product features and the high cost of development have also led larger companies to add value to their switch products through aggressive acquisition strategies. Small companies find a multivendor environment very costly; they must spend huge sums of money on marketing to bring their products to the attention of call centers. Under these circumstances, partnerships among vendors proliferate.

2.7   The Internet in the call center

A discussion of networks in the call center would not be complete without mentioning the significance and dramatic growth of the largest and most extensive network in the world—the Internet—which is available to the public and becoming increasingly important to the business community. It is hard to grasp how the Internet became so important to business in such a short time, and how dramatically it has changed many of the rules of conducting business. It has provided alternatives for how to work, where to work, how to communicate, how to keep informed, and how to communicate with customers. All of these aspects of the Internet have an impact on call center operations.

Customers have choices for how they communicate, and there are a number of them—some would say too many! There will always be some companies that want to stick to the older business models, but they will gradually be replaced because they will no longer be competitive. (see Figure 2.9)

Figure 2.9
Multidimensional customer contact.

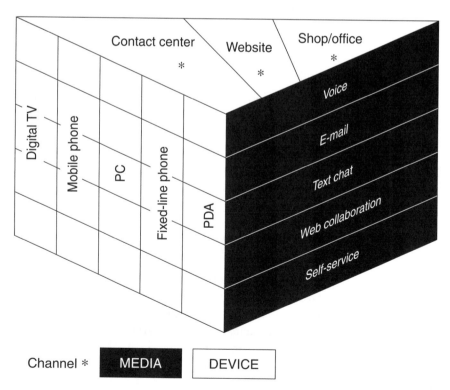

In the context of the Internet, the call center is revolutionary. Call centers are automated service delivery points, full of customer data and products, dedicated to one major objective: providing customers with whatever services or products they require. How does the Internet fit into the call center model? It is just one more communication channel for the customer, a channel that call centers need to manage at least as well as traditional communication channels.

The Internet is a relatively low-cost communication channel, easy to establish and manage and using many of the same network and communication infrastructures as the traditional communication channels. It provides a range of opportunities to CSRs operating from sites remote from the "home" call center and to customers with Internet connections on their home and office desktops. In this "cyberworld," each customer has the equivalent of the CSR terminal and can be provided with the same information as the CSR. However, CSRs must be in place to assist and guide customers who want to talk to a real person. The CSR represents the company's interests in a sales transaction and may pull or push the customer toward a product and (possibly) away from a problem. Customers usually need guidance at some point in a transaction, no matter how much information they have obtained from a Website. There may be confusing options or other procedures to be followed that need explaining, and the CSR can assure customers that their needs will be looked after.

Integrating the Internet into the call center

What is the best method for integrating the Internet into a call center that was designed as a telephony contact center? There are several options. The help desk was the first stage in the process in some companies. E-mail was a natural way to provide technical support to customers, enabling them to register their problems and track them as they were resolved. A second stage of integration occurred when the Internet became a tool for distributing technical documents to a wide community of problem solvers, sometimes including customers. This stage occurred in the late 1990s, when the Web had not yet reached predominance and was still not being considered in the planning for a call center. The e-mail model remains the basis for most real-life combinations of call centers and the Internet. It is the primary form of communication used by the Internet customer and the major form of non-telephony interactions in the center.

One of the problems in integrating the Internet and the call center is coordinating the multiple streams of input that are now available to callers.

If an unhappy customer sends an e-mail describing a problem and, after an hour or so without a response, then calls a CSR and begins all over, what happens to service statistics? Current generations of customer information systems can handle this situation, but in the early days of the Internet in the call center, it upset service statistics and caused problems for the help desk manager. One model of interaction based on the Internet gets around the problem of coordination. It involves customers who click on Websites to request either a call back or to initiate an Internet-based phone call with a CSR. The logic in this process is sound—the customer is already armed with information about the transaction, the reason the information is placed on a Website in the first place. This model can result in good customer interaction if the CSR is in the right place with customer information, if the telephony part of the transaction works perfectly, and if the call is placed within a reasonable time frame.

The products that make interaction over the Internet possible are examples of leading-edge technology that push the boundaries. Unfortunately, the vendor community is still in the process of integrating them into systems that work in the daily life of a call center. As time goes on, these applications will sort out into those that work and those that don't, and eventually some of them will find a place in call center operations.

Text-based interaction

Real-time, text-based interaction also demonstrates the power and capability of the Internet in the call center. In this scenario, a caller connects to a Website and asks for a CSR's assistance using a chat window. Removing the hardware and bandwidth necessary for voice communication permits live interaction, or what at least appears live to the caller. One benefit is that the CSR in the center can handle multiple callers at once because of the delay inherent in chat mode and can use scripts to speed up responses. The CSR is also able to guide the caller to a particular Web screen, share information, and participate fully in bringing a transaction to a successful close. Another, major benefit of this model is that the Internet/call center connection is moved from the service side to the sales side, and at a level of technology that is available to smaller companies. CSRs can guide a Web surfer to a sale or the next level of the sales process at the same cost savings as the more complex "call-me button" model of Web interaction. This is also one of the features available in call center/Internet integration but one yet to be accepted by call center managers, for reasons noted earlier.

The choice of which of the several methods of integrating the Internet into the call center for each organization will depend on several factors: the

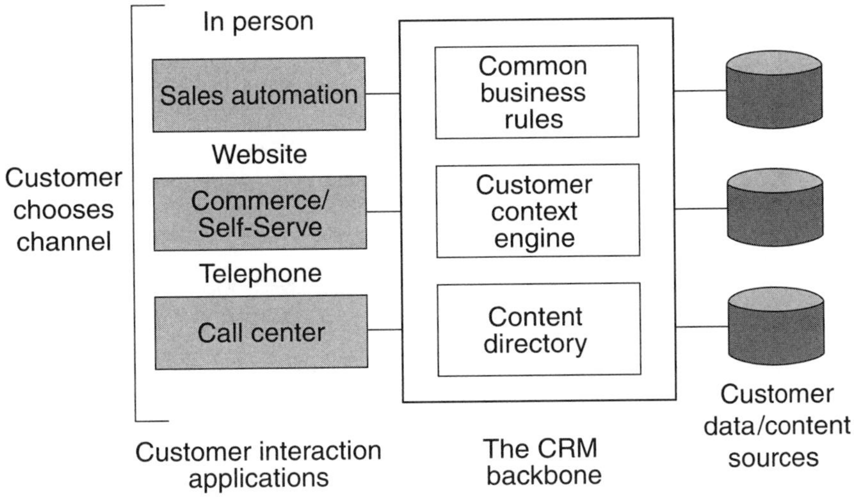

Figure 2.10
Data sources and customer interactions.

resources available, the comfort level with transitional technology, and, most importantly, the relationship between a company and its customers. (see Figure 2.10)

2.8   Database management technology

This section provides an overview of database management systems, in particular the relational database management systems (RDBMS) that are a component of most data warehousing systems, the technology that enables vast amounts of customer data to be stored, some of which will ultimately end up on the CSR's screen in a call center. This overview is not intended to be a definitive or detailed analysis of database technology; however, it does provide some selection criteria for and characteristics of this technology. The material is included in this book to illustrate its importance in the overall process of providing customer information to call centers.

Data mining, the process of extracting customer data from the data warehouse, is also reviewed and described, as is the importance of ensuring that only "clean" data are provided to the data warehouse.

Database management software is the technology that manages the data stored in the data warehouse and provides the tools for accessing and querying the data. In combination with the data warehouse, the repository of customer transaction data, this technology enables organizations to store, access, and manipulate customer data and to provide call center CSRs access to the data. (see Figure 2.11)

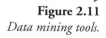

Figure 2.11
Data mining tools.

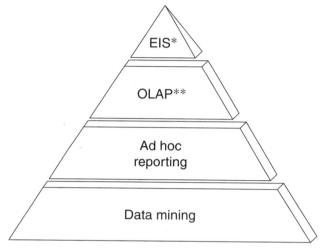

*Executive information systems   **On-line analytical processing

Database alternatives

There are several viable database management systems used in data warehousing. However, as is typical of the IT sector, vendors often offer products that are in the final development stages and ready for first release. There are, therefore, usually implementation glitches and code that doesn't work in these products.

Determining database requirements is one of the critical areas of data warehousing, and the impact of their selection will filter down to the call center, one way or another. Organizations often tend to select a database with the rationale that it is the "company standard," because it is expedient and it eliminates the need for support IS staff to learn another database. However, the selection of database products should follow the same rigorous evaluation process as for any other IT product. Database management software should be selected on its own merits, that is, because it meets the objectives of the type of data warehouse to be implemented—*operational data warehouse* or *informational data warehouse*—and for its contribution to the corporate CRM strategy.

Most RDBMSs are based on on-line transaction processing. These products can handle operational data warehouses and have short but high transactional volumes, a response time requirement, and a very limited amount of historical data. These characteristics contrast very clearly with database requirements for the informational data warehouse, which has low transactional volumes, no real response-time requirement, and a large amount of historical data. The access characteristics of these two data warehouse environments are completely different. Database management systems need to differentiate between these two types of data warehouses, so it is important when selecting the RDBMS to be aware of its architecture for providing effective data access to either or even both data warehouse configurations.

Data mining

Data mining and analytical tools, in combination with the data warehouse and database management technology, assist in increasing the return on investment (ROI) on stored customer data. In addition, they allow organizations to understand customer behavior patterns, rather than just grouping or segmenting them according to products they buy, age, or other personal characteristics, and highlight cross-selling opportunities and pinpoint the most profitable client profiles. These characteristics of the RDBMS are important to call center CSRs because they determine the ease of access and the usefulness of the customer data they will use in their day-to-day activities.

Integrating customer data and the call center

The information that can be gathered from the data warehouse and the RDBMS should form a ready source of customer data for the call center as well as provide information to marketing and salesforce automation programs. Conversely, customer information obtained in the call center should be continually fed back into the data repository. The more integrated the process, the closer the organization is to achieving one of the key objectives of a CRM strategy: *a single view of the customer throughout the organization.*

Data standards

Standards are necessary for the data stored in the data warehouse—consistent formatting reduces complications for data extraction. Ensuring that the highest quality of data is provided at the input stage promotes acceptance of the data and develops a high degree of confidence in it. Many corporate CRM strategies are thwarted by faulty, inconsistent data that prevent users from having a clear, unified profile of each customer. Disjointed data, blanks in some of the critical fields, and broken business rules are a few of the ways in which data can be corrupted, resulting in data integrity problems.

Integrating customer datasets is a challenge for any organization that wants to achieve a single view of the customer. Various departments—call centers, ordering, shipping, manufacturing, sales, and marketing—have customer contact and therefore customer information to contribute to the database. In a typical financial institution or insurance company, for example, there could be 50 to 150 different systems containing customer data. To have a single view of each customer to establish value levels and to meet customer needs, this data must be combined and integrated. Combining and integrating data to obtain a complete, current customer profile requires assembling different data stores, with data of varying ages, on different databases, and usually involving multiple programming languages and data formats. Vendor software is available that can assist in assembling and profiling data, as well as analyzing data before it gets stored in the data warehouse. Typically, these products locate different relationships in customer data from multiple sources, irrespective of source code and documentation, and provide information on how to clean and restructure the data.

Data clustering

Cluster analysis is an exploratory data analysis tool that uses statistical algorithms to identify distinct groups of customers that may not traditionally group together. It is used in segmentation not only to independently validate business assumptions but also to discover new interrelationships between variables that were previously not associated. This technique may be useful in call centers that have an outbound call requirement that targets certain demographics in a customer population.

2.9   Summary

This chapter has provided a detailed description of several important call center technologies, the features and services they provide, and the benefits they offer to call center operations. One thing that stands out about technology is that it is in a constant stage of transition, and today's advanced technology may be passé tomorrow. For call center developers and mangers, it is important to maintain an open mind on technology and to be always ready to examine, evaluate, and implement appropriate technologies that will assist in meeting call center and corporate CRM strategies.

3

Organizing and Managing the Call Center

You don't know what you don't know until you know it… the right solution is a continuous search for the right solution.

Dr. Ichak Adizes

3.1   Overview

The turn of the 20th century was the dawn of a new age in communications. A few decades earlier, in 1876, the telephone had been invented and telephone service was proliferating rapidly. As telephone services expanded, the public began to depend on and even expect reliable service from telecommunication providers.

As the subscriber base grew, telephone companies were contending with new resource-planning problems. Automated central offices hadn't yet been invented, so human operators were required to establish connections for callers. One big question was how many telephone operators were necessary to run the switchboard. Too few and service levels would be unacceptable to callers. But too many would be inefficient for telephone companies and would drive up costs for subscribers. Further complicating the issue was the fact that calls arrived randomly, driven by the myriad of motivations individual callers had for placing calls. (see Figure 3.1)

In the years that followed, many bright people would grapple with these resource-management challenges. One of the first was A. K. Erlang, an engineer with the Copenhagen Telephone Company, who in 1917 developed the queuing formula Erlang C. The formula is still widely used today in incoming call centers for calculating staffing requirements and is described in greater detail later in this chapter. Others who followed Erlang focused on developing disciplined forecasting techniques, scheduling methodologies, and system report parameters; advances in the development of forecasting and scheduling methodologies continue to be made.

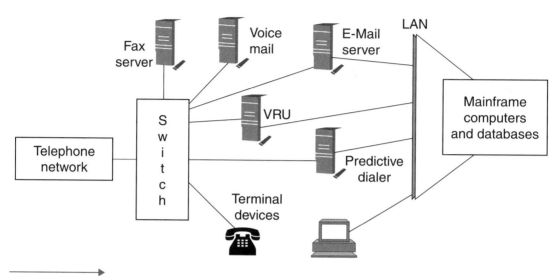

Figure 3.1   *Typical call center infrastructure.*

The management challenge

Managing a call center operation successfully requires a multitude of skills—managerial, troubleshooting, negotiating, and patience, not to mention a personality that works well under pressure and is able to handle the different types of CSRs who will work at the facility over time. Some familiarity with computer and communications technologies is an asset as well, although most internal call center facilities should have ready access to technical support for resolving hardware, software, and communications problems. The steady growth in the call center industry over the past 10 years has resulted in a requirement for new job-related management skills. As call center personnel have developed these skills, the position of call center manager has evolved and is now a portable, definable position, recognized from company to company and across different sectors of industry.

The global growth of call centers as a significant element of customer-centered business has led to the employment of a large number of people in call centers, estimated to be between 3 and 4 million, in North America alone. From a labor market perspective, the industry is not saturated, since the growth of call centers outpaces the supply of employees. Historically, the industry has had a difficult time attracting a steady supply of qualified workers. Turnover in the call center industry is a major problem as well. Turnover rates are significantly higher than those of other industries. A recent benchmarking study of call centers by the Purdue University Center for Customer-Driven Quality found that turnover is an industrywide problem. The survey revealed that inbound centers have an average annual turnover of 26% for full-time reps and 33% for part-timers. Nearly half of the centers said that part-timers handle 5% or less of their total calls.

This book cannot solve the turnover problem, nor can it make more employees available to the call center industry. However, in the context of the axiom that *"good management of human resources means happy, long-term employees,"* the guidelines and experiences of successful call center managers, as presented in this chapter and in Chapter 5 can assist new and existing call centers to manage the human resources that are so essential to their success.

Rising staff costs

Faced with the requirement of generating a profit, many businesses confront a major problem: rising staff costs. Over the next few years, management of call/contact center staff will move to the forefront of corporate concerns because

- The average call/contact center spends between 60 and 70% of its annual budget on staff salary.

- Globally, agent turnover rates average 22%, and approach 50% in some industries.

- Staff absenteeism is increasing and is as high as 17% in the health care industry, 10% in the telecommunications and consumer products markets, and averages 9% across all vertical markets.

- Over 80% of companies use external advertisements to search for agents and 72% use recruitment agencies, both of which involve significant costs.

- Call/contact center location clustering is increasing and has caused severe shortages of qualified staff in places such as Dublin (Ireland), Omaha, Nebraska (United States), New Brunswick (Canada), and Amsterdam (The Netherlands). In most countries with major call/contact center clusters, recruitment is becoming very difficult.

- There has been a rapid increase in the growth of the call/contact center industry.

- The growth of CRM and multimedia interaction will require skilled and experienced agents, and training costs will increase accordingly.

3.2   Management guidelines for a productive call center

Call centers need to tread the thin line between improving service, sales, and revenue on the one hand and controlling costs on the other. When the proper balance is struck by effective management of the call center, the result will be a company that is more efficient and more productive on all levels. To achieve these dual objectives, the cost of hiring, training, and measuring the performance of CSRs needs to be managed carefully.

The significant contribution of the human element to the success or failure of a call center operation, and the statistics just described, present call center managers with the following human resource challenges:

- Hiring competent, skilled CSRs

- Establishing competitive salary ranges

- Motivating and retaining CSRs

- Measuring CSR performance

- Maintaining CSR skills through appropriate training

This chapter focuses on the management aspects of call centers, including workforce management practices and processes, including CSR monitoring and performance measurement, call center structure, outsourcing resources, operator scheduling, and contingency and disaster recovery planning.

Chapter 4, "Selecting and Training Call Center Staff," provides insight into and more specific guidelines for another human resource aspect of call center management—staff selection and training—and the application of proven management techniques to ensure a productive call center environment and the effective management of the all-important human resource.

Workforce management systems (WFM)

One of the most important tools available to call center managers is the *workforce management system* (*WFM*). However, despite the wealth of technology available to manage call center operations and the critical nature of workforce management, workforce management systems are used in only about 10% of call centers, according to industry sources and surveys conducted over the past few years.

The first WFM applications were relatively unsophisticated compared to current products; however, they significantly reduced the time required to do simple agent scheduling. These applications were fed data from the ACD but were normally stand-alone solutions with limited or no integration, which meant the call center scheduler did not have a particularly accurate picture of what needed to be done. The WFM system did not improve the call center managers' knowledge so much as it assisted them in reaching similar conclusions more quickly.

Workforce management in the call center has been defined as *"the art and science of having the right number of CSRs available at the right time, to answer an accurately forecasted volume of incoming calls at the desired service level, with quality."* A number of software products are available to accomplish this objective, and their capability to accurately predict call volume and then staff accordingly is very attractive. More call centers should incorporate this software tool to make the task easier. The 10% of call centers that do use workforce management software are among the most advanced call center operations, with high call volumes, extensive use of technology, and high productivity levels. There are reasons why many centers do not use these productivity products, however, including the following.

Cost

WFM can be expensive; systems that predict call volume and match staff schedules to that volume can cost between $50,000 and $100,000 or more.

High maintenance

The perception that a fully configured WFM system requires scheduling, feeding data in, going over the data that comes out, and providing full-time supervision of the system may be true in some cases. When a system is complex, more training is required to run it, especially when scheduling and predicting are required across multiple sites.

Cultural barriers

Greater market penetration faces "cultural" barriers, in this case, the culture of the traditional call center where more emphasis is placed on managing the call and its flow through the system than on managing the workforce.

Limited promotion of WFM product capabilities

Companies that develop and supply WFM software have not provided a complete description of the benefits, perhaps because these vendors do not see the need, or because they do not have the level of competency or industry experience to appreciate the need.

Complexity

The disparity between the actual complexity required to develop the best possible schedule and the apparent simplicity of creating a schedule is often not recognized.

Call center managers have a range of options for creating a schedule, from a manual, back-of-the envelope calculation to using formulas in a simple spreadsheet with a special calculator to input the center's variables to ultimately using a five- or six-figure full-fledged computer program. Achieving the highest level of workforce productivity does require some powerful software, and it will be expensive.

Workforce management systems for multimedia centers

WFM solutions will become a key CRM-enabling technology in the multimedia call/contact center. It is an application that may provide a solution to both agent attrition and multimedia staffing. Businesses will be able to provide the right agents to the right customer and to leverage customer segmentation for a superior level of customer service. Without a means of accurately forecasting how much human resource will be needed to keep customers and agents satisfied while keeping costs to a minimum, businesses could have every sophisticated e-application available but fail to reach an acceptable service level.

The cost of running a contact/call center is considerable in most enterprises, and the center traditionally has been viewed as a cost center—a necessary evil. This perception has resulted in keeping expenditures on technology, people, and business processes to a minimum. The advent of the CRM approach and its impact on call centers, and vice versa, have meant that leading businesses in sectors such as financial services, retail, and telecommunications are beginning to view their contact centers as profit generators. Revenue growth is encouraged through cross selling and upselling support, and costs are kept low through implementing solutions such as IVR, predictive dialers, and other technologies that have been developed to streamline call center operations.

In the multimedia contact center, as in the traditional call center, the aim of workforce management software is to have the right agents available to help customers at the right time. A sophisticated yet easy-to-use solution, this software has become one of the most useful tools currently available to a call/contact center manager, from both the customer satisfaction and agent retention perspectives. Although WFM is not a total solution, it enables the business to resource the center as it wishes. The key attribute of superior workforce management software is its flexibility, particularly in a multimedia environment. The advent of CRM and multimedia customer contacts means that WFM is destined to play an increasingly important role in most major call/contact centers, supporting both the management of multimedia interactions and also allowing businesses to focus on customers' needs and resource the center effectively.

As previously noted, despite a relatively low profile in the past, interest in workforce management solutions has begun to grow. Leading companies are learning that there are major savings to be realized with WFM as well as opportunities to increase customer and agent satisfaction in a relatively cost-effective manner. Before WFM became available, call center managers spent days at a time working out agent staffing schedules with only a computer spreadsheet to help. A complex task requiring a great degree of skill to perform, the schedule was prone to error through last-minute changes of circumstance, lack of historical data, or plain human mistakes. Even when successfully accomplished, the level of detail and accuracy in the schedule often left something to be desired.

Advanced WFM to support multimedia and CRM

The primary reason for implementing a new workforce management solution in a call/contact center operation is multimedia contact and CRM. There is much more to implementing a multimedia contact center than simply offering e-mail and various flavors of live CSR assistance. In terms of cost and service levels, if a corporation is not able to support the new channels adequately, it would be better to offer only telephony. (see Figure 3.2) Similarly, a business determined to become CRM-focused must be aware of how it will be perceived by its customers if it promotes the use of new customer contact channels but does not maintain them.

One of the most interesting and important aspects of these new channels, from a call/contact center management viewpoint, is that they are outside traditional telephony queue theory. Multichannel and multidevice interactions—for example, those initiated by a phone call but requiring e-mail and Web collaboration to be completed successfully—mean that interaction management has suddenly become more complex.

Many companies invite customers to contact them by e-mail and then treat this channel of contact much as though it was an eye-catching postal address on correspondence. If these companies then fail to support the

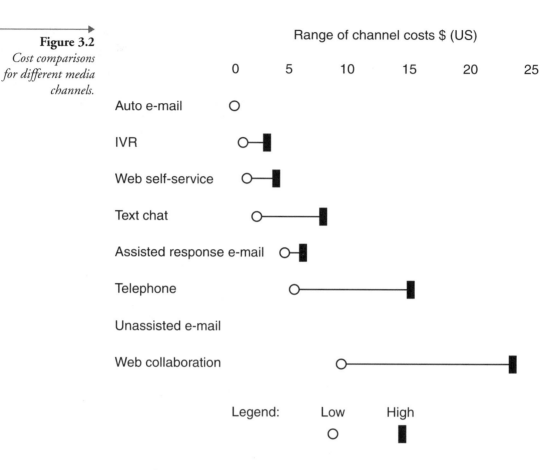

Figure 3.2
Cost comparisons for different media channels.

channel, then 70% of customer mail ends up in the dead letter department! Workforce management systems offer a very important solution to the challenge of providing and supporting superior levels of service across every channel.

The workforce management cycle

Fulfilling service levels while managing costs is an iterative cycle that requires several key processes to be completed. Feedback secured from each stage allows the enterprise to continually improve its efficiency and become more confident about its predictions. (see Figure 3.3) Workforce management systems should offer the following functionalities to support the modern customer-focused enterprise:

- Scheduling to meet service levels
- Adherence

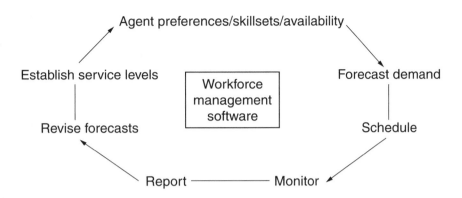

Figure 3.3
*Workforce
management cycle.*

- Reporting and forecasting
- What-if scenarios
- Virtual contact center/multisite support
- Compliance with employment law, rules, and union regulations
- Multimedia support
- Web-driven interfaces and tools

Scheduling to meet service levels

Scheduling is not as simple a process as it may appear. Knowledgeable organizations take CSR preferences and skill sets into account when scheduling. The "warm-body" approach to solving human resource issues—regarding one CSR the same as any other—will cause both agent-satisfaction and customer-service problems. Most companies using advanced workforce management software will have between 6 and 9 skillsets to work with, although a few contact centers use as many as 50. Business needs must come first, however, so a scheduler needs to find the best way to match the company's requirements with the skills of its employees. Scheduling can get particularly complicated in a multimedia environment, which usually has CSRs with multiple media-handling skills—voice, e-mail, text chat, and so on—and multiple business abilities such as sales, service product knowledge, and languages. Businesses must look for a solution that does not oversimplify the scheduling process, yet retains usability and the flexibility to make changes.

Prior to planning staffing resources, an organization needs to have an understanding of past history. A WFM system that provides historical data from all customer contacts, based on input from CTI as well as the ACD, means that scheduling can be more realistic. The WFM solution should enable organizations to factor in exceptions that affect staff workload—advertising campaigns, training, public holidays, and other special events and occasions—and determine the best time for a meeting or training session, as well as measure the impact on the overall operation of the center. Thus, an important factor in assessing the capabilities of WFM tools is *flexibility in forecasting functionality*, because situations can develop very quickly that make forecasts useless without the ability to alter schedules to reflect reality.

Adherence

Adherence is the ability to compare forecasts with reality and to use this information to correct problems. Sophisticated scheduling and forecasting is useless without the opportunity to improve the process through adherence monitoring. Real-time adherence allows managers to see exactly what is happening and can alert them to deviations from the expected activity, allowing them to make changes before problems occur. Adherence allows a business to fine-tune its call/contact center activity; the more it is used, the more accurate the forecasts and schedules will be.

The objective of call/contact center managers should be to look for a solution that is simple to understand so the staff will feel comfortable using it and that has the power and functionality to help the center manager understand what has happened and to make necessary changes quickly.

Reporting and forecasting

The ability of managers and supervisors to see exactly what is happening via real-time reports is key to the workforce management process. Reporting provides a measure of success in achieving targets. Standard reports that are important for determining efficiency include

- Speed of answer

- Average call-handling time

- Talk plus Not-ready plus Non-ACD

- Delay before abandon

- E-mail handling time

- Percentage of calls abandoned

- Number of interactions waiting

Workforce management systems can be excellent for gauging the efficiency of a center and also forecasting results, but including CRM-focused measures, such as customer satisfaction, increase in market share, and improvement in loyalty levels, is more difficult. These metrics are just as important as the queue-centric reports, and businesses should make sure they capture and extract this information from their systems. The more statistics from various sources that can be brought together consistently, the more accurate the view of customer-focused activity. There is no point in striving to achieve high levels of efficiency if customers remain unhappy with the service provided or unknowledgeable about products they should be buying. Taking into account and reacting to business metrics, as well as the service-level measures that workforce management systems are so effective at providing, is important to assessing the overall performance of the center.

What-if scenarios

One of the most useful tools for call/contact center managers, particularly in a multimedia environment, is the ability to see what will happen to service levels if an event occurs, before that event occurs. Sophisticated workforce management systems allow managers to try out what-if scenarios, at no risk to the center's operational ability, by providing a way to model various scenarios.

Using these modeling techniques, the contact center manager can, for example, understand how the center workload would change if the following events occurred:

- A new advertising campaign increases call volumes.

- A large number of untrained agents start work at the same time.

- A new multimedia channel becomes available to customers.

- A key product line is offered at a discount.

What-if scenarios are very useful in directing long-term strategies, such as planning, budgeting, and recruitment.

Virtual contact center/Multisite support

An increasing trend in some global enterprises, especially in larger markets such as the United States, the United Kingdom, Germany, and France is to have several call/contact centers servicing customers. This operational model has been driven by a number of developments, including

- Rapid call/contact center growth in particular areas that has caused recruitment and retention problems

- The increased number of call/contact centers for businesses involved in acquisitions or mergers

- Teleworking and remote call center locations that mean CSRs may never see their parent center

- The preference of some companies to offer a "local touch" to customers by basing centers in their area

- Improvements in networking and telephony that make it easier to establish virtual centers

- The increasing need of companies to serve global customers, requiring either operating contact centers in different time zones or paying overtime to CSRs to work covering hours

- The possibilities of operational redundancy and disaster recovery with multisite centers

Combining multiple smaller centers into one large center can provide significant economic benefit through simple economies of scale. Correctly staffing five 100-seat call/contact centers is generally more complex and less efficient than staffing a single 500-seat operation. This is especially true when skills-based routing via a universal queue is being used. All agent competencies are displayed to the scheduler, who can be more flexible simply because the available resource pool is so much deeper.

Compliance: union rules, regulations, and the law

Different countries have different labor laws, and a superior workforce management system has to be easily configurable to take into account union regulations, laws, and other rules applying to businesses. For example, companies based in the member states of the European Union must take into account the Working Time Directive, which specifies that employees must work no more than 48 hours per week and restricts working nights, holidays, and breaks. The monitoring of CSRs is regulated by law in Germany, where monitoring by name is considered to be an invasion of privacy. An evaluation of WFM systems needs to include whether or not a solution can be easily adapted to each specific country's regulations.

Multimedia support

Workforce management systems provide a significant benefit to call/contact center managers by answering one of the most urgent questions center managers ask themselves: *How do I staff my multimedia contact center?*

Many so-called contact centers simply give agents a few e-mails to deal with when call volumes decrease, but when call volumes rise, e-mails are forgotten. Contact center managers may be quite capable of efficiently managing telephony-only call centers. In many cases, their experience allows them to make good judgment calls on these operational issues, based on years of experience. However, managing the multimedia contact center challenges even the most seasoned call center manager, because multimedia contacts and transactions are fundamentally different from telephone calls and must be handled differently. This is a situation that can lead to staffing issues, for the following reasons:

- *CSR competencies have to be considered.* Good telephony CSRs may not have the skills required to be good at handling e-mail or text chat contacts, where quick typing speed is required along with strong technology skills and correct spelling, grammar, and punctuation. CSRs good at written customer service may not have the listening or verbal communication skills required for telephony service.

- *Customers have different levels of expectation depending on the channel they are using.* Most customers expect a response via e-mail within 24 hours, whereas a typical telephony service level is 80% of calls to be answered within 20 seconds.

- *Standard responses using e-mail can speed up the process considerably.*

- *Batch customer requests—e-mail, fax, and letter—are, by definition, not interactive.* Additional resources may be needed to deal with incomplete requests.

- *Telephone queues are essentially self-managing.* If the phone is not answered quickly enough, the call is abandoned and the phone queue decreases. With e-mail, contacts back up until they are dealt with, a situation that can present serious problems.

- *E-mails may get "stale-dated" because the customer loses interest, gives up on the e-mail, and calls the center for a verbal response.* This leads to a nonproductive, time- and resource-wasting cycle of answering dead e-mails while live ones go unattended until they too go out-of-date!

- *Costs increase as the unsatisfied e-mail customer rings the contact center to find out what happened to the e-mail.* Where e-mails are held separately from transactions—that is, in organizations where the universal queue and universal routing are not being used—the e-mail may remain live even after the issue has been resolved. (see Figure 3.4)

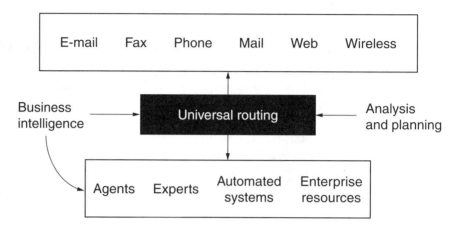

Figure 3.4
*Universal routing
and the universal
queue.*

- *In the early stages of multimedia contact implementation, extra time should be allowed for each nontraditional transaction.* CSRs will still be adapting to the process and the time per transaction should decrease as they become accustomed to the new environment.

- *Customers also need time to familiarize themselves with new contact methods such as text chat and Web collaborations.*

Experience has shown that many customers using Web collaboration for the first time enjoy the experience so much they spend longer than needed with each CSR.

Sales-focused call/contact centers will notice a rise in calls after a marketing campaign. In addition to the spike in calls after TV ads,

- E-mail advertising will produce a similar spike in inbound contacts with a range of different patterns.

- Interactive digital TV will produce major spikes in e-mail activity after TV commercials, which may well extend to text chat and Web collaboration as well, depending on how many channels the enterprise opens up.

- Different patterns of usage emerge from these new channels. Interactive TV is used more in the evenings, when most people return from work, whereas direct e-mail campaigns are likely to get an immediate response depending on where people access their e-mail.

The call/contact center manager has some advantages when handling e-mail, because supporting e-mail is not dependent on the time of day.

This means the scheduler has a considerable amount of freedom in trying to reduce the backlog. For example, some contact centers bring in students in the late evening to answer e-mails when most of the full-time CSRs have left the center. Others can answer e-mails through the night by employing people in other time zones—India, the Philippines, and Australia. In addition, the cost of e-mail is not location-dependent, given the resources available to the World Wide Web. It costs as much to route an e-mail around the globe as it does to send it to the person next door. And although telephone calls still have an associated long-distance cost, the difference between the two channels will become even less when VoIP becomes used globally. All of these points need to be considered when scheduling and forecasting for nontraditional types of contact. Additionally, how multimedia contacts will be handled must be decided. Will they be handled by dedicated agents or by blended agents, a process that could be more effective in a universal queue model and that has very positive effects on agent satisfaction?

A large number of operational headaches in call/contact centers are caused by not resourcing tasks correctly. New-generation workforce management systems will go a long way toward helping managers run things more smoothly and efficiently. Next-generation workforce management solutions will focus strongly on allowing call/contact center managers to plan long-term strategies. They will use these tools to model their operations based on various assumptions (for example, agent turnover at 20%, fixed agent career paths, 25% of workload being e-mail). Rather than having to react to external forces, the center manager will know how to resource the operation effectively before events actually happen as well as understanding their effects on the business.

WFM tools are very useful in assisting managers to prepare for sudden changes in call volume and other peaks and valleys that often come along without warning. For these situations, WFM can provide a warning, and it is often intuitive enough to see patterns in call histories and discern peaks and valleys that even experienced call center managers could not anticipate. A good example is holiday scheduling. Holidays bring together two divergent elements that most directly affect the call center. Calls surge up in unusual ways; however, they are predictable if the patterns that drive them are recognized. At holiday time, employees tend to have a variety of counterproductive demands, such as days off, flexible schedules, vacations, and time with families. WFM software predicts the call load for a given day from historical data. It provides information about how many calls are going to come in at any moment and allows managers to match that load effectively to the human resources available, even at times of unusual call patterns. Thus managers can act quickly to handle any divergence between people and calls, either days ahead of time or within a shift.

The preceding are just a few of the examples of improvements in efficiency and optimization of resources that WFM tools can provide, factors that take on new significance in a multimedia center. The following sections summarize the benefits of WFM and provide some guidelines for measuring the results obtained from WFM.

The major benefits of WFM

The major benefits of WFM tools are

- More efficient scheduling—managing changes in complex schedules and optimizing schedules

- Significant cost savings through efficient staffing levels and use of equipment

- Managing unexpected call-volume fluctuations

Other benefits of WFM

There are a number of other less tangible, but nonetheless important, benefits of WFM that also need to be considered when deciding to incorporate this tool into the call center, and at what level and cost. These benefits include the following:

Provision of threshold alert

Supervisors have instant information about intrashift variations that could cascade through the day and cause problems later. Schedules can be adjusted "on the fly."

Reporting on performance evaluation

Workforce management systems are not the only means of collecting performance data, but can be a means for making all the data coming from the ACD most relevant and meaningful. Coordinating the real-time and historical (short-term) views of activity is better than spreading that information and its analysis among different software tools, which creates islands of information that are harder to put back together later.

Discovering why service levels are not being met

WFM can provide information related to questions such as was an entire group's abandon rate higher because someone took lunch a little too early or because there were too few CSRs on hand for an expected spike? Or were there too many CSRs with a perfect service level at an unacceptably high cost? What would happen if 10 people were added to that shift? It can minimize unnecessary overtime payments, and provide calculations to justify making more CSRs available.

Coordinating among multiple sites

Integrating call center sites by pulling together agents from multiple sites into one virtual center provides all the workforce efficiencies obtainable with a single center with greater economies of scale.

Empowering CSRs by providing information

Schedules can be worked out to allow CSRs to understand the hows and whys of the decision-making process. Accurate call volume predictions and an automated scheduler that optimizes break and time-off preferences fairly lead to fewer complaints.

Simulating conditions and changes

Workforce management systems, when combined with simulation software, take existing or historical conditions and allow managers to adjust the parameters to conduct what-if scenarios. They can determine the effects of adding or subtracting people, changing group dynamics, and adding different technologies to the front end.

Providing competitive advantages in the workforce environment

The power to react to changing circumstances is a significant competitive advantage. Having a handle on costs, call volumes, and other variables in the call center operation mix can be a valuable aid to call center management. As well, it will ensure a better-managed, more-informed, happier workforce, making the call center more attractive as an employer, particularly in regions where skilled workers are hard to get and keep.

Currently, the penetration of the WFM tool in the call center workplace is so low that simply installing the software automatically confers a technology advantage over the competition. Although WFM tools may not be as fancy a technology tool as Web/call center technology combinations or

VoIP agents, they work well, have been proven over time, and can reduce costs and aggravation.

A Two-Step Reference Guide for Using WFM

- **Simulate conditions:** Use the software to create scenarios, for example, having two CSRs on vacation simultaneously, adding a part-time CSR for a few hours on Mondays, increasing call volume. Using software to simulate what-if scenarios lets you know how abandoned calls will increase and how long callers will be likely to wait in queue. *Simulation will demonstrate the effects of changes.*

- **Use reports wisely:** Try segmenting CSRs into workgroups based on similar salary levels and other attributes so that you can compare how each one is performing relative to others in the workgroup. *Reports provide analytical tools.*

Rationale for implementing WFM

In many companies, workforce management systems are not considered to be an essential element of call/contact center management resources in the initial setup of the center, despite the compelling rationale for installing these systems. When the pressure to cope effectively with the growth of customer interactions builds on the center, business users and operational staff must make a decision about which variety of WFM system is required.

Analysis of the cost and benefits of WFM systems indicates that the average time to breakeven on initial expenditures for workforce management solutions is 12 months using traditional workforce management systems in a telephony-based call center. Workforce management systems in multimedia contact centers will reduce the time to breakeven by about 50%, meaning that it will usually take six months from initial implementation, rather than 12 months.

The intangible returns must also be considered, because the call/contact center is an environment that can thrive or not depending on how well intangible aspects are managed. Happy, satisfied employees, reductions in recruitment and training costs through lower agent attrition, and increased upselling because of increased customer satisfaction are examples of intangibles that are important to the organization and that need to be considered by call/contact center management.

Review of functionality and benefits of WFM tools

Here is a summary checklist of features and functionality previously described that organizations evaluating workforce management systems need to consider. The WFM system should support the following features:

Forecasting

A core component of any WFM should take account of past operational data and be capable of assisting managers to plan exceptions.

Scheduling

Resourcing and supporting a skills-based environment is a critical function, and CRM-focused organizations have to take into account agent preferences and abilities.

Adherence

Key characteristics of effective WFM tools enable managers to see quickly whether activities are going as planned, and if not, to change them before it is too late.

Web-driven flexibility

Where remote working and "hot-desking" occur in a center operation, browser-based access via an intranet is a useful feature.

Reporting

Real-time reports are critical to the effectiveness of center operations, and flexibility and rapid report capabilities should be considered.

What-if scenario planning

Where major changes are anticipated—adding many new agents, channels, or advertising and marketing campaigns—what-if scenario functionality means testing the waters before embarking on a full-scale campaign.

Multimedia support

An important functionality to look for in new-generation WFM solutions is the capability to schedule and forecast across multiple channels and ensure service levels throughout the organization, especially at every customer Touch point.

Virtual contact center, multisite support

Allowing for growth and expansion to multiple centers should be a part of the WFM system. Running a virtual center rather than several stand-alone operations can increase the CSR competencies available and improve service levels.

Compliance with employment law, rules, and union regulations

As noted earlier, companies based in Europe, for example, must comply with the Working Time Directive. The selected WFM solution should be capable of easy adaptation to a specific country's requirements.

Available WFM systems

This section reviews the general characteristics of vendor offerings in workforce management tools, in particular, monitoring systems. A listing of specific vendors and the products they offer is contained in Appendix A, "Call Center Vendor Resources—Product and Service Offerings." This very robust and advanced area of technology offers a variety of products to serve different call center characteristics. A major contributor to advances in this area is the growth of the Internet, a technology that has made it easier to store and retrieve information across networks and in a variety of different media formats.

Monitoring systems

Monitoring is a critical part of the process of teaching a new CSR how to deal with customers, how to handle difficult situations, and simply how to follow a script and read a screen full of complex information. Feedback is important to improving the performance of CSRs. Even CSRs that have years of experience need constant skill assessment and additional training to update their phone skills and to keep them up-to-date on new technologies and how to use them.

Some telephone switches have a monitoring system built in, and some vendors provide sophisticated software for combined monitoring and quality assurance programs. Typically, these software tools collect data about agent performance and assess that data over the short or long term. Some products also automate the scheduling of agent monitoring for later review. Managers don't need to be present to monitor or to set up tapes.

Training headset models are also available that have a second jack on the amplifier to accommodate a "no-microphone" headset that a trainer could wear when sitting beside the trainee. A low-budget monitoring system can be incorporated by plugging a tape recorder into the jack.

Pros and cons of monitoring systems

There are two basic criteria for quality measurement in call centers:

- Ensuring the center has the best CSRs available, operating at the highest level they can personally achieve

- Enforcing a consistent standard of quality for customer contacts from the customer's point of view

Monitoring CSRs is still the best way to achieve quality in terms of both criteria. If handled with sensitivity, monitoring can be a benefit to CSRs because it helps them define and reach career goals, assess strengths and weaknesses, and make progress according to realistic standards. One technique used by some organizations is to involve senior management in the call center process. A call is monitored by a senior executive so that this individual hears directly the "voice of the customer." Although monitoring does have some negative implications, if properly presented to CSRs the benefits to both the individual and the center become obvious. The proper instructions for using monitoring products emphasize the benefits to both parties of performance monitoring.

One obvious benefit of monitoring, assuming that it is performed in the right atmosphere, is that it creates an objective standard of behavior that can be measured and one that can be repeated. It helps ensure delivery not only of good service but also of consistent service from each and every CSR. From a CSR's viewpoint, monitoring creates a way to measure performance that can be described in advance and critiqued intelligently. Results can be quantified and reps can see improvement over time. As well, it allows management to benchmark standards and ensure that all CSRs are treated fairly and by the same standards.

Excesses in monitoring

Some monitoring tools go too far in assessing CSR performance and can be a detriment to improving productivity. As noted previously, call centers typically have the problem of high turnover; one product that has a voice analyzer that dynamically analyzes the speech flow of either the CSR or the customer during a call would probably make this problem worse. The product advises supervisors about how CSRs are "feeling" during the call by reporting on stress levels and other psychological indices, the theory being that this information could then be used to enhance the management of customer relations within the call center. The vendor thinks that this product could be used in conjunction with a monitoring application that stores calls and then retrieves them on demand and runs them through the analyzer. It includes a suite of tools that can diagnose both real-time and off-line stress.

The types of data that are routinely captured by "quality monitoring systems," include, along with an audio message, the agent's screen activity or the Web page that the caller was looking at when completing the transaction. These data are combined to bring a new level of detail to the verification and quality monitoring process. Products such as these tread heavily on CSR sensitivities and they are very unlikely to enhance a CSR's performance. All CSRs experience stress, but there are a number of other, better ways from a human resource perspective to measure performance and reduce tension in the call center workplace. For example, some vendors offer screen monitoring and screen recording systems that provide tools with which supervisors can evaluate the interactions between CSRs and customers, evaluate CSR performance, and train new agents. Supervisors using these products have several monitoring options: They can view in real time one or more CSR PCs at the click of a button to see how they use the script and if they are using the system correctly. Or they can do a "round robin" among multiple PCs on the network, using a cycle mode, to systematically monitor a group of agents. There is also a "stealth" monitoring capability that lets supervisors monitor an agent's PC screen undetected. Supervisors can record any agent's screen at the click of a button and view and record one or more screens simultaneously. Later, they can play back these sessions, search to any point in the recording, and play back at any speed. These sessions can also be archived to accurately document performance on outsource contracts and to provide "proof of performance."

Selecting, installing, and using monitoring systems

Several useful guidelines, discussed in the next section, for monitoring systems should be considered before selecting a system and installing it in a new or existing call center operation. The newest technology tools are broad-based and make it possible for call center supervisors and managers to combine streams, allowing performance trends for both individual CSRs and groups to be analyzed from a variety of perspectives. Such an analysis can be scaled up to look at an entire center or groups of centers. Add information from accounts receivable, order entry, and other areas and a picture emerges that describes several characteristics about CSR performance. Thus, information on how much money a CSR or group of CSRs generates and whether a particular campaign is in trouble can be accessed.

Important guidelines for using quality monitoring systems

Here are three key pointers based on the experience of call center managers who have installed monitoring systems:

Select current recording and conversion technology

Two improvements in recording technology have occurred in the last decade. First, digital recording replaced analog, making it easier to store and retrieve specific calls; second, CTI links have made it possible to convert digital recording into data and combine it with other information about transactions.

Select software that works in tandem with core recording systems

Software products are available to help solve the problem of accessing disparate information throughout the enterprise by serving as a central repository for information from many sources, such as workforce management, human resources, predictive dialers, and ACDs. Combining, assessing, and exploring information from multiple sources is critical as call centers evolve into customer contact centers, because no one source has sufficient information to provide a complete performance picture.

Select an appropriate monitoring frequency

A CSR should be monitored for quality as frequently as is dictated by criteria such as how long that CSR has been on staff, what kind of traffic the CSR handles (inbound or outbound, sales or service), the sensitivity of the kind of customer interaction (i.e., financial services would monitor at a higher rate than telemarketing, etc.), as well as what kind of technology is used to do the monitoring.

Measuring results

In a Spring of 2002 survey of call centers, *Call Center Monitoring Study II Final Report*, a majority of call centers (93%) reported monitoring CSR calls, reflecting a 5% increase in the number of centers conducting monitoring two years earlier. According to this study, conducted by Incoming Calls Management Institute and A. C. Nielsen Co. of Canada, and based on a survey of 735 North American call centers, 4 out of 10 call centers monitor e-mail responses, 1 in 6 monitor fax correspondence, and 1 in 14 monitor Web text-chat sessions. This is a significant increase in the monitoring of e-mail and Web text-chat over two years ago, which no doubt reflects the increased popularity of these two channels.

Other key findings of the report are

- There is a wide variance in the number of calls monitored per month per agent. The most popular frequencies are 4 to 5 and 10 or more.

- More than one-third of call centers devote 1 to 5 hours per week to monitoring, and one-quarter devote 6 to 10 hours weekly. Larger call centers (200 or more agents) devote significantly more time per week to monitoring and coaching than the smallest call centers (fewer than 50 agents).

- Four in 10 call centers monitor both voice and screen. There appears to be a strong relationship between the size of the call center and monitoring voice and screen. As the size of the call center increases, the likelihood that it will monitor both mediums also increases.

- Overall, two-thirds of call centers surveyed share monitoring data/customer feedback with other departments within their company. Of the call centers that share monitoring data/customer feedback with other departments, almost one-third distribute this information on a monthly basis. One in 7 share monitoring data/customer feedback on a quarterly basis, and 1 in 10 on a weekly basis.

- The two most frequently cited reasons given for sharing monitoring data/customer feedback with other departments are "to improve quality of calls" and "to measure performance."

In general, call centers should tackle optimization and measurement questions based on a reasoned assessment of how the center relates to the rest of the organization and what the company expects from the center in relation to the competitive pressure in the rest of the industry sector. Expectations can vary across sectors. For example, airline call centers measure different performance characteristics than catalog order takers, and financial institutions have their own measurement criteria.

It is important to think in terms of results that impact on the call center objectives and how those results affect revenue. Call duration, for example, can impact both costs (telecom transmission charges) and customer satisfaction if the call is used to sell the caller some new product or service. Overall call center performance can be measured by using a workforce management system and keeping track of adherence to schedule—the closer to the predicted schedule, the more optimally the center has been staffed. This analysis helps to keep costs from ballooning out of proportion. The performance

of individual CSRs and groups can be measured by tying it to actual customer information. (This requires some CTI and/or backend integration
with customer data.) It is possible to generate a revenue figure for each
group or rep that weighs call length or number of calls taken by how valuable those calls are. A CSR who handles fewer calls involving premium customers with a high lifetime value to the customer is probably more effective
than an agent who handles more calls in a shorter time with low-impact
customers or callers who are not customers at all. (see Figure 3.5)

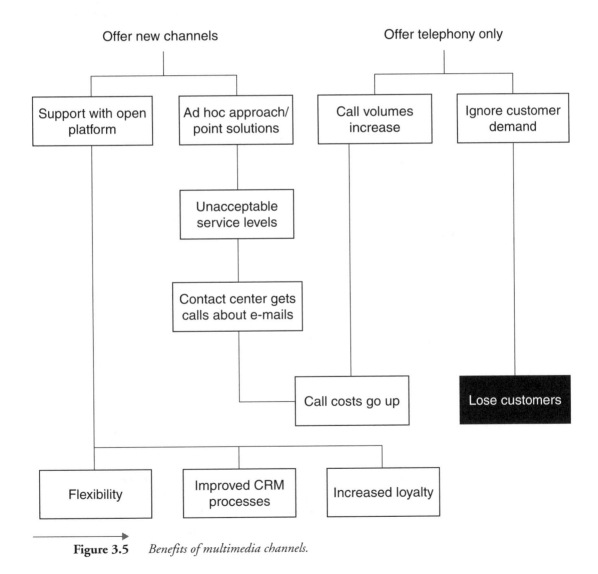

Figure 3.5   *Benefits of multimedia channels.*

Web-driven interfaces and tools

In today's call/contact center environment, managers and CSRs are not always in one central location. The existence of virtual multisite centers, teleworking, or dispersed call/contact center operations does not mean that workforce management systems cannot be employed. Businesses should look for a workforce management system that can be operated by remote users, if required. One approach is a browser-based application linked to the organization's intranet or the Internet, allowing scheduling, reporting, and management from any PC at any location with communication resources. In this configuration, CSRs also have the ability to access schedules, enter preferences, and request vacation time seamlessly and remotely.

Browser-based publishing tools also make collecting and sharing customer data within the call center and throughout the enterprise as easy as accessing a Web page. Call centers can publish customer contact information in a browser page format or "Web desktop," thus simplifying the transfer of customer information from the call center to the enterprise.

Departments outside of the call center can use these systems to get customized access to data necessary to make more strategic and timely business decisions. Data that can be accessed include digital call recordings and call center performance reports. Executive management, marketing, and product development, for instance, can track customer response to promotions, monitor service quality, and query customers through this system. Products such as these are part of an enterprise call center suite, an automated call monitoring system that collects and publishes information about customer contact with a company's CSRs.

Core elements of these Web tools include call evaluations and graphical comparisons of individual versus group performance. Supervisors can also add training tools, provide productivity reports, publish department-specific issues, and highlight morale programs, such as "CSR of the month," incentives, and other events.

Monitoring: summing up

The more automation, in theory, the less human monitoring is required because there is a better opportunity to obtain a true, random representative sample. If CSRs are convinced that monitoring is truly random, then their behavior smooths out and they are less likely to vary their responses between calls. The controversy over monitoring—how often, what tools, and how to address the issue with CSRs—is ongoing. Monitoring is essentially about judging people and their performance. Technology alone cannot make the monitoring process a success. Informed judgments need to be made by supervisors and managers, who must supply humanity to the application of technology tools.

3.3   Twelve characteristics of the best-managed call centers

Some call centers exude energy that may take one or more different forms: a feeling of community, pride of workmanship, and results that spring from good planning and coordination. Everyone in the center knows what the mission is and is focused on attaining the objectives. They are all pulling in the same direction, just like a well-trained sports team. A number of benchmarking studies address the subject of what makes a well-managed call center. But while these surveys report on the results obtained by these centers in terms of customer satisfaction and retention, service levels, planning accuracy, organizational structure, costs and revenues, employee satisfaction and turnover, they seldom describe *how* positive results were obtained.

The following 12 characteristics have been compiled from the experience of industry analysts and call center managers and represent a summary of those qualities that contribute to a well-managed call center. They are the attributes of some of the world's best-managed call centers, those that consistently outperform others in their respective industries based on commonly accepted measurement criteria, including customer surveys.

Recognize people as the key to success

Call centers that recognize the direction in which the business is going are continually cultivating CSR skills. They provide training and present attractive career paths to their people. They also consider the whole person when hiring and when rewarding for good performance. They pay attention to people's inherent talents and abilities, not just the job categories and specific duties.

Leading call centers also develop formal and informal communication channels in their organizations. Keeping people well informed helps them prepare for and accept change. Change is personal, and its meaning and level of acceptance are based clearly on how change is communicated and how it is perceived.

Receive support from the corporate culture

Corporate culture, often referred to as "the value principles" of an organization, tends to guide employee behavior and can either support and enhance the best-laid plans for organizational change or ruin them. There is no magic formula for creating a supportive corporate culture; however, managers in well-run call centers agree that shaping the culture of the organization is a primary leadership responsibility. They do not believe that this process should be left to fate, and they therefore devote considerable effort to understanding their organization and the people who are part of it.

Effective communication is a primary ingredient of a high-performance culture, creating meaning and direction for people. Organizations of all types depend on the existence of shared meanings and interpretations of reality, which facilitate coordinated action among employees. Many management training programs fail to appreciate the complexity and paradoxical nature of human organizations. Unfortunately, thought processes that should be involved in management principles give way to how-to-do-it formulas and techniques and slogans and homilies as the principle management guidelines. The most effective call center managers are comfortable with the fact that it is seldom possible to completely master interpersonal relationships and that compromises are necessary. Understanding this reality of life means spending more time on "people issues" than on anything else.

Focus quality on customer expectations

The best-managed call centers have a strong focus on evolving customer needs and expectations, and they are continually redefining quality around those expectations. They appreciate the fact that what worked yesterday may not necessarily work tomorrow.

Establish a collaborative planning process

A major objective of good call center planning is to "get the right number of people in the right places at the right time." Systematic planning accomplishes other positive objectives, however, including contributing to effective communication and creating a body of information that wouldn't otherwise be available. Call load patterns support the structure of schedules. Planning is the catalyst that encourages people to think about the future and see their contributions to the overall picture. Systematic planning is also important because it requires communication on issues such as resource allocation, budgeting, and workload priorities. Constant communication about these activities is a requirement for all active call centers.

Consider the incoming call center a total process

Call centers that consistently get the best results view themselves or "the operation" as a "total process" in the organization's day-to-day business activities. This view of the call center takes several forms and results in a number of desirable characteristics:

- Assisting in the development of an effective, collaborative planning and management process

- Enabling people to understand how the call center supports the organization's direction

- Ensuring that everyone in the call center and those with key supporting roles outside the call center have a basic understanding of how call centers operate

- Assisting managers to take the initiative in coordinating and relating to other departments

- Recognizing that most quality problems occur in the process stage and continually trying to improve processes

- Integrating the call center's activities effectively with other departments within the organization

- Providing the capability to respond to changing conditions

The days of the call center as an island unto itself, separate from the rest of the organization and considered simply as "the place where they handle sales and customer service," are fast fading. The true nature of the call center has become recognized—it is the "front wall" of the organization and an important part of a much larger corporate business process.

Establish an effective mix of technology and people

In the call center environment, personal contact with callers has to be reduced because there is simply too much caller demand for CSRs to handle routine calls or tasks that technology can readily handle. However, it is an important and fundamental aspect of good customer relations that callers are not relegated to machine responses when they need a real live person or when they prefer live answers to product or service questions.

Leading call centers continue to work to find the right mix of people and technology. Although technology can take an organization where it's going, very quickly, it's a good idea to be headed in the right direction! This means recognizing both where technology fits and the importance of the human element in making technology work effectively.

As noted in Chapter 2, new technologies are not passive; they are continually changing caller expectations, causing reallocations of resources, power shifts in call centers, and changes in the responsibilities of CSRs and managers. The challenge for call center professionals is to sort through the many choices, identify the technologies that can further the mission of the organization, and then implement them with the necessary foresight and planning.

Provide the correct mix of specialization and pooling

Pooling resources is one of the key characteristics of the incoming call center industry and is a primary function of technology tools such as ACDs, networks, and other supporting devices and systems. The advanced capabilities and increasing sophistication of intelligent ACDs and network services provide call centers with the means to mix and match the incoming call load in a variety of ways. The pooling activity that takes place in call centers that have the latest technology represents a continually changing mix of specialization and pooling. The technology available to handle each call according to its individual needs and characteristics requires call center planning, operation, and management to remain focused on cross training and broadening the skills of reps. There will be overlap, however, and contingencies in the operation that must be managed with intelligence and rationality. Leading call centers have an edge over other, less-productive call center environments because they have been able to strike the right mix of specialization and pooling—one of the reasons they obtain high marks for their successful operations. To accomplish this objective, they do the following:

- Expand responsibilities for CSRs

- Avoid unnecessary complexity in CSR group structures

- Improve information systems and training so that CSRs are capable of handling a broad range of transactions

- Implement a flowchart system and network programming to identify weaknesses in routing logic

- Hire multilingual agents, where possible

- Position the call center as close to the "pooled" end of the spectrum as possible

Leverage key statistics

The indicators of high-level call center performance include

- Average call value (for revenue-producing call centers)

- Successful forecasts of call load versus actual load

- Service level

- Cost per call

- Customer satisfaction

- Adherence to schedule

- Percentage of abandoned calls

- Errors and rework required

- Average call-handling time

Related to these operating statistics are three common characteristics of call centers that get the best results:

- They ensure statistical measurements are accurate, complete, and as unbiased as possible.

- Reports are viewed in relation to each other.

- They are aware that simply tracking high-level measurements won't inherently improve results.

They know that a single report, outside the context of the others, can lead to erroneous conclusions and that statistics can often be misleading. They prefer to work on the root causes of problem areas.

Receive budgets and support as needed

Often in call center operations, the budget is presented to call center managers before objectives have been stated and before anyone has agreed that objectives could be met within the assigned budget. It is much more logical for the "budgetsetters" in an organization to ask the individuals responsible for meeting defined objectives how much money they need, what other resources, and so on. A good analogy is the airline industry: Airlines couldn't possibly operate flights without a tangible connection between the results they want to achieve and the supporting resources. They start with an objective to fly a certain number of people to a particular destination and then budget to do this. The goal is a specific, predetermined outcome supported by carefully calculated resources. This is the way senior corporate management should consider call center operations—*specific objectives that require a certain level of resources.* The best call center managers decide on their objectives first and then obtain the necessary resources to support those objectives through careful planning.

Hurdle distance, time, and politics effectively

The evolution of computer and telecommunications technologies has resulted in the birth of new companies and the growth of existing companies that can span both geography and time. Fiber-optic cables crisscross the globe, and satellites provide virtually worldwide telecommunications service. Trends in the call center industry reflect these developments in the global marketplace. Distributed call centers, in which two or more centers share the call load, can span a region, a country, or the globe and are becoming commonplace. Telecommuting programs continue to proliferate at a growing rate. Call center personnel have been formed into cross-functional teams, with responsibilities for everything from forecasting the workload to improving quality.

Although new technologies have provided an increasing array of new capabilities, the natural barriers that exist between people who work in distributed environments remain, resulting in the following situations:

- People who work in different places and/or at different times often have difficulty seeing themselves as an integral part of a larger, unified team.

- Informal opportunities for relating to each other in traditional settings—lunchrooms, hallways, and break room—are only rarely available.

- Significant information may be exchanged outside the formal context of memos and meetings, resulting in an uneven distribution of this information among the dispersed group.

The changing workplace means that call center managers increasingly have the responsibility for managing people who work in different locations and don't report directly to them or don't work at the same time. Managers in the best-managed call centers recognize that the success of their operations depends on how well they master the art of managing and leading in a distributed, often widely geographically separated, environment. As some authors of leadership texts have pointed out, the key to leading a dispersed team to high performance levels is *building trust*. Unfortunately, trust cannot be bought or mandated—and there are no foolproof, specific formulae or rules for achieving trust. Like leadership itself, trust is hard to define and has no recipe for managers to follow to create it. Despite this fact, the experience of managers in the best-managed call centers has led to a set of guidelines—management processes that have been successful in many cases—to building a desired level of trust among employees, particularly in geographically dispersed centers. Following these concrete steps is more likely to create environments in which trust will flourish than taking no action at all:

- Create a clear vision for the call center and its objectives

- Ensure that everyone in the center receives key information at the same time

- Create opportunities for people in the distributed environment to get to know each other

- Make an extra effort to develop relationships among the more "distant" members of the group, whether the separation is due to time or geography

- Minimize the impact on call center staff of unnecessary hierarchies and cumbersome bureaucracies, which can affect distributed teams adversely

Be prepared and willing to experiment

Reassessing and reviewing operating procedures to determine how well the center is doing compared to its objectives is another hallmark of the most successful call centers. These reviews attempt to answer such questions as What areas can be improved? What activities can be terminated? What assumptions no longer make sense? What can be done differently? Is there an opportunity for outsourcing some call center activities?

Be capable of vision

The call center industry has come a long way in recent years. Customer expectations are high and call centers are gradually learning how to meet them. Most of the best-managed incoming call centers have learned how to deliver value to their organizations and its customers. Collectively, these organizations have invested billions of dollars and considerable time and effort in equipment, networks, and software, as well as in human resources, including many hours spent training and equipping call center staff to meet their responsibilities. Centers are now fully versed in the nuances of forecasting, staffing, and the behavior of queues. They have identified evolving customer needs, are constantly changing and improving processes to meet those needs, and finding new and better ways of operating in an increasingly competitive business environment.

Summing up the overall characteristics of well-managed call centers demonstrates that the best-managed centers are those that have excellent resource planning and management processes that are systematic, collaborative, and accurate and that result in the productivity, service level, and quality that make them industry leaders.

The future of call center management

Some call center mangers may view the future with some trepidation and may have reservations about the impact of the next wave of technology, but the future can bring many benefits. The growth of e-commerce and the changes it will require in traditional call center operations and processes will certainly have a significant effect on how call centers operate, as will the changing business environment. Call centers will therefore be required to handle an increasingly diverse mix of transactions. Managers wonder about how to keep up in an environment that is moving at a very rapid pace, in terms of changing technology, changing customer expectations, and heightened competition. But uncertainty also brings opportunities and challenges to overcome, and experienced call center professionals will be in demand by organizations that need people who can help them meet those challenges and make the transition into the new era of business.

3.4   The incoming call center

Incoming Calls Management Institute has developed a working definition of incoming call center management that is used in this book and was first stated in Chapter 3:

Incoming call center management is the art of having the right number of skilled people and supporting resources in place at the right times to handle an accurately forecasted workload, at a specified service level and with quality.

This definition leads to two major objectives for incoming call centers:

- Locate the right resources in the right places at the right times
- Provide a service level with quality

The capability of call centers to meet these objectives has evolved through three definable major stages:

1. *Service level awareness*—maintaining service level as calls arrive, with some correlation to service level in planning

2. *Seat-of-the pants management*—little consideration of service level in planning

3. *Correlating service level to the organization's mission*—choosing an appropriate service level and tying resources to achieving this service level

An eight-stage process for systematic planning and management

Many individual organizations have evolved through the same general stages and most now link service level to quality and the overall mission. Systematic planning and management are required to accomplish this important linkage and can be accomplished through an eight-stage process:

1. **Select a Service Level Objective** Service level is defined as a certain percentage of calls answered in a specified time frame, measured in seconds. The level should be appropriate for the services being provided and the expectations of callers using those services. Service level is the critical link between resources and results.

2. **Collect Data** ACD and computer systems are important sources of planning data because they provide call statistics and details such as number of incoming calls, duration of calls, call patterns, and changes in the call mix. Information about what marketing and other departments are doing, changes in legislation, competitor activities, and changes in customer needs and perceptions is also required.

3. **Forecast Call Load** Call load includes three components: call volume, average talk time, and average after-call work. A good forecast predicts all three components accurately for future time periods, usually in half-hour segments. In the modern call center, forecasting must go beyond inbound calls to reflect other choices customers have to interact with organizations—e-mail, faxes, and video and Web-based transactions.

4. **Determine the Base Staff Requirement** A formula commonly used for calculating staffing requirements is Erlang C. This formula

(to be described later in this chapter) is used in virtually all work-force management software systems and by many call center managers. Computer simulation programs also may provide solutions for staffing and a number of other management issues. New capabilities, such as skill-based routing and complex network environments, must also be taken into account when planning staffing.

5.   **Calculate Trunks and Related Systems Resources** Staffing and trunking issues are inextricably associated and must be calculated together.

6.   **Calculate Rostered Staff Factor and Organize Schedules** Rostered staff factor, also referred to as *shrink factor* or *shrinkage*, adds realism to staffing requirements by accounting for breaks, absenteeism, training, and nonphone work. Schedules are essentially forecasts of who needs to be where and when. They should lead to getting the right people in the right places at the right times.

7.   **Calculate Costs** This step projects costs for the resources required to meet service and quality objectives.

8.   **Repeat Steps 1–7 for Higher and Lower Levels of Service** Preparing three budgets around three different service levels provides an understanding of cost trade-offs, which is invaluable in budgeting decisions.

New opportunities and new challenges

In the marketing environment of the 21st century, there are enormous opportunities for interacting with customers. New services built around the World Wide Web, video capabilities, and other multimedia technologies are bringing new opportunities and challenges to the call center. Many inbound call center managers and CSRs are concerned about the new technologies and how they will affect their jobs and the call center industry in general.

The changing environment has caused the term *incoming call center* to be challenged on several fronts even as call centers are being accepted as an integral element of the business environment. The controversy is over the definition of this entity: Is it a center that handles calls? This concept hardly describes the incoming call center of today, of which there are hundreds in a variety of business sectors, from financial institutions to communications companies (see chapter 5, "Call Center Case Studies"). *Calls* are just one type of customer communication, and the word *center* does not describe the many multisite environments nor the growing number of organizations that have telecommuting programs. *Call center* has become an umbrella term for a variety of customer contact facilities, including reservation centers, help desks, information lines, and customer service centers, regardless of how they are organized or what types of transactions they handle.

Call center planning and management has also changed, not fundamentally, but in ways that are related to the new environment and the new technologies. With integrated Web services, customers and potential customers browsing a Website can click a button, be connected to the call center, and receive immediate live assistance. Planning and managing in this environment should involve the steps in the eight-stage planning and managing process described in the previous section. Planning for and managing video calls is another example. The process begins by choosing an appropriate service level objective, then collecting data, forecasting the video call load, calculating the base level of agents required, planning for system resources, and so on. The objectives are the same as for a more traditional call center operation: the right number of video-equipped agents and necessary technology resources in the right places at the right times, performing the right functions.

Changes to come

Changes in call center management practices related to the new types of transactions that need to be handled will be required. The new transactions will become increasingly complex as technology automates simple and routine tasks and leaves CSRs to manage interactions requiring the human touch. Customer expectations will continue to climb, and callers will not tolerate organizations that do not provide the choices and service levels they demand. The personal skills required of call center personnel, however, will not change: CSRs will still need good writing and customer service skills. Finding the right mix of technology and human capital will require an ongoing effort.

Since the early 1900s, there have been many advances in technology and the art and science of communication has been in the forefront, as described in Chapter 2. Technology has had significant impact on the call center: Operators, for example, are no longer needed to connect calls because the process has been automated. But managing the modern call center faces challenges similar to those faced by the telephone pioneers. Forecasting calls accurately, staffing appropriately, and getting the right people and other resources in the right places at the right times are continuing problems that connect today's call center to the past, as noted at the beginning of this chapter.

As telephone services matured, several solutions to resource management challenges were proposed. One of the first individuals to solve the problem of handling vast numbers of incoming calls and arriving at the optimum level of operator resources was A. K. Erlang. Erlang's queuing formula, *Erlang C*, still widely used today, gradually evolved into a programming language (Erlang) that has been used in a variety of mission-critical areas, especially in applications that must run continuously and across many machines such as air traffic control and, of course, call center operations.

3.5   Call centers—corporate business hubs

Recent studies indicate that in many sectors of the economy call centers have become a major factor in customer retention, competitiveness, and ability to adapt to changing markets. These operations are the "front wall" of the organization—often the first contact point for a customer. Senior executives are becoming much more aware of the significant contributions an efficient, customer-oriented call center can make to corporate business objectives and are supporting initiatives to attract the best people possible to their call centers. As call centers play an ever-increasing role in regional, national, and international economies, governments at all levels are providing tax incentives for call centers to locate in their jurisdictions.

Call center managers—professional skills

Those who aspire to call center management positions will need to develop a definable skillset to achieve success. These skills include

- *Communication*—writing, speaking, and interpersonal communication with all levels of management

- *Project management*—the ability to manage several projects at the same time

- *Training*—understanding the importance of training and the various training methodologies available

- *Leadership and management*—the ability to develop trust in employees and manage call center activities

- *Performance assessments*—the ability to review and assess employee performance

- *Quantitative analysis*—the ability to analyze statistical reports

Call center managers who successfully meet these challenges have significant opportunities for advancement. As noted previously, call center management has become a recognized management position and has cross-industry applications and thus the same job mobility opportunities as other industry management positions.

Knowledge requirements

In addition to a skillset, there are some other attributes which might be called *knowledge requirements.* These are personal experience and background characteristics that might round out the abilities of a call center manager. The knowledge requirements include

- Customer service

- Forecasting

- Staffing and scheduling

- Caller behavior

- Random call arrival

- Queuing theory

- Systems and software

- Organizational behavior

- Ergonomics and workplace environment

- Industry vocabulary

Staying in tune with industry developments through attendance at conferences, call center associations, and generally participating and contributing to industry events is important for call center managers. Continual personal growth and development will also be of benefit to a career. Keeping abreast of evolving technologies and developing a network of other professionals and resources available to assist in resolving job-related problems are other activities that can help the manager along a career path.

3.6   Service level—a core value

At the heart of effective incoming call center management is the principle of *service level.* A service level objective can be used to determine the resources required and the effectiveness of the center in its impact on the corporate business goals. Here are some of the questions that can be answered by establishing and monitoring a specified level of service:

- How accessible is the call center?

- How much staff is required?

- How does the center compare to the competition?

- Can the center handle the response to marketing campaigns?

- How busy will the CSRs be?

- What will the costs be?

Defining a service level

Service level is often referred to by various terms. In some call centers, it is the *telephone service factor*, or TSF. Others refer to it as *grade of service* (GOS), although this may be confused with the term for the degree of blocking on a group of trunks. Service level is also referred to as *accessibility* or *service standard*. Typically, the term *service level* is used to refer specifically to transactions that must be handled on arrival at the call center. Response time, often called *speed of reply*, may even be called *service level* as well. To avoid confusion, response time will be used in a specific sense in this book, to describe *the level of service assigned to transactions that can be handled at a later time and do not need to be handled "on arrival."*

The most widely-accepted definition of service level is based on the percentage of calls answered in a given time frame, for example, 90 percent of calls answered in 20 seconds. Some managers define service level as a percentage only or as an abandonment rate. Others refer to the percentage of the time the service level objective is met, whatever that objective may be. And there are those who define service level as "average speed of answer" or longest delayed call.

The various interpretations and other definitions of service level often lead to misunderstandings and mismanagement. By its nature, service level should be defined as a specific percentage of all calls answered in a specific time frame, as previously noted. Planning should be based on achieving this target. Choosing an appropriate service level objective is one of the first steps a call center manager should take to ensure effective planning and management of the operation and to establish budgets.

Establishing a service level helps to link resources to results and measures the degree to which customers are being transferred and handled by a CSR. Service level is a tested and proven criterion in call centers worldwide for transactions that must be handled when they arrive—most commonly inbound phone calls. However, as customer contact methods change, new multimedia services—video calls and calls integrated with the World Wide Web—may also become part of the service level criterion. Because of its universal acceptance as a primary call center criterion, service level will remain an important objective to the next generation of call centers.

Other response categories

In addition to the "immediate response" category, most incoming call centers are required to handle transactions that belong in a second category, those that don't have to be handled at the time they arrive. Some examples of these transactions are

- Postal correspondence (snail mail)
- E-mail
- Faxes
- Voice mail
- Video mail

These transactions allow a larger window of time for the call center to respond. It is as important, however, to establish specific response time objectives for these interactions as it is for the first category of transactions. All categories of transactions can contribute to meeting the service objectives of the call center if appropriate priorities are established.

Other response criteria

Average speed of answer (ASA), another often-used response criterion, is related to service level because it is derived from the same set of data. However, ASA is often misinterpreted. In any set of data, it is generally assumed that the average lies somewhere in the middle or that "average" represents typical experience. This is not true for call center purposes. Although mathematically correct, the average does not represent the experience of individual callers. In a call center, most callers get connected to a CSR *much quicker* than the average, but some wait *far beyond* the average. For example, with an average speed of answer of 15 seconds, about 70 percent of callers get answered immediately, but a small percentage of callers will wait three or four minutes in the calling queue. Although ASA is useful in calculating some call center requirements—for example, in calculating trunk load—service level is a more reliable and more telling measure of a caller's experience.

Abandoned calls

Considering call abandonment rates alone as a measure of whether staffing levels are appropriate can be quite misleading. A high abandonment rate is probably a symptom of staff problems. But a low abandonment rate doesn't necessarily mean the center is optimally staffed. If abandonment rates are unacceptable, call center managers need to evaluate the situation to determine what is wrong. It is most likely that the evaluation will reveal a too low service level. When service level is being achieved, abandonment rates tend to take care of themselves.

Unanswered calls

One important consideration about service level is what happens to calls that don't get answered in the specified service-level time frame? Most Erlang C and computer simulation software programs can calculate the answers to this question and others. For example, for a service level of 80 percent answered in 20 seconds, experience indicates that about 30 percent of callers end up in the queue, that the longest wait will be around three minutes, and that the average speed of answer will range from 10 to 15 seconds. This example points up the obvious fact that different callers have different experiences with call centers, even if they are part of the same set of data measured by service level, ASA, and other measurements. The reason for this is "random call arrival," a reality of call center operation and a factor that needs to be considered when deciding how to measure quality of service. Service level is the single best measure of quality, largely because it enables the center to determine what happens to different callers.

Inbound transactions—priority levels

There are two major categories of inbound transactions, with two priority levels, that a call center needs to handle:

- Those that must be handled when they arrive (e.g., inbound calls)—
  Performance objective: Service Level

- Those than can be handled at a later time (e.g., correspondence)—
  Performance objective: Response Time

The rationale for a service level

Establishing a service level based on calls answered in a specified time as opposed to percentage of calls answered or percentage of calls abandoned or even average speed of answer provides a clear-cut indication of a caller's experience when contacting the call center. Service level is the most stable measurement of the inbound call-in queue. The importance of a defined service level can be summed up by examining the effect on customers and call center operations as it relates to the following factors:

- Agent burnout and errors

- Levels of lost calls

- Customer goodwill

- Links between resources and results

- Focus on planning activities

Applying service-level metrics

It is important that service level be interpreted in the context of call blockage, that is, calls not getting through. Any time some portion of callers is getting busy signals, no matter whether generated by the system resulting from a limited number of staff and lines during a busy period, service level reports only report on the calls that are getting through. Reports based on service level and average speed of answer can be configured to look very impressive simply by limiting the number of calls allowed to get through.

Service level is obviously a time-dependent parameter, and daily service level reports may often conceal important information. Service level may be down in the morning; however, if staff levels improve and every call in the afternoon is handled immediately, the daily report will look very good against service-level objectives. On the other hand, the level of service from a callers' perspective is a different story. It is not difficult for managers accountable for daily reports and meeting service-level objectives to "fudge" these reports or call center activity to make the situation look better than it really is. If the morning service level was low, they may keep CSRs on the phones through the afternoon when the call load drops, just to make reports look better. This is a waste of valuable time and resources and provides inconsistent service to customers.

Consider this: If daily reports are potentially misleading, the longer the time frame between reports, the more misleading they can be. Therefore, monthly averages for service level are virtually meaningless, because they don't reflect the day-by-day, half-hour–by–half-hour realities. Even so, monthly reports are a popular way to summarize activity for senior management, although there are more meaningful methods of reporting call center activity.

ACDs and service level

There are a number of alternative methods to calculate service level using ACDs. Following are some of the most common calculations used, although some ACDs allow users to specify other definitions of service level using a variety of other call center parameters:

1. *Calls answered in* Y *seconds divided by calls answered:*

$$\frac{\text{CA}(Y \text{ sec})}{\text{CA}}$$

This is a very simple but incomplete measure of service level. It is not recommended for a definitive analysis because it considers only answered calls. It is an incomplete recognition of call activity and, therefore, not a good measure of service level. For example, call abandonment is entirely ignored in this calculation.

2. *Calls answered + calls abandoned in* Y *seconds divided by (total calls answered + total calls abandoned):*

$$\frac{\text{CA} + \text{CAB} (Y \text{ sec})}{(\text{TCA} + \text{TCB})}$$

For most situations, this alternative is preferable because the calculations include all traffic received by the ACD; therefore, it provides a complete picture of call center activity. The combination of total calls answered (TCA) plus total calls abandoned (TCB) is often referred to as *total calls offered*.

3. *Calls answered in* Y *seconds divided by the sum of (calls answered + calls abandoned):*

$$\frac{\text{CA}(Y \text{ sec})}{(\text{CA} + \text{CB})}$$

This alternative tends to be the least popular among call center managers because calls that enter the queue but then fall into the abandoned category drive service level down. It is appropriate in situations where calls enter a queue *after* callers receive a delay announcement. It is not recommended in situations where callers enter a queue *before* they receive the delay announcement.

4.   *Calls answered before* Y *seconds divided by (calls answered + calls abandoned) after* Y *seconds*:

$$\frac{\text{CA(before } Y \text{ sec)}}{(\text{CA} + \text{CB})(\text{after } Y \text{ sec})}$$

With this calculation, abandoned calls only impact service level if they happen after the specified Y seconds. This measurement provides a way to avoid "penalizing" the service level due to callers who abandon quickly, without ignoring abandoned calls altogether.

Turning service level into quality of service

As many call center managers have discovered, it is important not to confuse service level with *quality of service.* It is possible to regularly and continuously meet service-level objectives and at the same time create extra work, have low productivity, and provide a poor quality of service to customers. A narrow focus on service level will not necessarily provide quality. CSRs can have an excellent service level but still make some or all of the following mistakes that may not be reflected in service level because they are content related and not traffic related:

- Relay the wrong information to callers

- Make callers upset

- Fail to accomplish call center objectives

- Record incorrect information

- Miss opportunities to capture valuable feedback

Service level—a limited measure

Service level is a limited measure of overall call center performance because it indicates only that "not too many callers had to wait longer than a certain number of seconds before reaching a CSR." Unfortunately, service level measurement devices such as those provided in an ACD cannot measure whether callers and the organization achieved their mutual goals. It is important not to play the "numbers" game and to keep the primary objective in mind.

Optimizing service level with quality is an ongoing consideration in every call center. If service level is the only characteristic that is being measured and managed there can be too much emphasis on it. A good service level is an enabler for other important objectives—calls are coming in and being answered so that the organization and callers can achieve their mutual goals: getting information on product or services, selling products, or providing other customer-oriented information.

On the other hand, a poor service level reduces call center productivity. As service deteriorates, more and more callers are likely to complain when calls are finally answered. CSRs will spend valuable time apologizing to callers and will not be able to answer as many calls as the service level deteriorates. Costs will increase and revenues will likely be affected negatively. Other negative situations will also develop. Calls will get longer because CSRs will eventually pace themselves differently. And they will take breaks when they are on calls if they are so busy they cannot take breaks between calls, because the "in-between" time no longer exists. In the longer term, as service level starts to slip and continues to decline, CSRs often try to clear up the queue. If they are not able to do this, they eventually adopt work habits that are detrimental to the call center. Call handling time goes up and employee moral is affected and turnover and burnout increase, along with recruitment and training costs. This is obviously a disastrous spiral for a call center environment.

The impact of a poor service level will ultimately be felt in the quality of service offered. When CSRs are overworked due to constant congestion in the queue, they often become lazy and can also become less "customer-friendly." Callers are telling them about the difficulties they had getting through to the center, and CSRs make more mistakes under these conditions. These mistakes contribute to repeat calls, unnecessary service calls, escalation of calls, and complaints to higher management, callbacks, and so on—all of which drive service level down further, again illustrating that a poor service level is the beginning of a vicious cycle.

Based on this discussion, it is apparent that quality should never be considered as an attribute that is *opposite* to service level—the two must go together.

Choosing a service-level objective

The number of staff needed to handle transactions and the schedules should flow from the service-level objective. (see Figure 3.6) Imagine that the call center receives 50 calls that last an average of three minutes in a half-hour period. If there are only two CSRs answering calls, the delay time for

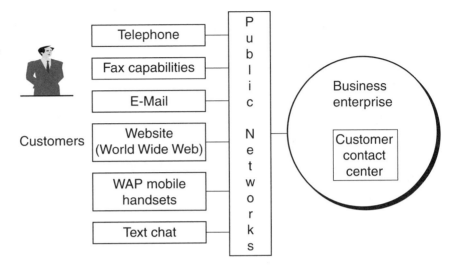

Figure 3.6
Customer inputs to a multimedia call/ contact center.

most callers will be long, and abandonment rates will be high. Adding CSRs will reduce delay times. An acceptable rule of thumb is reduce the queue to an acceptable level for both the call center and the callers. The number of CSRs required to provide this degree of service then becomes the service-level target and defines the correct level of resources to meet that target.

There are no generally accepted industry standards for service level, but there are several factors, mostly subjective, that affect service level:

- Value of the call

- Fully loaded labor costs

- Trunk costs

- Caller tolerances

- An organization's desire to differentiate products or services by level of service provided in the call center

An industry standard would have to be based on all call centers placing the same values on these factors, which would be difficult, if not impossible, to achieve. However, some regulated industries have defined service levels. For example, service levels are defined by regulation for cable TV companies in the United States and for telecom call centers in some countries. These levels of service may be regulated through a service-level agreement (SLA). In Canada, Bell Canada service levels are regulated by the CRTC (Canadian Radio and Telecommunications Commission).

It is reasonable to conclude from the discussion here that the correct service level for a call center, apart from legal regulations, is the one that meets the following conditions:

- Minimizes expenses
- Keeps abandonment to an acceptable level
- Maximizes revenue
- Meets caller needs and expectations
- Minimizes agent burnout and errors
- Is agreed upon and supported by senior management

Guidelines for determining service-level objectives

There are a number of methods for determining service-level objectives, but the following four approaches have been distilled from the collective experience of call center managers:

- Minimize abandonment
- Take the middle of the road—follow the crowd
- Relate to competition
- Conduct a customer survey

Each approach requires some subjectivity and judgment on the part of management personnel.

Minimize abandonment

No single service level would satisfy all situations affecting how long callers will wait for a CSR to respond. A number of factors influence caller tolerance, including

- How motivated callers are to reach the call center
- What substitutes for a telephone call are available
- The competition's service level
- The caller's expectations based on past experiences
- How much time the caller has
- The conditions at the locations callers are calling from
- Who is paying for the call

The first approach to choosing a service-level objective essentially involves asking the question, *How low can response times go without losing callers?* This assumes that a higher level of service means lower abandonment and vice versa; that is, as long as callers don't abandon, service is acceptable. But that is not always the case—abandonment is not static and will fluctuate as the seven factors of caller tolerance change. Abandonment is difficult to forecast, and choosing a service level around abandonment is one of the least desirable ways to establish a service level.

Take the middle of the road—Follow the crowd

The "middle-of-the-road" method defines service level as *percentage of calls answered in so many seconds, for example, 80 percent answered in 20 seconds.* The 80/20 objective has been cited in some ACD manuals as an "industry standard." However, it has never been recognized as such, even though many early call centers used it. The 80/20 objective is still fairly common because for many call centers it is a reasonable balance between callers' expectations and the practicality of having enough staff to meet the objective.

Benchmarking the competition

Another popular method for choosing a service level is to benchmark competitors or other similar organizations and then use this information as a starting point. This can be done informally by simply asking for the information or by conducting a formal benchmarking study. Whatever the approach, keep in mind that the results reported and those actually achieved may not reflect the actual situation. Human nature tends to "color" the truth on the positive side, especially when the competition may have access to the responses! Cases have been documented where companies with the same service level objectives—80 percent of calls answered in 30 seconds—achieved very different results.

A more formal way to determine the potential impact of abandonment on overall costs is *incremental revenue analysis*, a variation of the benchmarking approach. Traditionally, this approach has been used in revenue-generating environments, for example, airline or railway reservation centers and catalog companies, where calls have a measurable value. It is more difficult to use in customer service centers and help desk environments, where the value of calls can only be estimated. In incremental revenue analysis, a cost is attached to abandoned calls and assumptions made as to how many calls would be lost at various service levels. CSRs and trunks are added as long as they produce positive incrementals, either marginal/additional revenue or value, after paying for the initial costs. As long as the assumptions are clearly understood and communicated to management, this approach can be very useful when combined with other approaches.

Customer survey

A fourth method for choosing service level is to conduct a customer survey. This involves analyzing caller tolerance.

It is always a good idea to know what callers expect, but random call arrival means that different callers have different experiences with a call center. Even for a modest service level such as 80 percent answered in 60 seconds, over half the callers will get an immediate answer. Some may still be in the queue for three to five minutes (assuming no overflow or other contingency). This significant range of response times means that many callers in a set would claim that the service level was great, while others would describe it as totally unsatisfactory!

There are variations in customer survey methodology. Some managers take samples of individual callers and then compare the responses to the actual wait times for their calls. Others conduct general customer surveys. These samples indicate that waits of up to 60 to 90 seconds are acceptable to a fair percentage of the callers surveyed.

3.7   Creating value through workforce optimization

Call center managers need to understand that successful management means understanding the complex trade-offs inherent in the sophisticated call center operating environment, where the proper allocation, dispersal, and treatment of the human resource are fundamental requirements. Quantifying and increasing the value of workforce optimization solutions is important and needs to be addressed. Typically, analysis focuses on software and infrastructure investments that will yield greater efficiencies resulting from automation. Some call center product vendors, however, take a different approach that assesses the return on investment in the human resource, the employees in the call center.

Assessing value creation

Personnel costs usually account for 70 to 80% of overall operational expenses in contact centers. Leveraging these personnel resources efficiently through workforce optimization solutions can potentially provide significant returns. However, most models for assessing value creation only consider the benefits derived from streamlining the processes of forecasting and

Figure 3.7
*Ascending levels of
CSR skills
experience.*

scheduling call center staff to meet service goals. These models may result in significant gains through the automation of various functions, but they fail to address the real complexity of workforce optimization and are far too simple to portray accurately the real meaning of workforce optimization.

The major factors involved in managing and maximizing CSR productivity and the quality of customer interactions while maximizing the number of contacts handled per agent hinge on the ability to match the volume and type of customer contacts precisely. These factors include availability of agents by skill type and contact media type (e.g., e-mail, phone, or fax). Done effectively, the returns for each call can be maximized and result in a maximization of returns for the entire call center. (see Figure 3.7)

Staffing and customer service

To paraphrase a well-known authority on workforce optimization, Dr. Richard Coleman, founder of Coleman Consulting Group, it takes an organization as sophisticated as a contact (call) center to show how developing strategic staffing plans relies on understanding the complex trade-offs inherent in each staffing scenario. The effects of seemingly insignificant staffing changes are far-reaching. Staffing plans dictate the kind of service customers receive and, ultimately, the profitability of customer relationships. The implementation of best practices and an understanding of the mathematics behind workforce optimization, as described previously in this chapter, are essential to successfully leveraging the center's human capital.

Most call centers lack the tools to assess the rationale behind their service-level agreements effectively. As noted previously, government regulation dictates the service level required in some industries, for example, public utilities. Missing the service commitment in these industries can result in fines and subsequent damage to businesses. In other, unregulated sectors, most organizations set service goals according to industry benchmarks, which can be a somewhat arbitrary process. However, the difference between 70 and 80% of calls answered in 20 seconds is recognized by customers who communicate with the call center. On the other hand, the marginal benefit to the customer of moving from 91 to 93% of calls answered in 20 seconds may have significant cost implications and not make much tangible difference in the quality of the customer experience. What is also lacking from these arbitrary models is the ability to quantify the significant *customer loyalty* and *profitability gains,* above and beyond efficiency gains, that an enterprise can expect to achieve by optimizing its workforce.

The customer experience

The automation of workforce measurement is intended to ensure that customers remain loyal, that a mutually profitable relationship exists and is retained, and that the impact of workforce optimization will not lead the company into an unprofitable or nonviable direction. These objectives can be realized by establishing and sustaining a strong customer experience. The process begins with the people who most frequently interact with customers—call center employees—the mangers, supervisors, and CSRs who are the front line of customer contact.

The call center employee environment

By strengthening the link between employees and customers, workforce optimization enhances profitability. The call center is often the only means for the organization to regularly interact with customers. Unfortunately, the typical working environment of a call center does not foster a harmonious relationship between the company and the call center employees, for several reasons:

- High stress

- Limited work space

- Pressure

- Intense and fast-paced activity

- The perception of most employees of their function within the enterprise, a perception that often belies the important role of the call center employee in the organization.

Working in a call center can be a thankless job, and a reflection of this fact, noted previously in this book, is the extremely high staff turnover relative to other industries—ranging somewhere between 20 and 35% annually. In many centers, CSRs are treated as nothing more than an overhead cost rather than as critically important to increasing enterprise profitability. This view is changing as corporate executives realize the importance of customer relationship management (CRM) and the call center role to corporate CRM strategy. (Chapter 6 describes in detail the contribution of call centers and call center employees to an organization.) Organizations that are able to channel the human potential of the call center realize a significant benefit from this corporate resource. Those that succeed in positively influencing employees' attitudes about their jobs begin by including more flexibility and improving job recognition. *Employee job satisfaction has been demonstrated to be one of the most significant determinants of the quality of customer relationships.*

Training, recognition, and employee empowerment

Many call center employees believe that they have little control over their own schedules and even less over how their current position might translate into a career path with future growth opportunities within the organization and beyond. When questioned about what can be done to improve their job satisfaction, the vast majority of employees cite *increasing recognition for the important work they do and providing more flexibility in scheduling to allow for outside commitments.* Most CSRs would also like to have the opportunity to schedule their own enrichment training, to improve their skills, or to learn about emerging technologies or products that may assist them to advance in their field of employment. They also want to be able to move into higher-paying or more strategic positions within the organization. In some centers, higher-skilled positions command higher salaries; for example, CSRs trained to handle e-mail customer contacts often earn more than those responsible for phone communication alone.

Naturally, a certain percentage of CSRs will always perceive their work as a short-term job rather than as a career, but improvements in working conditions can substantially impact the turnover resulting from CSRs changing jobs for slight improvements in their work environment. Anecdotal evidence from a Gartner research report indicates that 85% of CSRs who leave their organizations leave of their own volition, while only 15% are terminated due to poor performance. Of the agents who leave on their own, some move on to other opportunities for reasons beyond employer control, for example, a career change. It would be impossible and even undesirable to eliminate the natural turnover of the poorest performers and those employees looking for different opportunities. In many cases, however, CSRs don't leave companies, they leave managers!

The experience of call center managers and the results obtained form research reports point up the fact that a significant amount of employee turnover can be influenced by the employer. Experienced call center managers know that the nature of the call center industry will always produce a higher turnover rate than other industry sectors. The Gartner research report concludes that call center turnover for nontechnical agents will probably never fall under 10–12% per year because of natural turnover. If this statistic is valid, there is still a substantial percentage of employee turnover that falls into the category of *controllable turnover*. Call center turnover in some industry sectors ranges as high as 50%; the controllable turnover percentage is therefore quite significant. The challenge for call center management and for the corporation's human resources department is to determine the personnel policies that are most effective in reducing employee turnover.

Responding to employee needs

One of the keys to reducing the controllable turnover percentage is to understand and respond to the changing way employees view their jobs. There is a requirement for a new approach to employee concerns and, to paraphrase Peter Drucker, it is change in the way companies need to treat employees … organizations need to market membership (employment in) their companies at least as much as they market products and services. People need to be attracted, recognized, and rewarded. In the call center environment, increasing flexibility and allowing for a career path are two ways that turnover can be curbed and a reputation as an employer of choice can be gained—a reputation as an employer with such high levels of employee satisfaction that employees refer the business to potential customers and employees alike.

Some workforce optimization systems offered by vendors of call center services and products provide the tools and best practices needed to increase efficiency and improve employee satisfaction while meeting business goals and objectives. By empowering employees to manage their own time and providing some information on how their day-to-day activities relate to their longer-term career goals, these solutions increase employee satisfaction and loyalty. Some workforce optimization products have a training component as well that offers opportunities for training on new systems or products—within defined parameters—to meet customer service demands and to satisfy employees' desires for more control over their careers. These products include training for new and existing employees, giving them the skills necessary to meet the requirements of critical positions that need to be filled. This pays off in greater efficiency for the organization because it spends fewer resources on recruiting for new positions.

Call center analyst Paul Stockford of Saddletree Research has described how CRM has made companies realize that customer interactions with contact or call center employees have strategic value. As a result, the strategic role of these employees is rapidly being recognized. The result of a well-managed scheduling program—one that considers both customer and agent attributes—has the extended effect of building loyalty among contact center agents as well, with the resulting economic benefits flowing straight to the bottom line.

The impact of employee loyalty

The long-term effects of increased employee loyalty often have a greater impact than the profitability gains resulting from more effective use of training and recruiting dollars. Long-term employee loyalty is critical to retaining loyal, satisfied customers. Satisfied employees are more likely to refer an organization to friends and family, with the potential for new customers as well as sources for recruiting new employees.

As noted, the average annual turnover in call centers is between 20 and 35%, and companies spend an average of $6,000–$8,000 on recruitment and training per agent. Even a marginal improvement in employee loyalty has the potential to generate considerable cost savings. But significant as these numbers are, they do not begin to quantify the tremendous financial benefits of the productivity gains that result from employee tenure. Especially during periods of economic uncertainty, when shareholders of publicly traded companies look critically at costs and earnings, controlling labor expenditures becomes even more important. Because loyal employees have critical customer and corporate knowledge, the benefits of their loyalty during these times quickly spread throughout the organization. Thus, using effective human resource practices and policies to keep employees satisfied results in knowledge and skills staying within the organization and their continual leveraging to serve customers.

Categorical knowledge

Employees with what Aberdeen Research refers to as *categorical knowledge* are able to immediately recognize customer needs and act decisively and appropriately to satisfy them. These employees are far more likely to resolve issues on the first call or contact than less experienced agents with the same skill. Even the most talented new employee lacks the intuition and skills that come only from experience. Veteran employees are valuable because their experience and corporate knowledge translates into less time spent on each contact and greater overall productivity. A recent study by the University of Calgary further confirms the connection between customer satisfaction and employee training and tenure. The study showed that highly trained generalist agents pulled in a 22% higher level of customer satisfaction, and agents with even more specialized training average 11% higher customer satisfaction than generalists. These results demonstrate that *training is very important and advanced training is even more important!*

Employees with categorical knowledge are of benefit to the organization because they have gained experience and a solid understanding of the company's business as a result of the years spent with the company. Their knowledge and ability to satisfy customers transform the call center into a profit center through significant improvements in upsell and cross sell abilities. According to some studies on customer retention, it costs 5 to 12 times more to acquire a new customer than to retain an existing customer. Therefore, keeping customer-focused, seasoned employees is necessary to the overall success of the enterprise. Customers recognize the importance of good service as well. In surveys, customers repeatedly cite the level and quality of customer support as the most important variables in determining whether to do business with companies on an ongoing basis. This finding can be translated into an important axiom for call center management: *Keep the CSR and retain the customer!*

Customer loyalty and profitability

Customers who are not completely satisfied may defect, particularly when offered a better deal, a more convenient location, or the promise of a higher level of service from a competitor. When customers are fully satisfied with a company's service, they will return time and again to make new purchases and to expand their relationship with the organization. The secret to obtaining and retaining that elusive *customer loyalty* is long-term, seasoned employees. They have the power to truly satisfy customers and extend their loyalty—they know the company, the customers, and how to build lasting, profitable relationships.

Although solidifying relationships with employees and customers may be difficult, the effort expended will bring long-term benefits. In fact, reducing customer defections by as little as *5 percentage points* can double profits. Studies show that, over time, companies with higher customer retention rates are more profitable. Incremental increases in retention rates have significant impact on profitability over the long term. Many have written about this correlation between customer loyalty and company profitability. The proof can be found in some of the world's most successful companies—companies like Charles Schwab, Cisco, and General Motors, to select a few household names—where a direct relationship can be established among employee/customer satisfaction, loyalty, and company success. These are also companies that have well-earned reputations for listening to both employee and customer needs and working hard to maintain relationships with profitable customers and with seasoned employees.

Conclusion: managing the primary assets

Many organizations have made significant investments in automating and managing the customer experience in the call center and at other customer contact points, but they have often forgotten the most important element: *the people who actually determine customer loyalty and subsequently, enterprise profitability.* Call centers are the places where many of these people are located and where the customer frequently has the first contact with the company.

By properly managing the most important component of a call center—the human resource—and influencing how employees view their jobs and how they perform their jobs in a positive way, sound personnel management practices and workforce optimization systems can begin a chain of value creation that leads to closer relationships with employees and more profitable relationships with customers. By assisting call center managers to manage their primary assets effectively—the call center employees who are behind customer interactions—workforce optimization systems are unique in their ability to impact relationships between employees and customers.

Following are some convenient guidelines for evaluating how well a corporate call center is optimizing the potential of its human resources with good management practices. They indicate how the implementation of workforce optimization systems can benefit the organization.

MAXIMIZING THE RETURN ON HUMAN ASSETS

Performance Criteria for Call Center Managers

- Optimize business practices to ensure employees are working in the most effective ways.

- Incorporate employee enrichment effectively into employee work times.

- Establish the true marginal cost of a labor hour.

- Use workforce optimization software to optimize and schedule employees.

- Ensure employees have schedule flexibility while meeting service-level objectives.

- Ensure that the first call/contact resolution rate meets objectives.

- Ensure that the cost and efficiency implications of customer service goals are fully understood by call center staff.

- Establish the appropriateness of operational service goals and ensure they are cost-effective.

- Establish overlapping CSR schedules to minimize the impact of absenteeism and lateness.

- Be prepared to incorporate new customer contact channels into the call center.

- Organize and arrange physical resources as well as CSR schedules—office space, computers, and so on—to optimize effective and efficient sharing.

- Involve employees in managing their own schedules and designing flexible shifts.

- Recruit and hire the right employees with the right skills at the right times.

- Determine who the best customers are and quantify the lifetime value of these customers.

3.8   **Disaster and contingency planning in call centers**

An important aspect of managing a corporate facility—one that includes resources, equipment, and people—is disaster and contingency planning. There are several reasons why a disaster and contingency plan should be put in place by every call center operation, and should be rehearsed, like a fire drill, periodically. Not the least of these reasons is maintaining call center services in the face of natural or human disasters. Many problems or contingencies can arise that result in a call center being shut down and customer communication lost, possibly for an extended period, if alternative arrangements have not been made.

Downtime

Several situations can result in call center downtime: natural disasters—storms, snow, flooding—can keep people from getting to the center; construction, often the bane of those who need to maintain continuous communication services because of frequent disruptions to power, cable, or telephone lines; fire; power spikes; cable cuts; computer crashes; and network outages—all can very quickly cut communication links to the outside world. While these disturbances may be localized, affecting only a small number of centers, the cost of downtime to any center hit by a temporary shutdown can be enormous. This is why it is critical for call centers to invest in disaster contingency planning, with the hope that it may never have to be implemented but if required the center and staff are well prepared.

Coping with emergency situations

The following procedures for coping with emergency situations have been developed from the experience of many call centers.

Identify key systems at risk in a disaster or emergency situation

Some of these systems are obvious—switching technology, data processing equipment, and so on. How vulnerable is the business if the package delivery/courier service is not available? Labor trouble in these service organizations can shut a business down. Orders may be taken over the phone, but if they can't be delivered, customers may stay away. Because all organizations depend on other companies, every service that is outsourced is particularly vulnerable, especially order fulfillment, personnel supply, and service and maintenance on internal equipment.

If outside services are critical to continuous operation, there are essentially two choices for setting up a contingency plan:

- Single-source services, ensuring that vendors have enough redundancy or extra capacity to handle defined contingencies

- Multisource services to provide backup in case the primary vendor has difficulty meeting contractual obligations

As noted, contingency planning needs to be applied to every service, from courier services to communication resources such as long-distance services. Organizations that are service providers need to inform customers of contingency plans to ensure continued service in case of snow, fire, or other short- and medium-term emergencies.

Conduct a cabling/wiring/power assessment

Map out every wire and connection in the center with a pictorial interconnection diagram showing the connections between technologies. This will make it possible to check the power protection status of every server, PC, switch, and node. A critical assessment will identify which items are covered by UPS (uninterruptible power supply) units, which have hot-swappable power supplies, and which systems require these resources.

Telephone systems are particularly vulnerable to lightning strikes, and a protection mechanism should be in place to prevent outages in phone service. A lightning strike could short out all phone sets and headsets, leaving CSRs with working computers and incoming ACD calls that cannot be answered.

Identify manual work procedures

A contingency plan should provide for manual order taking if the computer systems go down. Make sure there are always enough hard copies of current product or service catalogs for every inbound CSR so that basic pricing and ordering information can be given to a caller. CSRs also need to be trained in procedures for handling customers when customer data are not available. In addition, contingency planning should provide backup resources as well as procedures for handling the sudden flood of calls that come into the center when the IVR or auto attendant is down.

The Internet can pose another type of contingency planning problem. Can the center react to an increase or decrease in contact volume through alternative means, such as e-mail or text-chat? The more access methods customers have, the more points at which a sudden change can cause problems that may not be disastrous but may require special consideration. On the other hand, the more avenues a customer has to contact a company, the less likely the company will lose that customer to a disaster.

Identify key personnel

It's important to know who will be on call during a problem situation and the specific responsibilities of those personnel. Every staff member should be briefed on his or her responsibilities in an emergency.

Any working group convened for call center contingency planning should include members from other departments, especially people from IT and the facilities management departments, in order to share knowledge. They need to be made aware of the impact call center failure could have on the entire company and on the company's revenue stream. Personnel from other departments need to provide coordinated responses to problems that affect data processing, order processing, shipping, the availability of human resources—in fact, every aspect of the business.

Explore secondary operating sites

Sometimes, the only way truly to prevent disasters is to replicate call center functions in another location. If there's a flood, fire, or natural disaster that affects the central operation, CSRs can continue to operate from another location. Doing this could be as simple as using non call center assets (basic office space, for example) or as complex as arranging to buy contingency services from organizations that provide disaster and contingency services. There are also companies that offer to operate an entire call center from alternative sites in any location, for a substantial fee. These "call centers on call" are not traditional outsourcing services. User organizations pay a retainer to have access to their services as required, such as in an extreme emergency. Disaster-oriented services can provide a range of resources, including equipment, temporary (often mobile) facilities, and data processing and backup functions, as well.

These are only a few of the options available. It is important to remember that the continued operation of a call center depends on a complex set of connected technologies that are vulnerable to circumstances outside the control of call center management.

Power protection

Power is one of the company's most serious resources that require protection. When a call center goes down, company revenues stop flowing. Call center downtime, whether caused by natural or human disasters, is to be avoided at all costs. Downtime means customer calls are not coming in, orders are not being taken, and customers are getting impatient, even angry. They will turn to other companies to meet their needs. Thus, protecting the center from power outages is an important function that must be performed from the first day of operation.

One of the most common causes of downtime is failure of the electrical power system, often without warning, an event that will take a call center "off the air," usually for some time. Backup power sources are mandatory to prevent downtime due to power outages. The IVR (interactive voice response) system is a good example of a technology resource that will be out of service in a power failure. Once a call center has become dependent on IVR, it becomes a crucial part of the enterprise—handling a substantial amount of call traffic, promoting customer satisfaction, and generating revenue. In some cases, the IVR system handles all inbound calls, either directly or by passing them back to CSRs through an ACD. In this situation, loss of IVR would be as serious as loss of phone service.

Some facts about power problems that can help a call center manager prepare for power outages in the most effective manner are

- *Power problems are the single most frequent cause of phone and computer system failure.* Surveys indicate that the average IVR system has a significant power fluctuation (spike, surge, or brownout) approximately 400 times a year. Increasing consumption in regional power grids will only exacerbate the problem.

- *Power-related damage is one of the most difficult types of damage to recover from.* This form of damage creates two problems: It can destroy hardware, often necessitating costly, time-consuming replacements, and it wipes out data.

- *Multiple connections to trunks, networks, peripherals, and so on increase the number of access routes for power surges.* The more components that are interconnected, including data sources, the more vulnerable the center is to a power outage.

Uninterruptible power supply (UPS)

An uninterruptible power supply (UPS) is a battery system that provides power to a telephone switch or computer. Surge protectors control high voltages that can surge down power or telephone lines, destroying delicate equipment. Power conditioners remove noise, adjust voltage levels, and generally deliver clean power to telephone switches and computers. There are high-end UPS systems available that combine all of these functions in a single unit. Some UPS systems are marketed specifically for telecommunications applications; however, the UPS specifications for power protection of telephone systems are essentially the same as for a computer system.

Power management software is a recent development in the management of electrical power. These products allow users to track power conditions throughout the network from a workstation and provide UPS with more sophisticated features, including the capability of shutting down unattended equipment.

Power protection is an inexpensive form of insurance for call centers. The technology is proven and the added cost ranges from 10 to 25% of the hardware's value, excluding the value of the data that power protection will preserve in the event of a power outage. In fact, call center data are usually far more valuable than the hardware, which can be replaced.

Auditing disaster and contingency plans

There are two major components to a successful disaster and contingency recovery strategy. The first is *contingency planning*, which involves identifying all the elements critical to the call center operation: people, processes and equipment. It also means planning for situations where these elements will not be available with backup strategies for a variety of emergency conditions. The second component is *installing a technology net* that includes power protection, backup power supplies, redundant trunks and carriers, and duplicating any other resources that may be required in an emergency.

To ensure complete protection of the call center, an audit of disaster and contingency plans should also include the following activities:

- *Document every aspect of the center*—from wiring runs to home phone numbers of all critical personnel. This activity includes putting all plans on paper so they will survive a network crash. Staff members need to know where the plans are stored and have quick access to them.

- *Conduct emergency drills involving all staff*—so they are well prepared for a real emergency. They need to know their roles and how to keep the center operating.

- *Identify potential risks*—depending on the geographic location of the center, there may be greater likelihood of an emergency involving a snowstorm than an earthquake.

- *Conduct a power audit*—UPS devices are designed with the assumption that building wiring will provide proper routes to ground and has sufficient load capacity to control diverted power surges. Ensure that building power circuitry meets this requirement.

What needs to be protected? Identify exactly what systems are particularly critical and which are less critical and nonessential in the short term to the continued operation of the center. Establish priorities. Is it more important to be able to take orders? Or provide service? Thinking about these priorities will provide useful insight into the way the call center fits into the company's overall business process.

The key objective in disaster and contingency planning is to take precautions to ensure a minimum continuity of function and connection to customers. The call center is one of a company's most vulnerable departments because it has several complex core technologies and the loss of its operational capabilities means being cut off from customers; therefore, its recovery should be a top priority.

3.9   **Outsourcing the call center**

Setting up an outsourcing vendor for a corporate call center is a complex task. Putting all of the company's corporate eggs in an outsourcing basket may give many call center managers some uneasy moments. It's difficult enough to ensure that a company's own employees are managing customer relationships correctly. The outsourcing organization is being asked to handle an extremely valuable corporate asset: *the customer relationship.* The importance of this aspect of a corporation's business operations cannot be overemphasized, as will be shown in greater detail in Chapter 6, "Building Customer Relationships with Call Centers."

Market studies and analysis of the views of call center managers regarding outsourcing reveal widespread concern over the benefits of outsourcing. In one recent user study, users reported higher satisfaction levels with in-house call centers than with outsourced call center services. Nevertheless, another report from IDC on the worldwide call center services industry indicates that it will grow to $58.6 billion by 2003 based on three segments of the call center services market: consulting, systems integration, and outsourcing. Outsourcing was reported to be the largest segment, with 74% of the total market, or $42 billion by 2003.

Call center outsourcing will continue to grow at a strong pace; however, the growth comes with a price tag. Users of outsourcing services are concerned, as they should be, with "staff competence," "flexibility," and "the caliber of operations" at their outsourced centers. The outsourcing business has grown rapidly over the past several years, however, because, by and large, outsourcers do provide good service, and companies need the service, the expertise and the technology provided by these organizations.

Outsourcing and maintaining customer relationships

The outsourcing sector is a very large component of an even larger call center industry, and it is undergoing continual change. Just as in-house call centers need continual monitoring and upgrading, so do outsourced centers. As well, managers who opt for an outsourced call center are beginning to realize how critical customer relationships are and are understandably concerned about losing control over corporate strategies. Turning sensitive service and revenue tasks over to an outside vendor creates stresses that are reflected in tentative satisfaction ratings. It is important for clients of outsourcing operations to manage their relationships just as if the centers were in house.

The fragile business of outsourcing

Outsourcing companies are a major component of the "teleservices" industry and are often the subject of adverse reports in the media, especially if they are public companies. In general, outsourcing centers are larger than in-house centers and are often comprised of networks of interlinked centers. As noted, they are subject to the same human resources problems—high turnover and employee burnout—as any other sector of the teleservices industry.

Growth in the outsourcing business has brought pressure to bear on these operations, requiring them to be very productive and to reflect the corporate cultures of their client organizations. For a variety of reasons, outsourcing services are a fragile element of the call center service market. Outsourcers must cater to a customer base that demands the highest levels of technology and insists that outsourcers provide very sophisticated off-premise technology that can be integrated into their own existing systems. The services provided by outsourcers are a luxury for many client organizations and will be scaled back during bad times to reduce costs and will likely become very price competitive. All of the negative business factors that affect in-house call centers have an even greater impact on outsourced centers: shortage of qualified labor, capital costs of keeping pace with demand and new technology, and the introduction of unproven, innovative technologies, such as Web/call center combinations.

For these reasons, it is difficult to turn a profit in the call center outsourcing business, yet many organizations are attracted to the business opportunity and are willing to "buck the odds." The business opportunity that attracts outsourcers is the growth of new businesses that require some form of call center or customer contact service in their formative stages. Often, when a company is growing the only way to keep up with an expanding customer base is to rely on outside resources. Traditionally, outsourcers have functioned as a bridge—handling high call volumes during peak seasons or during product launches.

Outsourcing is a good technique for testing new concepts, products, or services without incurring capital expenses. A new campaign can be tested on an outbound list without incurring the costs involved in buying communications equipment or hiring additional employees. Outsourcers can offer the latest technologies in the most sophisticated implementations and can readily handle short-term requirements very well.

Managing the relationship

The relationship between a company and its outsourcer needs to be managed in the same way as the relationship between a company and its customers. Organizations that use outsourced call centers can take some specific steps to ensure they get the most out of their relationship with the outsourcer.

The first step is to clearly define the responsibilities and goals the outsourcer is expected to achieve. An outsourcer is a partner, one who makes, or should make, a concerted effort to understand the goals of the client organization if the relationship is to be a long-term one. Some outsourcers have a tendency to put all their clients in the same basket—assuming that the same services will suffice for all business sectors, a belief that is far from the real-world situation. Different businesses need different types of call center services—one size does not fit all!

Organizations evaluating outsourcing services should pay close attention to the experience and special brand of services offered by potential outsourcers. A major consideration should be whether the outsourcer is experienced in conducting business in the same way as the client company. And if so, are they coming into the relationship with preconceived notions of how the business should be run? The evaluation should include checking references and calling in to centers to see how calls are handled. Staff training of outsourcer personnel is another important element in selecting the right outsourcing service provider. Is there a regular program for refreshing the knowledge of CSRs? What are the turnover rates? Other issues that are important to clarify are the following:

- What physical centers will be used for campaigns?

- What is the turnover rate at those centers?

- How skilled and motivated are the outsourcer's CSRs?

- What kind of career path is available for agents—do they get promoted to supervisor?

- How long is the average tenure?

Making the move

Moving to an outsourcing facility is a business decision that is often difficult to make due to "fear of the unknown." When an organization manages its own in-house call center, the strengths and weaknesses of people working in the center are known and managers have learned how to use these characteristics for best effect. Also, acknowledging the necessity to move to outsourcing, especially for the smaller, growing company, can be dispiriting. The sense that you are losing touch with customers, not to mention having to rely on outsourcing personnel who represent an unknown human resource quantity, can be an unsettling experience, not only for the call center manager but also for other internal department heads charged with the responsibility of contracting with an outsourcer and working with that organization.

Some pointers for outsourcers

The outsourcing/client relationship is an extremely important one and should be well thought out before any agreement is signed. The successful outsourcing organization needs to emphasize the connection it offers between the client company and its customers and prospects. They need to rely on their experience, and that of their CSRs, to develop confidence among their client organizations.

Outsourcers have access to a range of technology tools that enable their client companies to closely monitor their communication with the client company's customers closer to the point of interaction—real-time reporting tools are one example. A client sees the results of calls (inbound or outbound) without having to take those calls itself. Other tools—monitoring and quality assurance systems—can deliver complete voice and data records of each call to the client, if required. Like any other service organization, outsourcers must take responsibility for the quality and nature of their services, and should be held accountable by their clients for any errors of commission or omission.

Telephone companies as outsourcers

Telephone companies, also referred to as *telcos* or *carriers* in this book, are a major component of the teleservices industry. They provide the communications infrastructure—cable, satellite, networking facilities, and other equipment essential to every form of electronic communication—and carry voice, data, or video data, both digital and analog. Using their vast networks of communications resources, telcos often provide call center outsourcing facilities as one element of their communication services to customers. There is some advantage to using a telephone carrier to provide outsourcing. For one thing, they undoubtedly have available the most current communication, networking, and call-management technologies. The communications business is highly competitive, and no telco wants to be left behind in the race to offer the latest technology in its core business areas.

Telco service offerings

Often, the outsourcing services offered by telcos are quite comprehensive and may include

- Order fulfillment

- Call handling

- Transaction processing

- Consulting services to improve efficiency

- Methods of using the center to support the company's strategic goals

- Offloading some or all of the in-house call center volume

A full outsourcing service contract with a telco could also include handling every aspect of an in-house call center operation, from call distribution and management, queuing, routing and call processing to each and every customer contact, from the first IVR interaction to faxing back order confirmations. Contracting these functions to a telco-based call center offers a considerable benefit to companies looking for a complete outsourcing package that will be maintained at the highest technological level.

Outsourcing is a natural extension of the basic business of telcos. Much of the communication expertise is already present as part of the telco's core business. They know how to handle calls and call centers, and some of their centers are among the world's busiest. Long-distance carriers have long used their own centers as test beds for their own new technology, including some of the enhanced network services that make their entry into the outsourcing field possible.

Increased revenues for telcos

For the carriers, the economics of providing outsourcing services are extremely attractive. Carriers generate much of their revenue by selling telecom minutes to call centers as well as to others. The 800 number traffic, the bread and butter of call centers, is also a key component of their revenue. Anything they can do to generate usage of their networks will enhance their revenues. Both providing a call center with an off-premise solution for IVR or a multisite option that lets the company hold calls in the network while waiting for an agent to become available are services that generate time usage. Discounts that bring long-distance costs closer to zero cents per minute may be offered to telco call center customers who elect to contract for these value-added services. (see Figure 3.8)

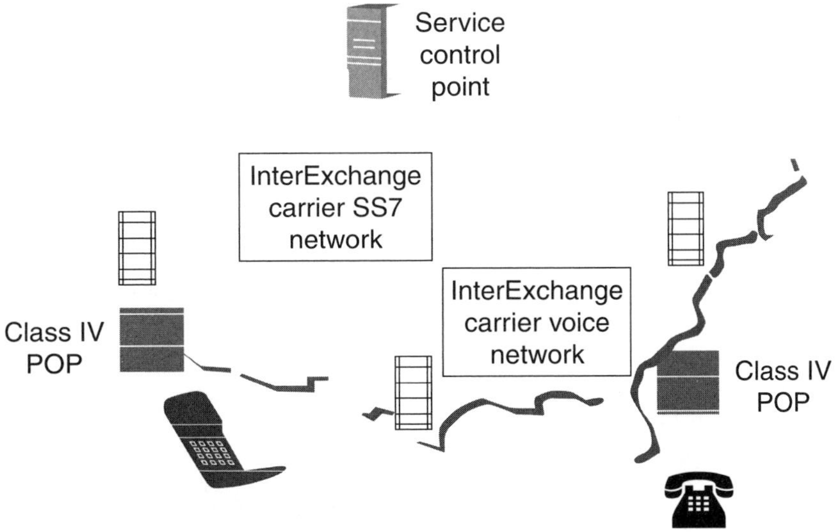

Figure 3.8
The 800 network.

Over time, carriers will gradually enhance their call centers by including agents and will eventually provide the same services as any other outsourcer. Some carriers have already taken on the role of call center "consolidators"—combining all the technology pieces under one contract.

Benefits of telcos as outsourcers

To reiterate, the attraction of carrier outsourcing services to the user organization is that they provide the opportunity to get up and running quickly with a center that the organization will help them build. Users can pick from a large menu of service offerings and hardware and software vendors to supply the applications. The carrier takes contractual responsibility to certify that all of the components integrate completely and successfully, and there is a one-number call for multivendor technical support.

Carriers have taken on an increased level of functionality, of the kind normally provided by an outsourcing organization. The advantage carriers have, as noted, is that they can configure their offerings, can push other vendors into working relationships because they are large organizations, can set standards, and have much closer relationships to call centers than the traditional outsourcer.

Choices to benefit the outsourcing customer

The more choices that call center users have, the better. The next few years will probably see a tremendous boom in the types of services a call center can outsource to a carrier network. Carriers will offer all the automated front-end transactions, especially IVR, and routing will be well handled outside the call center.

As a result of carriers "getting serious" about the outsourcing business, outsourcing will become specialized. For example, if a call center application has more to do with routing and automated call handling, the carrier may well be a better choice than the outsourcing vendor. On the other hand, if the application is more agent-oriented and involves customer-sensitive services like selling or servicing existing customers, a traditional outsourcer may be better qualified to provide the service.

Value-added services from carriers

Network services are being provided by the network carrier in the telecom network outside of traditional premise-based call center equipment. This can be a significant source of revenue for carriers because they can reduce toll-free services to a very low level and more than make up the difference by selling other services as value-added features. Networked services can provide virtual or distributed call centering, dispersing CSRs among many centers and routing calls among them as if they were all located at one site. Also included under the network services umbrellas is IVR, which extracts the customer input from the network, then uses this input to determine how to handle the call.

Web integration services

Web integration services are another burgeoning area of activity for call centers that network carriers can help them with. The technologies involved and the expansion of customer contact points pose significant contact management problems for call centers. Managers now need to cope with the technical and human resources issues that have cropped up from the explosion of Web access channels to the center. Live text-chat, call-me buttons, and even simple e-mail messages can create additional handling requirements for CSRs and managers alike.

Using the network to provide some automated handling of evolving customer contact channels—particularly IVR—is something telcos have been doing for years. They have always had the technology and the equipment to do this. When Centrex ACD facilities and the increasing demand for multisite centers are added to the picture, telcos are in an enviable position to offer a range of outsourcing services. For a call center, outsourcing network-based services, paid for either monthly or by transaction, offers a way to be more flexible in the face of unpredictable volume and varied access pathways.

Predicted growth patterns for the first five or more years of the 21st century indicate that there will be a lot of voice over IP (VoIP), even at the desktop, and a shortage of available and qualified CSRs to work in call centers, which will lead to an increase in home-based, telecommuting CSRs in some sectors. Pressure will therefore come from both call center organizations and the outsourcing community to move to network-based services. The growth of e-commerce and the electronic forms of communication that are a part of this business environment will make it extremely difficult to predict how many transactions will be handled electronically, rather than by live CSRs. From the carriers' perspective, increased competition is forcing them to look at service offerings as a way to differentiate their organizations from others in the business.

Ultimately, all of these new methods of conducting business, along with their technologies, will represent an opportunity for call centers to play mix-and-match with their technology and outsourced services. Network-based services will offer a suitable and acceptable alternative to premise-based equipment for a lot of centers and result in new ways of managing the call center operation.

Outsourcing and network-based call center services

Network-based services are any agent-support systems that traditionally occur within the center: call routing, transaction processing, database lookup, screen pop, among others. Over the next few years, there will be some amalgamation of call center outsourcers, not to mention mergers that will undoubtedly occur in the telecommunication sector. There will be competition to offer Internet-based transactions and video-enabled call centers. With these new offerings to expand the range of options for customers to contact call centers, there will be a wide variety of new and improved services, and call centers will be the beneficiaries. One researcher has reported that network-based call center services have been the biggest growth segment in the call center market, estimating that these services will generate more than $4 billion in annual revenues for service providers by 2005. This report further states that 35% of call center agents worldwide will use some type of network-based call center service, with nearly half of those using network services as their primary call distribution method.

The high-tech outsourcers

Another interesting development in recent years is the evolution of some high-tech companies into major outsourcers, largely due to the requirements of their customers for consulting services relating to their products or services.

As call centers become more widely distributed and provide more business functions, the companies that provide products and services to call centers will also change. There is considerable emphasis within outsourcing organizations on the advanced computer telephony integration (CTI) technology described in Chapter 2 as well as technology for linking call centers with other back-office operations. Outsourcers are becoming "engines of growth" in the call center industry.

Outsourcers and specialty niches

Outsourcers often provide an entrée into specialty markets, either geographic or language-oriented. Some of them provide multilingual capabilities to enable organizations to conduct campaigns in other countries and often globally. As noted, other outsourcers provide services to specific industry sectors, such as retailing, financial institutions, fundraisers, collections, communication, and high technology.

The future of the traditional outsourcer

Traditional outsourcers will continue to be a mainstay of the industry. Although carriers are superbly positioned to provide outsourcing services, this business component is not their main focus, and it is unlikely that carriers will ever replace outsourcer organizations that make outsourcing their core business and therefore concentrate on providing call center services to their customers. Further evidence of this is that opportunities for outsourcing have been available for some years, yet only recently have carriers discovered the market for enhanced services, and they do not have a good track record of developing products from technologies. Traditional outsourcers will undoubtedly retain the competitive advantage.

Carriers tend to be slow to enter new markets and develop new products. This appears to be a characteristic of the telco marketplace and is probably a relic left over from the monopoly positions they held for many years in the communications industry. No need to hurry, there is no competition anyway! Carriers are often referred to as "Ma Bells," an oblique reference to the fact that they have a tendency to "mother" their services and products far too long before introducing them. As a result, they are often left behind by competitors who are not encumbered by the traditions of the monopolies once held by the telcos.

In the past, outsourcers were considered to be primarily outbound entities, providing a range of telemarketing services to organizations that did not have their own telemarketing facilities or that needed some additional resources to run a marketing campaign or customer survey. From this basic entrée into the call center market, outsourcing services have evolved and become much broader and more sophisticated. In fact, outsourcing services now offered go well beyond the original concept of an outsourcing organization. Back-office functions are now offered by outsourcers, and their range of services may include inbound and outbound call handling, customer tracking, quality assurance, fulfillment, data processing, and even help desk customer support—a considerable enhancement of their traditional services.

Customer support or, as it has become known in many industry sectors, the *help desk*, is one area that more and more companies are contracting to outside experts. This is especially true in such industry sectors as personal computers and home electronics, where there may be a high volume of customer support inquiries following purchases that the vendor is not staffed to handle. The advanced technologies that enable calls to be routed and tracked make the help desk function easier and more cost-effective. As postsales customer support becomes simultaneously more important and more expensive, companies are looking for lower-cost alternatives that don't force them to compromise on the quality and level of response.

Challenges and pressures

As noted previously, outsourcers have the same challenges and pressures to manage as in-house call centers. As a group, they have always been in the forefront of technological and operational change in the call center industry and will continue to be good indicators of where the business is going. Several emerging trends and technologies will change the way outsourcers do business in the next decade, and the following paragraphs provide some insight into these factors.

Over the next five years, it is unlikely that the outsourcing environment will change dramatically, despite changes in technology and the operating procedures that these changes will introduce. Although there are several trends pushing the call center in virtualized and various directions, the physical nature of today's centers—rooms full of people, talking into headsets, looking at screens—is unlikely to change in the immediate future.

Any changes in the outsourcing industry in the next few years will reflect changes in the rest of the call center industry—what happens within in-house call centers. The pressure to improve productivity and deliver more and better services directly to the end user will continue unabated and possibly be even more apparent, as customer demands increase and become an increasingly strong component of the competitive business environment. Organizations are continuously working to provide more "self-service" methods of interaction—letting customers interact with and search databases for answers to their own problems—for example, automated systems to transfer funds, travel-oriented services, and Internet front-end banking services that are integrated into those services, with back-end database tools. An evolving series of power technologies will continue to become available to call centers; some will be new, while others will be enhancements of existing technologies. For outsourcers, it will be important to stay ahead of the competition—to use these new technologies to improve efficiency and to differentiate their services from the competition—and to remain profitable businesses.

Summarizing the benefits of outsourcing

From the preceding description of outsourcing, it should be apparent that the benefits to organizations choosing the outsourcing route for their call center operations are not many; they can, however, be significant in content. The following summarizes the three major benefits:

- *Access to advanced technologies*—capital investments in switches, dialers, and workstations and upgrades to hardware and software are all managed by the outsourcing organization, which is generally equipped with state-of-the-art call center systems. Costs can be spread over multiple clients.

- *Vertical expertise*—specialized industry-oriented expertise is offered to meet the needs of financial institutions, fundraising organizations, and retailers, among others. In fact, outsourcers for most industry sectors know how vertical markets function and how to treat customers in those markets.

- *Speed*—seasonal or even more frequent fluctuations in the number of CSRs that a particular marketing program may need can be addressed quickly.

4

Selecting and Training Call Center Staff

This chapter describes recommended selection criteria for call center CSRs, supervisors, and managers as well as training course content and syllabus topics for all three categories of staff. The number of personnel in each of these categories and the training requirements in a given call center will obviously depend on the size of the call center, that is, how many "seats" there are in the center.

Staff selection and training are important aspects of every call/contact center operation and can be significant determining factors in their effectiveness and productivity. CSRs are the prime human resource focus of the call center, as they should be, because they are the first point of contact with the customer. Supervisors are usually responsible for managing a certain number of CSRs, and managers may have the overall responsibility for the call center operation. Managers and supervisors responsible for operating the sophisticated environment of the modern call center need to be knowledgeable in many areas, including business, team leadership, motivation, counseling, mentoring, scheduling, complaint handling, and incentive programs, as well as being able to communicate an organization's business and objectives. Most centers do not train their supervisors in these skills, nor do they evaluate candidates for these skills during the candidate selection process. This situation has to change if the call center operation is to be successful in meeting an organization's business objectives and its customer relationship strategy. This chapter provides recommended evaluation criteria for new call center employees, as well as specific course outlines for staff training sessions.

4.1   Overview

The type of training that most successful centers provide to CSRs, supervisors, and managers heavily emphasizes business training and handling a wide range of call situations. Supervisor and management training programs should not be the extent of the learning process, however. Ongoing learning should also include attending industry conferences and reading trade publications. Networking with other call center supervisors and managers is also a good source of learning and acquiring useful knowledge.

Testing the waters

It is easier for CSRs to make the transition to supervise if they have been well prepared during their time on the front lines. CSRs who exceed performance objectives, demonstrate leadership abilities, communicate well, are technically competent, and have high-level customer service skills should be offered the opportunity to learn other functions and to move into management positions. Call center managers should continually seek out CSRs who are interested in learning and should find learning opportunities for those CSRs who express an interest in a particular area. For example, for CSRs who express the desire to become trainers, managers should provide opportunities for these individuals to help out with the training group, either by assisting in training development or even conducting a training session. Other occasions for these CSRs to try out their management or training skills occur, for example, when a supervisor is out of the center for an extended period of time (e.g., on maternity or medical leave or holidays). On such occasions, a senior-level agent could be asked to be an interim team leader. CSRs aspiring to management roles can also be encouraged to represent their call centers in organizationwide, cross-functional project meetings.

Developing formal and informal methods of nurturing and growing aspiring CSRs into call center supervisors and managers may be time-intensive, but it is also necessary to ensure a successful transition into management. It is difficult for people to be placed in a leadership situation when they are not prepared for the role, either formally or informally.

Motivating call center employees

The aspects of the work environment that motivate call center employees are the same ones that motivate employees in any other work environment, plus some that take into account the special responsibilities of call center staff.

These motivational factors, not necessarily in order of significance, can be summarized as follows:

- Wages

- Working conditions

- Work challenges

- Management appreciation

- Job security

- Promotion and career path opportunities

- Involvement in planning

- Employer loyalty

- Tactful human resource policies

- Coaching and training

Training provides CSRs, supervisors, and managers with the critical knowledge and skills to make a measurable contribution to strategic goals. Appropriate training for center staff can improve productivity and service levels by more than 15%. A training and development plan for the next 12- to 18-month period should be established and should include ongoing training programs for all staff in areas of customer service, sales, and systems/ processes. Additional training requirements will be dictated by what business system/applications are in place—customer service, sales, and help desk, among others.

Some general training issues

In general, it is important to develop a knowledge and skills matrix and curricula that identify the initial and ongoing training needs of CSRs, supervisors, and managers. A reevaluation of skills should be done on a regular schedule to ensure that adequate training is being provided and that there are reference points for defining "subject expertise." It is also important to ensure that call-handling guidelines and other procedures be well documented and available at the CSR's desktop for quick reference. Specific training requirements may differ from one organization to another; however, there are a number of common, key elements that should be incorporated into any initial training program, including

- Knowledge of the organization, including its mission, vision and core values, key performance objectives, office values, and business strategies

- Product knowledge—products and services of the organization, including key use, benefits, and pricing (if appropriate)
- Customer knowledge, including customer profiles
- Communication skills, including voice skills and call-handling strategies, use of voice mail and e-mail
- Guidelines for procedures, escalations, quality calls, and monitoring
- Customer escalation procedures
- Computer systems
- Office procedures and hours of operation

An induction and training manual should be developed and should document the entire training program, including lesson plan, facilitator's guide, overhead transparencies, and workshop manuals.

Managers and supervisors/team leaders should undergo management training to provide them with an in-depth understanding of call center management principles. This knowledge is essential for effective day-to-day management of a well-run center and should cover the following topics:

- Performance management
- Service-level management
- Cost of call management
- Monitoring, analyzing, and coaching

In addition, all call center staff, including supervisors, managers, and support staff, should undergo customer service and sales skills training as part of their initial training programs.

Training strategies

A wide variety of training methods can be employed to facilitate training: classroom activities, call observation, product knowledge tests, one-on-one coaching, and on-line tutorials. Self-paced training aids should be provided for individual reference and self-learning; some training aids, often referred to as *tool kits*, (described later in this chapter) are specifically designed for the call center environment and written in the form of modules with workbooks and audiotapes. Most centers employ several or all of these methods, depending on the training curriculum.

Supervisors and managers are promoted from within in many call centers, being selected from among the best agents and those who demonstrate leadership qualities. These leaders will provide CSR staff with the "voice" of the organization. They need to be well trained and brought up-to-date frequently. It is therefore important, as an investment in the future of the organization, to provide ongoing training to both new and upcoming supervisors. This training should include a thorough grounding in how to run an effective and efficient call center—from communication skills and workforce measurement techniques to using tools such as Erlang C for measuring service levels, as well as the range of technologies available.

The following sections describe recommended selection criteria for call center staff as well as training guidelines for each level.

4.2   Staff selection criteria

The high cost associated with the staffing, training, and relatively high turnover rates in call centers makes it extremely important that recruiting processes ensure the best possible hires. The first major decision is whether to conduct the search internally or externally, using a recruiting agency, or to use a combination of both. If an organization has no experience in the recruitment and selection of call center personnel, then one option is to use a specialized recruitment agency. There are many general recruitment agencies, but it is important to select an agency with extensive experience in selecting call center personnel.

Call centers have unique selection and hiring challenges. Distinct skills and abilities are required when a brief telephone conversation or typed response to an e-mail is the only contact. Call center CSRs must listen, speak, read, type, and analyze all at the same time. Supervisors, team leaders, and managers must possess many of the same skills, along with business/staff management competencies and experience. They will also need to understand voice systems, data collection and interpretation, contact flow, and cost per call.

Telephone interviewing of candidates for all three levels of call center jobs is an essential part of the selection process. The aim of the telephone interview is to establish candidates' work experience, communication skills, telephone voice skills, and selling ability (if applicable). It will also reveal their attitude, enthusiasm, and the creativity of their telephone performance. Another important part of the selection process is role playing, which provides an opportunity to assess how good the applicants are at communicating and selling themselves. Three different role-play scenarios should be used to test the extent of a candidate's customer service orientation, communication skills, ability to handle complaints, and phone selling skills.

The following sections list some of the special skills and competencies that are important skillsets for the call center operating environment and provide some criteria for recruiting and selecting of CSRs, supervisors, and managers.

CSRs

- Above-average oral and written communications skills
- Refined sales and customer service abilities
- Ability to multitask in a fast-paced environment
- Keyboarding and computer skills
- Comfortable with intranet and Internet, e-mail, and use of headset
- Pleasant telephone voice and manner

The recruitment and selection process for CSRs should include

- Telephone and e-mail screening
- Behavioral interviews
- Simulation/role-playing exercises
- Testing for keyboarding and written communications skills
- Evaluation of sales and customer service aptitude
- Screening of references provided

Supervisors/team leaders

Recruiting supervisors/team leaders is similar to CSR recruitment but will emphasize different skills. For this level, experience in leading and managing teams within a call center environment is an important criterion. Interview questions should address these skills and the interview should include role-playing based on specific scenarios involving motivating, coaching, and counseling team members.

The following skillsets are important attributes for supervisors and team leaders:

- CSR skills and competencies
- Call center monitoring skills
- Ability to set up and interpret call center performance measurements
- Experience with workforce management tools

- Exceptional mentoring and coaching abilities
- Working knowledge of voice systems and other call center applications
- Proficiency in the preparation of reports and charts

The recruitment process is similar to that for CSRs.

Managers

The strategic importance of the call center manager to the establishment and effective operation of the center requires special consideration in recruitment and selection, which may therefore involve an executive search or external recruitment agency that specializes in this type of recruitment. Call center managers should possess the following skillsets:

- Ability to effectively lead and manage the call center
- High-level communications skills
- Ability to achieve agreed-upon targets and key performance indicators
- Ability to effectively manage resources within defined budgets
- High-level focus on continuous improvement

4.3   Training CSR staff

As noted previously, a wide variety of training programs and methods for call center training programs exist, including,

- Classroom activities—workshops, seminars
- Call observation
- Product knowledge tests
- One-on-one monitoring and coaching
- On-line tutorials
- Tool kits

Call-handling guidelines should be fully documented and communicated to CSRs on a continuous basis. Documentation should be included in initial CSR training and available at the CSR workstation for quick reference. These standards become part of individual and center performance measurements and are the basis of CSR assessment using call monitoring or other performance measurements. In addition to initial training, CSRs should have ongoing training, which may focus on new technologies, sales or help desk skills, collections, or other topics that can improve the knowledge and skill level of CSRs.

Examples of recommended CSR workshop topics for half-day, one-day, and two-day training sessions are provided next. The CSR workshops described are examples of training syllabuses that provide participants with the foundation knowledge and skills required for individual and team success. Along with an emphasis on handling a variety of customer communications, are included the "why" of customer relations, customer requirements, the changing demands and expectations of customers, good and bad customer service, and how to exceed expectations.

4.4   Recommended topics for CSR workshops

The CSR workshop examples provided here are based extensively on training and curriculum information provided by Bell Contact Centre Solutions, a division of Bell Canada, and are included with permission. There are five recommended CSR workshop categories in the series, which cover a range from basic customer service, sales, and listening skills to help desk and collections. A summary description of each workshop is provided, with details of each workshop syllabus shown in the exhibits that follow.

1. **Excellence in Customer Service (One Day)**

    - Communication skills
    - Call control
    - Handling customer complaints
    - Maximizing the call
    - Personal effectiveness

2. **Contact Center Sales Skills (Two Days)**

    - Attitudes for success (belief in self, goal-oriented)
    - Skills for success (call preplanning, cultivating, discovering, presenting recommendations, why people buy)
    - Skills practice (applying skills learned)

3. **Building Effective Listening Skills (Half Day)**

    - Effective listening
    - Listening skills
    - Role of listening
    - Ten common faults
    - Developing a personal action plan

4.   **Customer Service Skills for the Help Desk (One Day)**

- Behavior leading to a positive customer experience
- Understanding the difference between basic and excellent service and the effect it has on customers
- Communicating with and understanding customers, using effective listening and questioning
- Addressing and satisfying a difficult or irate customer
- Dealing with different personalities
- Declining with diplomacy
- Negotiating mutually positive outcomes
- Learning how to manage stress

5.   **Collecting Overdue Accounts (One Day)**

- Proactive customer account management
- Collections call processing
- Handling difficult customers
- Skills practice
- Action planning

Details of each workshop are provided in Exhibits 4-1, 4-2, 4-3, 4-4, and 4-5.

Exhibit 4-1   Excellence in Customer Service (One Day)

Objectives

This half-day, six-module workshop focuses on developing the following skills:

- Enhanced telephone professionalism

- Adapting individual communication styles

- Applying active, empathetic listening with question techniques for complete understanding of customer needs

- Managing conversations with an assertive, action-oriented approach

- Effectively addressing and satisfying a difficult or irate customer

- Identifying revenue opportunities for maximized customer contacts

- Improving personal effectiveness through time and stress management

(continued)

Exhibit 4-1   continued

By learning and applying superior customer service techniques on every call, CSRs will strengthen their customer relationships, resulting in long-term loyalty. How effectively CSRs manage calls directly impacts a customer's perception of the company.

Module 1: Workshop Introduction

- Objectives
- The call center CSR's role:
    - meeting and exceeding customer expectations
    - best telephone practices (greet, hold, transfer, close)

Module 2: Communication Skills—Voice

- Developing rapport through speed, articulation, tone, and modulation
- Customers with an accent

Module 3: Communication Skills—Listening

- Listening effectively
- Acknowledging and empathizing

Module 4: Call Control

- Question types and how to apply them
- Managing conversations that go "off topic"
- Assertiveness techniques
- Professional phrases

Module 5: Handling Customer Complaints

- A 10-step process for handling customer complaints or other difficult calls
- Handling callers who shout, swear/threaten, become sarcastic
- Declining with diplomacy
- Controlling emotional reactions

(continued)

Exhibit 4-1   continued

Module 6: Maximizing the Call

- Identifying revenue opportunities for maximum contact return

Module 7: Personal Effectiveness

- Stress-management techniques
- Time-management skills

Exhibit 4-2   Contact Center Sales Skills (One Day)

Objectives

This one-day call/contact center sales skills workshop will teach CSRs fundamental telephone skills and proven sales techniques to strengthen their ability to deliver superior customer service and maximize sales on each and every customer contact. CSRs will learn

- The consultative sales call flow strategy
- The skills and behaviors required to be successful at consultative selling
- The steps to identifying buying motives and triggers
- How to effectively apply their product knowledge during a sales call
- How to use benefits, advantages, and features to recommend solutions and techniques for neutralizing objections
- Effective techniques for closing the sale

Module 1: Workshop Introduction

- Overview
- Personal vision statement
- Critical teleselling skills

(continued)

Exhibit 4-2   continued

Module 2: Initial Approach

- Effective call opening—inbound/outbound
- Quality standards
- Voice dynamics to capture the customer's attention
- Establishing rapport and securing the customer's interest

Module 3: Determining Needs

- Question types and when to ask them
- Listening effectively to pinpoint needs
- Positioning information gathered to present effective recommendations

Module 4: Recommendations

- Linking needs uncovered to benefits of product/service
- Matching benefits to customer needs
- Checking for customer approval

Module 5: Answer

- Preparing to overcome common objections
- Proven techniques to remove the objection
- Moving the customer to a buying position
- Recognizing buying signals
- Knowing when to close
- Asking for a commitment
- Using voice dynamics to close

Module 6: Call Completion

- Recap agreements and next steps
- Apply quality close standards
- Note callbacks/follow-up

Exhibit 4-3   Building Effective Listening Skills (Half Day)

Objectives

This interactive workshop will provide CSRs with the skills required to determine customer needs, gather important information, and avoid misunderstanding and frustration, resulting in positive customer perception and increased customer loyalty. It includes both individual/group exercises and role playing. Participants practice their newly acquired skills by applying them to their own simulated job environments. This course will enable CSRs to

- Assess their listening style and identify areas for improvement

- Avoid the most common faults of poor listeners and use the accompanying prescriptions for better listening

- Apply and practice empathetic listening

- Listen "nonvisually" and "nonverbally"

- Take notes and process information effectively

Key Topics

- The role and value of effective listening in the overall communication process

- Listening skills and habit, self-assessment

- Understanding the role of listening in the perception, reception, and attention equation

- Ten common faults or barriers to effective listening and the solutions for improvement

- Understanding key characteristics of the "Five Levels of Listening"

- How to listen "nonvisually" and "nonverbally" and why these skills are important

- How information processing and note taking can help with effective listening

- Developing a personal action plan to apply and build on improved listening skills and habits

Exhibit 4-4   Customer Service Skills for the Help Desk (One Day)

Objectives

This interactive one-day workshop is designed for the special needs of help desk personnel to effectively manage SOS calls in a friendly, yet focused manner. Emphasis is on understanding callers' needs and maintaining call control. It includes both individual and group exercises and role playing. Participants practice examples, phrases, and approaches to apply during caller duress. By learning and applying superior customer service techniques, this workshop will help CSRs strengthen their customer service relationships, resulting in long-term loyalty to the business. The specific skills learned will include

- Behavior that leads to a positive customer experience

- Understanding the difference between giving basic "core" service versus excellent "more" service, and the effect it has on customers

- Discovering how to communicate and understand customers by using effective listening and questioning techniques, proper words and phrases, and the all-important voice tone

- Learning how to address and satisfy a difficult or irate customer

- Acquiring techniques on how to deal with different personality types by identifying your own and understanding the characteristics of other types

- Declining with diplomacy and negotiating mutually positive outcomes

- Learning how to manage stress

Exhibit 4-5   Collecting Overdue Accounts (One Day)

Objectives

The objectives of this workshop are to train CSRs to do collection calls on outstanding company accounts.

Module 1: Workshop Introduction

- Overview

- Introduction to the collections call process

(continued)

Exhibit 4-5   continued

Module 2: Being Proactive in Customer Account Management

- Understanding the time value of money

- Why collections policies are important

- The telephone collector's role and qualities for effective performance

- Seven commandments in collections

- Eight common mistakes in collections

- Personal privacy: collections and the law

Module 3: Communication Skills

- Comparing face-to-face with telephone communication

- Setting an effective telephone speech rate

- Why it's important to reflect the customer's communication style

- Enhancing voice quality through tone, volume, inflection, and elimination of jargon

- Overcoming listening barriers; listening effectively using active/interactive skills

Module 4: The ABCs of the Collections Call Process

- Reviewing the collections call process

- Planning and preparing for the collection call

- Identifying and assessing "at-risk" accounts

- Setting call objectives and making the call introduction

- Asking for payment: the call to action

- Handling excuses or reasons for nonpayment

- Selling the benefits of prompt payment and negotiating a payment plan

- Confirming commitments and ending the call

(continued)

Exhibit 4-5   continued

Module 5: Handling Difficult Customers

- Handling a customer's complaint

- Using assertiveness skills

- Handling anger from a personal and customer perspective

- Applying principles of empathy

- Tactics for getting to "yes"

- Enhancing customer relationships through the "law of reciprocity"

- Overcoming frustration and call reluctance

- Techniques for handling stress

Module 6: Experiential Skills Practice

- Role-playing exercises that allow participants to practice collection skills by applying them in a simulated on-the-job environment

Module 7: Action Planning and Workshop Review

- Reviewing key workshop lessons

- Setting an action plan for improved job performance

- Establishing an ongoing improvement process

- Workshop evaluation

4.5   Tool kits

Typically, tool kits are self-paced programs consisting of a number of modules that CSRs can use to study alone or in small groups. Using workbooks and audiocassettes, a CSR can complete a module and be back on line in less than 45 minutes. In some instances, working through the exercises alone is all that's necessary; in other cases, a CSR will work with a coach or peer to obtain feedback on his or her progress. The kits include a matrix describing the specific skill or knowledge gaps each module covers. This means that a CSR's training efforts can be focused on particular area(s) of need. Tool kits are available to assist CSRs in developing and refining the following skills:

- Effective listening

- Overcoming language barriers

- Preparing to take the call

- Telephone professionalism

- Improving voice quality

- Asking the right questions

- Identifying social styles and selecting strategies

- Identifying skills and maintaining call control

- Offering solutions and ensuring customer satisfaction

- Emotional self-control

- Handling difficult calls

4.6   Advanced CSR training

Longer workshops, typically lasting three days, can further develop CSR skillsets. Some recommended objectives and course content are shown next.

Objectives

- Understand standards required for effective teamwork

- Establish personal learning goals

- Recognize the importance of attitude ownership on quality of contact

- Understand why self-motivation is part of customer satisfaction

- Acquire increased telephone professionalism and self-confidence

- Adapt individual communication style through voice, speed, and tone to suit different customers

- Apply active, empathetic listening with questioning techniques for a complete understanding of customer needs

- Manage customer conversations with an assertive, action-oriented approach

- Effectively address and satisfy a difficult or irate customer

- Improve personal effectiveness through time and stress management

A typical course outline for a three-day advanced CSR workshop to meet these objectives should contain the following elements:

- Teamwork
- Personal goal setting
- Attitude and motivation
- Excellence in customer service
- Meeting and exceeding customer expectations
- Best telephone practices
- Developing rapport through speed, articulation, tone, and modulation
- Listening effectively using active/interactive skills
- Managing customer conversations that go "off topic"
- Assertiveness techniques
- Professional phrases
- Handling difficult customers
- A process for handling customer complaints or difficult calls
- Handling callers who shout, swear/threaten, use sarcasm
- Declining with diplomacy
- Controlling emotional reactions
- Personal effectiveness
- Stress-management techniques
- Time-management skills

4.7   Training supervisory and management staff

The benefits of promoting CSRs to supervisory and management positions from within the call center have been mentioned previously. This process will be successful providing internal or external training programs are made available to these employees to assist them in following a call center career path. The primary benefits to the organization of promoting from within are that employees who have gone the CSR route know the business, customers, staff, and corporate culture. As most organizations will understand, an internal career path is a great motivator for other CSRs—particularly when support is provided to their former peers to help them succeed in their new roles. Whether or not CSRs are promoted from within, or brought in from outside the call center to fill supervisory or management positions, however, training should be made available to help these individuals perform their new roles effectively.

Leadership skills training is critical

For centers with a career development program that provides CSRs opportunities to regularly move "up the ladder," it is essential to develop a formal curriculum and time frame for supervisory training. Adapting to a supervisory or management role in an environment where the individual has been a peer to other CSRs can be a difficult transition. Supervising former fellow CSRs and becoming a team leader, instead of just a team member, is not easy for some. However, the transition needs to be made by those CSRs who want to follow a career path in call center management in order to move into supervisory or management positions. Although not every CSR will aspire to a supervisory or management position, there should be a recognized and well-established career path for those who do.

In addition to the more specific training required for call center supervisory and management personnel, additional leadership training, which includes managing tasks as well as leading people, is essential.

Personal development topics for managers and supervisors

Any supervisory training program, whether formal or informal, should include such call center management topics as forecasting, workforce management, planning and scheduling, and using technology in addition to training in basic leadership skills. The following key areas for personal development of supervisory and management personnel are recommended in a supervisory training program:

- Customer interaction
- Employee interaction
- Team leadership
- Decision making
- Employee motivation and recognition
- Communication
- Systems manipulations
- High-level problem solving

- Company process knowledge
- Company HR policies and procedures knowledge
- Conflict management
- Reports and data analysis
- Monitoring and coaching
- Performance-management processes

Planning the curriculum

Developing a curriculum for supervisory and management personnel is a complex task; however, when broken down into its components, it is much easier to manage. For instance, if the company has a training department, an initial step would be to request that this department collaborate with center management to develop a career-path training program for supervisors and managers. This program should be broken down into modules that allow individuals 12 to 18 months to complete the curriculum.

With the assistance of the training department, a range of topics, selected from the following list, should be included in a training program:

- Forecasting and scheduling
- Understanding metrics and reporting
- Workforce management
- Communicating with CSRs
- Motivating CSRs
- Customer relationship management (concept and/or technology)

Follow-up, information-sharing sessions with supervisors should be conducted to get their input. The training program should provide consistent development in all key areas of call center management, and future training needs should be considered. The curriculum must be expandable, with the capability to add new training sessions as they become necessary.

If a company does not have the training expertise in-house, there are other training resources available (see Appendix A, "Call Center Vendor Resources") as well as other methods of learning besides the training received in an instructor/student environment. Self-development learning resources include tool kits, industry conferences and seminars, Web seminars, white papers, and books.

Staff input

Once an initial training plan has been developed, consult with a team of call center managers, supervisors, CSRs, and in-house trainers, if any, and analyze the training requirements. Determine where opportunities lie and then prioritize them, based on the following guidelines:

- Select training topics that will provide the biggest return in the quickest amount of time
- Schedule training sessions for mutual availability of training resources and call center staff

List the top-five training opportunities for supervisors and then determine the best way to deliver the training. To test the training plan, select a pilot team to undergo the training and act as a focus group to review and modify the curriculum.

The experience of many call center managers points up the importance of defining expectations in order that CSRs can fulfill them. If they demonstrate they can do this, then it's really in the best interest of the customer, the employees, and the company to move these people into positions of more responsibility—because they've demonstrated they can do the job. They can also bring the customer's perspective with them to the supervisory or management role.

Develop clear performance guidelines

In addition to training and providing early growth opportunities, management can ensure the success of new supervisors by developing clear, consistent guidelines and expectations. These expectations should be objective and measurable and provide feedback to frontline staff on what their performance gaps are and how they can work toward closing them. Opportunities should be provided in the call center to actually develop competencies in a way that shows people are ready for additional assignments or responsibilities.

Supervisory and management workshops

Exhibits 4-6, 4-7, 4-8, 4-9, and 4-10 are recommended topics for supervisory and management workshops. The topics have been derived from workshops developed and presented by Bell Contact Centre Solutions.

Exhibit 4-6   Managing Performance (Two or Five Days)

Objectives

This supervisory and management workshop addresses the following performance issues:

- Productivity
- Quality
- Agent performance
- Service levels

This workshop will prepare CSRs aspiring to move up the ladder to supervisory or management positions to apply the "best practices" of successful contact centers. It will identify the types of performance and service-level reports to focus on, and why, as well as unleash the power and potential of the center's enabling technology.

The content is the same for both workshops; however, the five-day workshop goes into more depth in each area; analyzing the data, providing training on the Excel templates for productivity and service-level management, quality call calibrations, and other topics.

Exhibit 4-7   Service-Level Management (Two Days)

Objectives

The objectives of this workshop are to teach supervisors and managers the following skills:

- Using the mathematical queuing model
- Working with key variables such as average talk time, average idle time, and average not ready time, and how they impact service levels
- Examining incoming call load factors including: daily call volumes, cyclical call volume variations, call volumes during emergency events
- Creating and analyzing service-level measurement charts, including daily volume and ASA trends, hours of worst abandonment rate, and ASA and staffing levels

(continued)

Exhibit 4-7   continued

- Making service-level measurements that are meaningful

- Forecasting call loads

- Resource planning using industry-accepted Erlang C formulas and industry staffing methods

- Scheduling staff

- Handling customer impatience and the cost of abandoned calls

- Managing in real time

- Contingency planning

Exhibit 4-8   Coach Development (Four Days)

Objectives

The coach development workshop is designed to develop the following skills:

- Understanding and supporting the performance model

- Understanding measures that are indicators of behavior patterns

- Coach to behaviors, in support of skill- and knowledge-gap analysis

- Defining the difference between coaching to "what I heard and/or what I saw" versus coaching to metrics

- Understanding the role of a coach—lead, support, and develop

---

Exhibit 4-9   Monitoring, Analyzing, and Coaching (One Day)

Objectives

This workshop is designed to develop monitoring and analyzing skills that can assist supervisors to manage CSRs more effectively. The following topics are included:

- Defining, monitoring, analyzing, coaching, and performance standards within the call/contact center

(continued)

Exhibit 4-9   continued

- Exploring the role and benefits of monitoring and coaching in contact centers

- Types of call monitoring

- The 5 Ws of call monitoring: Who, What, Where, When, and Why

- Setting call performance standards

- Developing a call-monitoring worksheet

- Understanding the holistic versus tabular approach to monitoring

- Gaining broad-based support and acceptance for call monitoring

- Defining and creating call standards

- Developing a call-monitoring strategy

- Taking a process-driven approach to call analysis

- Prescribing the appropriate action to improve call handling

- Turning the coaching process into a positive and valuable event for both CSRs and management

- Developing a personal monitoring and coaching action plan

Exhibit 4-10   Coaching for Results (Two Days)

Recommended topics in this two-day workshop will provide call center supervisors and managers with the skills and know-how to coach effectively. Five modules are included in this workshop:

Module 1: The Principles of Coaching

This module describes coaching and how it differs from mentoring, training, and counseling. The benefits of coaching and why some managers avoid it and the skills required to perform the coaching job are discussed. Examples of employee performance problems are examined.

Module 2: The Coaching Continuum

The "Coaching Continuum" is a four-step approach to coaching. The process is discussed in detail and participants role-play to solidify understanding. Role-play sessions are tape-recorded to allow participants to review and critique their work.

(continued)

Exhibit 4-10   continued

Module 3: Coaching One-on-One

This module discusses how to overcome resistance when employees do not want to be coached. Role-playing sessions are tape-recorded, reviewed, and critiqued by the participants. Emphasis is placed on coaching as an ongoing commitment from both the manager and employee. Learning points are reinforced through professional adult-learning-based facilitation, as well as individual and group activities. The transfer of learned skills to actual skills on the job is enhanced through a series of coaching simulation exercises. These exercises allow the participants to apply and practice their new skills within a simulated job environment.

Module 4: Essential Coaching Skills

This section of the workshop highlights the skills that are critical to a successful coaching session:

- Listening and questioning techniques
- How to effectively motivate employees

Module 5: Setting the Stage

The final section of the workshop describes how to introduce coaching into the participant's organization, which is applicable to a company that is just starting the coaching concept. Participants practice their newly acquired skills by applying them to their own simulated job environments through experientially based exercises, enhancing the transfer of skills learned to on-the-job performance.

Monitoring and coaching guidelines

As noted previously in this handbook, monitoring is a sensitive issue with CSRs and should be carefully planned and implemented. Therefore, once the monitoring/coaching program has been designed, it needs to be discussed and agreed upon by both CSRs and management to ensure mutual understanding and acceptance.

One commonly accepted rule of thumb for monitoring is that it should be done on the basis of 10 calls per rep every two weeks. Some of the issues that need to be addressed in monitoring and coaching CSRs are

- *Why monitor?* Will it identify areas for additional training, enhance individual skills, and improve quality and productivity?

- *How will monitoring be done?* Will it be remote and/or side-by-side, will calls be taped, what is being monitored (voice, desktop, or both)?

- *What is being evaluated?* Quality of problem resolution, tone of voice, ability to capture important detail, questioning techniques, sales and customer service skills?

- *Who will be monitoring?* Manager, supervisor, trainer, peers?

- *When will it be done?* Random, daily, one call per rep per day?

- *How will performance be measured?* Metrics, scoring, accuracy, objective versus subjective, cumulative results rather than one-time event (unless specific coaching is required at that time)?

- *How will feedback be given?* Frequency, what data, one-on-one?

- *How will personal calls be handled to ensure privacy?*

4.8   Summary: meeting objectives

The overall goal of selecting the right individuals for the call center operation, managing the center efficiently and effectively, and establishing an extensive, well-planned training program is to meet corporate objectives for customer service and to support the organization's overall CRM strategy. To accomplish these objectives, there are two important requirements, which apply to every call center operation in every business sector. These are summarized next.

Meet customer needs

Meet the needs of the customer by following these guidelines:

- Fully identify the caller's need or problem.

- Take ownership of the call—if possible, resolve the caller's need during the call itself.

- Complete all steps to call resolution before taking another call.

- For items that take longer than five minutes but are not a high priority, handle during a lower call volume period, but before the end of the day.

Meet business requirements

Satisfy the needs of the business by adhering to these criteria:

- Thorough and efficient follow-up after calls
- Updating all information
- Understanding the goals and mission statement and applying that understanding to every customer contact

Call Center Case Studies

5

This chapter presents a broad range of international call center case studies selected from both the public and private sectors. These case studies illustrate how one or more of the following processes are used by organizations to enhance productivity and maintain effective customer relationships: Managing their respective call centers, applying best-practice human resource policies, using appropriate technologies, and implementing vendor resources. For every case study, the term *call center* may also mean *customer contact center*.

The case studies are presented in a traditional business school format, beginning with a brief corporate profile, the challenge for the call center, a description of the call center operation, the technologies and vendor resources used, where applicable, and the benefits achieved. The amount of detail in each case study varies and is based on the amount of information available from each organization.

Businesses in a number of industry sectors as well as government organizations at all levels have either established new centers or expanded existing call center operations over the last several years. These have either been in-house centers or one of the outsourcing organizations listed in Appendix A, "Call Center Vendor Resources," or carrier organizations that recognize this business as an adjunct to their main communications business. The 25 organizations selected from around the world for these case studies have successfully implemented or upgraded call center operations and have demonstrated this success by meeting recognized industry criteria of service levels, reduced staff turnover, enhanced profitability, and a high level of customer satisfaction. The following sectors and businesses within each sector are represented in this chapter:

- **Communications**
  - Axtel
  - CLEAR Communications
  - diAx
  - Group Telecom
  - GTE Telecommunications Services
  - Nokia

- **Energy**
  - PPL EnergyPlus West

- **Financial Services**
  - The Depository Trust Company (DTC)
  - Liberty Funds Group
  - Metlife Investors Group
  - Nordea, Merita Bank
  - PNC Bank

- **Government**
  - Toronto Community Housing Corporation (TCHC)

- **Health Care**
  - Delta Dental Plan of Kentucky
  - Philips Oral Healthcare
  - University of Alabama Health Services Foundation, P.C.

- **Real Estate**
  - Oxford Properties Group

- **Retail**
  - Bargain Network
  - Borders Group
  - HSN

- **Technology**
  - 3COM
  - SGI (Silicon Graphics)
  - Crystal Decisions
  - Primavera Systems

- **Travel**
  - Thomas Cook Direct

5.1   Communications

Company: Axtel

Profile

Axtel is a provider of integrated telecommunication solutions in the recently liberalized Mexican market; it has 300 CSRs in its Monterrey contact center and handles over 18,000 calls per day.

Challenge

Axtel's workforce management system is fed information about the operation's activity, including key data such as peak call times, call duration, and agent workload. The system can then predict what will happen when advertising campaigns run and how exceptions such as these will affect the day-to-day operation of the contact center. The aim is a fairly simple one: increase the volume of calls handled without employing more agents and maintain the service level at 80% of calls answered within 20 seconds.

Solution

Axtel will soon be turning its Monterrey call center into a multimedia contact center and will use workforce management to ensure that the center has current performance measurement tools to obtain high levels of productivity and customer service.

Benefits

Benefits achieved include

- More efficient measurement of call center performance
- Capability to operate a multimedia contact center

Company: CLEAR Communications

Profile

CLEAR Communications is a New Zealand telecommunications services provider, founded in 1990, with call centers in Auckland and Christchurch. Surveys have indicated that CLEAR customers are impressed with the company's service; however, as the company has discovered, when customer service is improved, customers quickly progress through four stages: They appreciate it, they get used to it, they expect it, and they demand it.

Challenge

With strong competition in its marketplace, CLEAR posed this question to a group of managers and supervisors participating in a series of workshops: How do we stay ahead of the competition and meet customer expectations?

Solution

The results of the workshop session pointed to the critical requirement to continually assess current and future customer expectations. Leveraging customer feedback was considered important as the company moved into service innovations and improvements. Modest improvements were made to ensure that the organization was continually moving forward and therefore staying one step ahead of customer expectations.

Benefits

CLEAR has achieved about 20% market share in the New Zealand telecommunications sector because of its high level of customer service and favorable word-of-mouth advertising.

Company: diAx

Profile

diAx is a rapidly growing European telecom provider based in Switzerland. With its four contact centers and 720 agents, it takes up to 35,000 calls per day from its 1.3-million customer base.

Challenge

Implementing a virtual contact center has meant that each of the 38 agent skillsets available (such as language and specialized knowledge) has increased, as these skill pools are no longer location dependent. In a country like Switzerland, where the population speaks Italian, French, German, or English, the ability to present customers with as large a pool of CSR language skills as possible is critical to the success of the business.

Solution

The company's four contact centers were integrated to form a single, virtual contact center. Customers are given one telephone number, which gets routed correctly in 95% of cases from the calling-line identity (CLI).

Benefits

The following benefits were achieved:

- The solution implemented was supported by an open architecture.
- ACDs from separate leading manufacturers were integrated seamlessly into the virtual contact center infrastructure.

Company: Group Telecom

Profile

Group Telecom is a Canadian local exchange carrier offering next-generation telecommunications solutions to Canadian businesses. The company specializes in data, Internet applications, and voice products and services designed to improve the reliability of communications and the productivity and profitability of its customer's businesses. Group Telecom's portfolio of products and services of advanced business communication tools is provided over the company's own national fiber network and switching equipment.

Challenge

Group Telecom focuses on providing efficient support and excellent customer service and building a reputation as a leader in the telecommunications industry. The company needed a powerful call-management solution that would enhance customer support capabilities and reduce call-handling and call-transfer times. The software solution had to be flexible and scalable to support existing contact centers in Calgary, Vancouver, Toronto, and Montreal, and it had to be able to handle future growth.

Solution

Group Telecom chose the LGS Interaction Management Solution (IMS), based on the Apropos Multimedia Interaction Management Solution, to facilitate the company's vision of ECARE for its customer service contact center. This vendor solution was selected for the following reasons:

- Ease of use
- Ease of integration with existing switches
- Capacity for multimedia interactions (voice, e-mail, and Web inquiries)
- Rapid deployment (six-week target)

Using the queuing and distribution capabilities of Apropos, Group Telecom quickly routes callers to the proper department and most suitable agent.

Using a visual queue for inbound calls, voice mails, and e-mails, CSRs can identify priority customers and the reason for their call. It also captures information on abandoned calls so that CSRs can call back.

Benefits

The advantages of the IMS solution are

- One fully integrated solution residing on one platform with one central point of administration, reporting, and databasing

- Visual queuing that allows CSRs to preview calls and always routes calls to the best available agent, increasing both CSR and customer satisfaction

- Skill-based routing allowing agents multiple queues

- The ability of supervisors to monitor the call center from their desktops in real time, including call load, call disposition, and the activity of individual CSRs, and to allocate CSRs among queues in real time

- Analysis of calls to improve operations

- Flexibility to utilize many different switching platforms in a number of different locations and customer transactions

- Significant increase in CSR productivity

- Simple administration—one server to handle incoming calls and e-mails

- Insight into quantity and purpose of calls through robust reporting tools

- Insight into the efficiency of its contact center

- Increased customer satisfaction

Company: GTE Telecommunications Services (GTE TSI)

Profile

GTE Telecommunications Services, based in Tampa, Florida, is a global supplier of interoperability solutions for wireless paging and Internet service providers. In addition to operating the world's largest wireless data clearinghouse, GTE TSI's broad array of products includes interstandard wireless roaming solutions, intelligent network services, fraud management solutions, and other types of service bureau applications that simplify the complex technical and business relationships existing in today's competitive global telecommunications industry.

Challenge

GTE TSI needed to easily communicate through various media types, including e-mail, inbound and outbound calls, and voice mail. In addition, the company could only track and monitor calls but required a system that could easily interface with customers on a more personal, prioritized basis. Finally, the company was challenged with the inability to produce adequate reports or measure sufficient data from multiple interaction types, and it needed these business metrics and tools to further optimize the customer support hotline center.

Solution

GTE TSI selected and successfully implemented the Apropos Multimedia Interaction Management system. The Apropos system routes, tracks, and reports on all inbound and outbound interactions. In addition to Apropos, GTE TSI uses Remedy's CRM application to provide agents with "screen pops" containing customer information. To complement the Remedy system, Apropos prioritizes and escalates each interaction according to business rules, providing the capability of managing each interaction based on its value to the business. The Apropos system also includes a comprehensive reporting system that fully supports management's requirements and assists in delivering superior service to customers.

Benefits

- Full caller data and prioritization—enhances the CSR's ability to deliver a quicker and more efficient response.

- Reporting across all media types—enables the center to improve service levels and increase productivity

- Fully integrated multimedia capabilities—allows customers to effectively communicate through various media types and increases the capability to satisfy customers as they contact the center

Company: Nokia

Profile

Nokia, headquartered in Irving, Texas, is a world leader in mobile communications. Backed by its experience, innovation, user-friendliness, and secure solutions, the company has become a major supplier of mobile phones and mobile fixed and IP networks.

Challenge

Nokia's Information Management Group realized the need to have better insight into the types of calls received by the contact center. Nokia needed a solution that would provide insight into all support center activities and easily create and generate reports. Improved call-routing capabilities and a system that could handle fax services were also required. The solution had to meet current needs and business challenges and be capable of integrating with existing systems.

Solution

The Apropos Multimedia Interaction Management Suite was chosen for five of Nokia's contact centers throughout the world because of its intelligent, skills-based routing feature that automatically directs customers to specific customer support representatives for personalized handling. The system also provides the capability to manage and monitor all customer interactions and includes comprehensive reporting.

The initial implementation included voice, voice mail, and fax-back features, which enabled CSRs to fax information from the desktop. Shortly afterwards, Nokia also implemented the e-mail application, an enterprise-class solution designed specifically for e-commerce, to provide a unified mechanism for blending, prioritizing, and escalating e-mail interactions in the flow of all customer interactions within their support center.

Benefits

The selected vendor solution provided the following benefits:

- *Intelligent, skills-based routing*—assigns calls to the appropriate agent, delivering a more efficient and quicker response

- *Comprehensive report tolls*—measures service and performance levels and enables management to make well-informed business decisions

- *Multichannel solution*—allows customer support representatives to respond to and effectively serve their customers regardless of how they choose to communicate with the center.

5.2   Energy

Company: PPL EnergyPlus West

Profile

PPL EnergyPlus is a Fortune 500 company headquartered in Allentown, Pennsylvania. The company markets and sells wholesale and retail energy in 42 states and Canada and delivers energy to nearly six million customers in the United States alone. Started 80 years ago, the company believes that the future belongs to energy companies that understand customer needs and are dedicated to providing competitively priced energy.

Challenge

Whenever an agent is required to negotiate a price over the phone, that agent is essentially creating a verbal contract. PPL EnergyPlus realized that it is critical that those verbal contacts be recorded and archived for liability purposes. By recording calls from their digital Nortel PBX, the company found that they could eliminate or settle disputes and head off costly non-productive litigation. However, its reel-to-reel recorder had problems with line noise.

Solution

Voice Print International (VPI) was contacted to assess the call center environment; it created a custom solution that records clear, crisp audio. This vendor solution solved a number of issues for PPL EnergyPlus. VPI's system is based on an open architecture that the company was able to integrate easily with its existing system. Maintenance is completely hassle-free because the system is very reliable and replacement components are available at any computer store.

Benefits

The following benefits were achieved with this vendor solution:

- Calls that used to take 10 to 30 minutes to retrieve can now be retrieved in seconds using a database "query" to find calls

- Significant savings in time and money in the call retrieval process

5.3   Financial services

Company: The Depository Trust Company (DTC)

Profile

DTC, headquartered in New York, is the world's largest securities depository, holding nearly $20 trillion in assets for its members and their customers. DTC is a national clearinghouse for the settlement of trades in corporate, municipal, and mortgage-backed securities and performs asset services for its participating banks and broker/dealers.

Challenge

With only 30 CSRs supporting over 3,500 internal and 30,000 external customers at its help desk, DTC was challenged with providing the support necessary to efficiently manage the large volume of calls received daily. The company realized that it had no way to monitor the types of calls received, and agents were managing different types of customer requests without any advance notification of who was calling or why. It was also difficult to measure or gauge the center's level of service because there were no real-time reporting tools or capabilities. DTC needed a solution that would address these continuous challenges and that would also integrate easily into its existing database application.

Solution

The Apropos Multimedia Interaction Management Suite seamlessly integrated into DTC's existing database application, allowing for up-front automation and identification of callers. This enabled CSRs to access and view information about callers so that their response was more accurate and efficient.

Apropos prioritizes and escalates each interaction according to business rules, which gave DTC the ability to truly manage interactions based on the value to the business. By storing and displaying the interactions in a multimedia queue, the system assisted in the effective management of the numerous calls received. In addition, the real-time reporting feature allowed management to examine help desk activities and assisted in making better-informed business decisions.

Benefits

The vendor solution provided the following benefits:

- *Cradle-to-grave reporting*—provides full insight into center activities, allowing management to make better, more informed decisions based on actual business data and improved productivity

- *Prioritizing and escalation rules*—accommodates unique business and service-level requirements, delivering a more personalized and effective response

- *Improved visibility of caller information*—ensures that customers will receive more efficient service, increasing customer satisfaction

Company: Liberty Funds Group

Profile

Liberty Funds Group is an integrated asset accumulation and management organization. Its operating companies manage $66 billion of assets for investors worldwide through an array of fixed, indexed, and variable annuities; private and institutional accounts; and mutual funds. Liberty Funds brings together the investment expertise of a select group of money management firms known throughout the industry for their strong track record of success.

Challenge

With locations in Colorado and Boston and over 200 agents who were being recorded daily, Liberty Funds Group had decided to upgrade its recording system from a removable media-based system to an on-line storage-based system. It was important that the new solution could directly integrate digitally with the existing Aspect ACD and Northern PBX systems and be easy to use. As well, because Liberty Funds Group is required by law to store all recordings for up to seven years, the company required a long-term, network-attached storage solution.

Solution

Liberty Funds chose Voice Print International (VPI) because it needed to store all of its data on-line in the most reliable system with the largest on-line storage capacity. VPI's standard solution provides the client with over 11,000 channel hours of on-line storage for instant playback of audio files stored in compressed .wav format. VPI compresses the audio files using industry-standard GSM compression. Because GSM compression is Microsoft native, standard media players recognize the GSM codes and can play back the attached .wav file without additional software downloads.

Benefits

The following benefits were achieved:

- CSRs can quickly and easily find a record and display it.

- The company can define how thousands of hours of recorded transaction activity can be effectively managed to meet their strategic operational information management needs.

- Whether voice or screen capture video or the two synchronized together, the client dictates where the record is archived, how long it is archived, how it is retrieved, and how it will be used in the future.

- The RAID5 storage configuration used by VPI allows clients to store as many hours as its business or the law dictates, while offering high reliability through redundancy.

Company: MetLife Investors Group

Profile

MetLife Investors Group is an affiliate of MetLife, America's largest life insurer. MetLife serves 1 out of every 11 American households and 86 of the Fortune 100 companies. The company offers a full line of financial products, state-of-the-art technology capabilities, and high-touch service, with a primary goal of making business easier for the intermediary. The company is comprised of two insurance groups, as well as an investment management entity. MetLife Investors' products include a range of variable annuities, distributed through registered investment advisors, financial planners, regional broker-dealers, wirehouses, and banks.

Challenge

MetLife Investors' CSRs must be equipped with the necessary tools to ensure they are servicing their customers in the right manner. This means making it possible for customers to contact company investment agents via any communication medium they choose—phone, fax, e-mail, or Web— and enabling agents to effectively and efficiently service customers while properly managing all interactions. Additionally, MetLife Investors recognized that efficiently handling customer interactions was not enough. CSRs must derive value from every customer interaction, making each and every interaction matter.

Solution

In addition to seeking a contact center solution that supported multichannel forms of communication, MetLife Investors needed a comprehensive solution to support its two customer service centers, encompassing its sales and administrative departments, located in Newport Beach, California and Des Moines, Iowa. The two centers supported 250 CSRs, more than 150,000 financial brokers, and millions of consumers who contact the company to obtain account information. MetLife Investors was seeking a fully integrated call center solution to meet the following requirements:

- Skills-based routing and intelligent routing with alerts based on business parameters

- Informing agents about the interactions waiting to be handled

- Identifying callers

- Enabling investment agents to form strong relationships with customers

- Continuously improving service

- Keeping costs down when implementing a new solution

The Apropos' Interaction Management Solution was chosen to help manage all customer interactions, and Channel Parity was selected to design and implement solutions for multi-channel centers. Together with Apropos, these two vendor solutions enabled MetLife Investors to facilitate a single consistent view of customers across all communication channels.

Benefits

The benefits to the company were several, including the following:

- Helped drive millions of dollars in revenue by supporting customer interactions

- Enabled the core business to function efficiently and effectively

- Provided an efficient and consistent level of customer service—regardless of how they chose to communicate with the company

- Increased CSR productivity by providing intelligent call routing to the appropriate agent group or individual, based on CSR skillsets, customer history, and so on

- Improved visibility of customer information allowing agents to sustain high call volumes while providing high-quality service.

Company: Nordea, Merita Bank

Profile

Nordea, Merita Bank of Sweden runs eight contact centers in its home country and four in Finland and two in Denmark. More than 1,000 CSRs deal with 120,000 contacts per day from a customer base of nine million individuals and 700,000 companies.

Challenge

To improve efficiency and customer service levels by adopting the latest call center technology.

Solution

The company's operations are heavily oriented around IVR—which amounted to 85% of contacts—and, increasingly, the Internet. If customers wished to speak with a CSR, they could do so and all IVR-captured information was passed along with the call. To manage the high customer contact volume, the company created virtual contact centers and augmented its existing technology with advanced call management and routing systems.

Benefits

The virtual contact center infrastructure provided the following benefits:

- Dynamic load balancing across sites, making the workload fairer

- Improvements in call center operation for both customers and CSRs

Company: PNC Bank

Profile

PNC Bank is a major U.S. bank with over 770 branches and more than $77 billion in assets. Incoming contacts to the call center are identified and segmented according to specific customer attributes. The contact is then passed to a consultant, who not only helps the customer with a particular need but also introduces other financial products.

Challenge

The company needed to streamline its call management process and to provide more information directly to its CSRs and outside consultants.

Solution

The company used the universal queue model for cross selling financial products and found that this call management process provided significant benefits.

Benefits

The benefits achieved include the following:

- Customer and product information now appear as a "screen pop" on the agent's screen as the call arrives.

- Call times have decreased by between 12 and 30 seconds per call, depending on the type of contact.

- Customer satisfaction ratings and profits have increased.

5.4   Government

Company: Toronto Community Housing Corporation (TCHC)

Profile

Toronto Community Housing Corporation (TCHC) is a municipal government organization that manages 57,500 residential rental units in the city of Toronto. TCHC sees the key to its success as the ability to operate at the community level to respond to customer issues quickly and effectively. Inquiries include housing availability, waiting list status, rent payments, maintenance requests, and safety concerns, among a variety of other tenant-related issues.

Challenge

After years of striving for a better operational model, TCHC recognized it required a community-based approach to service more effectively its diversified client base brought about by the amalgamation of two municipal housing organizations. TCHC faced the challenge of providing personalized, responsive service from multiple locations at a lower cost, which required an innovative solution to address the infrastructure requirements, increase the level of customer service, and provide flexibility for future change while mitigating the associated costs. In addition, TCHC wanted to eliminate the numerous phone numbers it currently listed for contacting the company, thus making it easier for customers to get in touch.

The company has 16 community offices throughout metropolitan Toronto supported by one central response/contact center. The challenge was getting a call to the "right resource the first time" with minimal effort. A superior enterprisewide call management solution was needed to provide seamless information flow regardless of physical location and to provide the capability to track, report, and analyze all customer interactions.

Solution

TCHC needed a long-term, flexible, and expandable system. It selected the Apropos Interaction Management Solutions (IMS) to meet its challenges. With its sophisticated call-handling features, IMS enabled the organization to manage the following business activities:

- Route calls across Toronto to the best resource using just one phone number, regardless of whether that resource was located at a central or remote site.

- Facilitate amalgamation and decentralization to community offices by reducing negative customer service impacts but without reducing CSR productivity.

- Change the number of locations and size of the community offices/contact centers in the future without significant infrastructure costs.

- Provide 24-hour service with live CSRs via a virtual contact center without the need to operate all 16 community units after hours.

- Manage a centralized system by installing a single point of configuration and administration.

- Gain openness and flexibility by integrating with existing infrastructure and allowing migration to new systems resulting from amalgamation.

- Gain PBX independence by interfacing with existing PBX and Centrex lines.

- Route calls effectively through an integrated, robust ACD.

- Identify the client through calling line identification (CLID) and route the call to the appropriate community office based on data in the corporate client database.

- By identifying callers through CLID, find matches over 70% of the time, saving staff time and providing the added "security" that staff are speaking with the correct party.

- Through the caller preview function, allow agents to preview caller information, such as caller name, building, and suite number, prior to answering; agents know at a glance who, why, how many, and how long customers are waiting in queue.

- Integrate with the corporate database applications to provide an application-specific screen-pop of the customer's data on the legacy system.

- Determine instantly in the visual queue which building is experiencing an emergency and is calling over the special phone line that deals specifically with elevator emergencies. Since emergency calls are taken out of queue and dealt with immediately, agents can speak "live" with persons who may be trapped inside the elevator and keep them calm until help arrives.

Benefits

The integration of the Apropos solution has greatly improved customer service and productivity at TCHC. The solution has had a positive impact on TCHC's services in these specific, main areas:

- The volume of calls is down from 17,500 per month to 15,000 over a 12-month period, mostly because of improved client interactions resulting in reduced repeat calls.

- Busy signals have been eliminated.

- Average hold times have been reduced by 50% over the last 12 months.

- 85% of TCHC tenant callers receive automated, personalized service.

- Rapport with customers has improved.

- Flexibility allows menu options designed to meet the characteristics of each community.

- Clients need to dial just one phone number to get answers to their inquiries.

- The centralized database makes it easy to track customer issues, thus constantly improving service and ensuring a consistent and seamless flow of information.

5.5   Health care

Company: Delta Dental Plan of Kentucky

Profile

The company manages dental plans for a broad range of client companies. In just a few months, Delta's customer service call center dramatically improved productivity by changing its call center performance metrics.

Solution

The company decided to revamp its use of existing technology, implement a stricter schedule-adherence policy, and introduce new incentive, quality, and team-building programs for its CSRs.

The first task for the call center's manager of customer service was to review how calls were handled. The 10-agent center takes about 30,000 calls monthly from plan providers, members, group administrators, and insurance brokers and agents. Initially, callers enter an interactive voice response unit where they can get automated information, such as the status of their claims. If they opt out of the automated system, the center's ACD routes the calls to CSRs.

One of the problems with the manner in which the center was handling calls was that CSRs were making decisions themselves as to how much time they needed to spend on after-call work. Calls were routed from the IVR to the CSR's phones, but each agent could decide when to answer these calls. The solution was to change CSR priorities.

A stricter schedule-adherence policy was introduced, requiring all CSRs to work on seven-and-a-half-hour shifts and be available 95% of that time. As well, a tiered structure for routing calls through the ACD was introduced.

Benefits

Specific benefits that were realized include the following:

- The average speed of answer dropped from more than 200 seconds to less than 20 seconds.

- Call abandonment, previously more than 12%, virtually disappeared, to less than 2%.

- Long-distance costs dropped by 20%, in spite of a 10% increase in call volume.

- Fewer angry callers meant agents were less stressed, which has improved overall morale.

- Formal performance-based programs for both individuals and teams were organized, with appropriate awards ranging from gift certificates and gift baskets to time off.

- Call-handling and off-work time were scheduled more efficiently, and a formal call-quality program was established to ensure continuous top performance.

Company: Philips Oral Healthcare

Profile

Philips Oral Healthcare, Inc., formerly Optiva Corporation, located in Snoqualmie, Washington, manufactures Sonicare, a high-tech toothbrush that uses patented sonic technology, fluid dynamics, and electromechanical design to aid in dental care. The company sells its products in the United States through warehouse clubs, mass merchandisers, department stores, and other outlets as well as distributing its products in Canada, Europe, and Japan.

Challenge

In the early days, Optiva's Customer Support Group consisted of 5 CSRs who received about 8,000 inbound calls per month. Its CRM solution was DOS-based, limited in functionality, and lacked reporting capabilities. From 1996 onward, Optiva experienced exponential growth and increased the number of CSRs to 52. A solution was required to manage customer relationships better and the large volume of calls and increased number of accounts contacting the center.

Solution

In 1997, Optiva implemented the Onyx Customer Care Solution, and in the following year, selected the Apropos Multimedia Interaction Management solution to provide the additional functionality needed and to integrate seamlessly with the existing Onyx database. The Apropos system increased the visibility of the center's activities, enhanced management's ability to extract data, and provided robust reporting capabilities.

Benefits

The benefits of the combined vendor call-management software included the following:

- Caller ID, intelligent routing, and screen pops of information

- Access to pertinent caller data

- Reduction in time of call handling by an average of 30 seconds

- CTI capabilities that enable CSRs to call back customers who may have abandoned the multimedia queue

- Robust reporting capabilities providing real-time information and business metrics to improve overall productivity and enhance the customer's experience

Company: University of Alabama Health Services Foundation, P.C.

Profile

The University of Alabama Health Services Foundation, P.C., is a non-profit physician group practice that is a member of the University of Alabama at Birmingham (UAB) Health System. Since its beginning in 1973, the Health Services Foundation has grown to include almost 700 faculty, fellows, and physicians offering services in 33 specialties. These services are reinforced by the research and educational programs of UAB's Academic Health Center, resulting in patient care that is innovative, medically advanced, internationally renowned, and highly compassionate. The physicians of the Health Services Foundation are affiliated with UAB Hospital and the Kirklin Clinic at UAB, which houses most outpatient activities. The foundation formed the Management Services Organization in 1999 and consolidated operations and systems to manage activities related to revenue cycle, including billing and receivables management.

Challenge

Approximately 30% of the foundation's small-balance patient accounts cost more to collect than the actual payment. With limited resources available for collection, these balances often were referred to collection agencies.

Solution

The foundation selected two products from Avaya: Proactive Contact Management and Self-Service Solutions, which were combined to provide a solution to the collections problem that gained additional revenue while freeing resources for other important tasks. With these solutions, the foundation created a virtual payment center designed to automate outgoing calls to patients via predictive dialing and immediately provide patients with an avenue for self-payment using interactive voice response.

Benefits

The following benefits were achieved:

- Maximization of the collection center's performance at the lowest cost

- An additional $50,000 in revenue each month

- Happier customers and better financial performance

- Reduction by 27% in the number of agents needed to handle complex inquiries

- All incoming calls regarding billing questions directed to the interactive voice response system first

- The option for patients to quickly, independently, and confidentially manage their requests

5.6   Real estate

Company: Oxford Properties Group

Profile

Oxford Properties operates an extensive building maintenance organization that services over 25 million square feet of premium office space across Canada.

Challenge

Good tenant relations is a key to success in the real estate business. The extent of Oxford's real estate holdings required its maintenance staff to respond to building maintenance requests quickly and efficiently. A recent tenant satisfaction survey indicated there was room for improvement in the following areas: ease of contact, response times, and satisfaction with problem resolutions.

Solution

To provide the best possible service experience for their tenants, Oxford's management team identified three primary objectives:

- Eliminate confusion by consolidating three regional centers into a single, multichannel center

- Adopt a service level commitment for the contact center to answer 90% of calls within 10 seconds.

- Establish a target of having a service person on site within 30 minutes 95% of the time.

To realize these goals—and to ensure that their building maintenance group was a positive asset that would strengthen tenant loyalty—Oxford selected Bell Canada's call center project management resources to assist its internal team in designing an innovative program, called 310-MAXX, to manage the 30-minute service mandate on orders coming into its building maintenance organization.

With the 310-MAXX program, Oxford tenants simply make a service request call to 310-MAXX from anywhere in Canada or log on to Oxford's building maintenance Website. To turn their vision into reality, Oxford Properties also partnered with Bell Contact Centre Solutions to assist in the start-up and management of the contact center.

The first phase focused on preparing the new, centralized, multichannel facility to handle the increased traffic. This included adding or upgrading the following elements:

- Megalink Access Services

- PBX

- 310 service

- In-house cabling

- A Symposium server and Symposium set installation

It also involved providing extensive professional services to help with the hiring of CSRs and supervisors, initial CSR training, metrics to measure and manage advances in the center, change management to involve contact center staff in implementing "best practices." This major corporate effort was supported by having all of the key ingredients in place, including top-down sponsorship from the president and CEO, a dedicated team of over 45 people who implemented the changes, the involvement of every telephone agent, and training to close any gaps in knowledge and skills.

Benefits

The modified call center and enhanced communication resources were up and running in seven weeks and provided the following benefits:

- Customers can now submit service requests directly, 24 hours a day, via phone or Web and can track the status of their service request on-line or by calling 310-MAXX.

- Once the job is complete, customers receive confirmation via e-mail.

- Tenants and Oxford Properties alike can use the Web-enabled tracking system to monitor request patterns and predict future maintenance needs.

- 92% of customer calls are answered in 10 seconds, on a daily basis.

- Productivity has increased by 106%.

- Quality has increased by 100%.

- Purdue University's Call Center Benchmarking Study ranked Oxford's improved system #4 in its industry group.

- A national disaster contingency plan was implemented.

5.7 Retail

Company: Bargain Network

Profile

Bargain Network specializes in locating "distressed sale" opportunities for its network members. It is one of the leading merchandise search engines for real estate foreclosures, government-seized merchandise, and live auction events. The company offers live agents to assist customers on a 24-hour basis.

Challenge

For a contact center such as Bargain Network, customer service is top priority. With a call volume of 12,000 calls per day, supervisors understand the need to monitor, record, and store all communications between agent and customer for both liability and quality assurance. The company had been recording critical communications using simple cassette tapes and off-the-shelf tape recorders. As the business grew, the quality of the recording and archiving was not meeting the high standards required, and the company was not able to realize the full potential of recorded information. The challenge was to find and implement a cost-effective, reliable, and easy-to-use solution for real-time digital data recording.

Solution

Bargain Networks selected Voice Print International (VPI) to upgrade its call and data recording systems to meet the challenges. VPI's system allowed the company to optimize the time used servicing customers.

Benefits

The solution selected by the company provided the following benefits:

- Capability of monitoring both verbal and electronic communication between agents and customers

- Re-creation of the customer experience and evaluation of CSR performance by reviewing communication via phone, fax, e-mail, and/or the Web

- Archiving of calls to DVD-RAM, a reliable, long-term storage media enabling CSRs to locate data with pinpoint accuracy within seconds

Company: Borders Group

Profile

Borders Group, a Fortune 500 company, is a leading global retailer of books, music, movies, and other related items. Through its affiliates, Borders operates over 340 Borders Books and Music stores in the United States as well as 17 international Borders stores, approximately 860 Waldenbooks locations, and 32 U.K.-based Books etc. stores.

Challenge

The seasonal nature of Borders' business combined with its multiskilled contact center made optimizing its workforce a formidable challenge. The company plans for its staffing needs well in advance of the holiday season, when customer expectations are higher than usual and business volume is high. During this period, there is an over 35% surge in call volume, making optimizing available resources and staff essential. Overstaffing costs could significantly cut into profit margins, whereas understaffing at such a critical time of the year would be disastrous.

In addition to planning for significantly increased call volumes, Borders Group had a variety of complex criteria to be considered in developing the optimal schedule, which included 15 contact center skills, employee work preferences, and seniority-based scheduling.

Solution

The company chose Blue Pumpkin software to resolve its call center management requirement and ran a series of "what-if" staffing scenarios to design a workforce optimization strategy that accurately reflected all of Borders' business goals. Based upon a staff selection plan generated by

Blue Pumpkin software, Borders Group knew exactly how many seasonal workers to hire as well as both the number of hours and skills required, making the hiring process much easier.

Benefits

The following benefits were achieved:

- Reduced turnover of nonseasonal employees from 15 to 10%

- Reduced overall recruiting and training expenses by 25%

- Increased agent productivity by 53%, with a 33% reduction in expenses by allocating agent time more effectively over operating hours

- Achieved customer service levels of 88% during the holiday period, with most calls answered in less than 10 seconds

- Reduced costs and delivered a high level of customer service

- Improved skillsets of seasonal staff and enabled them to get on the phones 33% faster, allowing them to be productive in one week instead of three

Company: HSN (Home Shopping Network)

Profile

HSN is a division of USA Networks Inc., a leader in TV and Internet-based direct retailing. The company received more than 68 million sales and service calls in 1999 and generated $1.2 billion in sales.

Challenge

When HSN's two contact centers became too busy at peak times, a percentage of calls were routed to a third-party provider. This percentage could only be changed every 15 minutes, which meant that agents in HSN's contact centers could be idle while the calls were still being routed to the third party. As well, HSN elected to route calls from frequent customers to a specific CSR to strengthen relationships and loyalty.

Solution

To resolve this situation with the third-party provider, HSN installed a load-balancing system for multiple call center sites. Routing calls to a specific CSR was accomplished by using intelligent voice recognition (IVR) and an analysis by a voice-print-enabled IVR. This feature enabled the company to check security and provide the customer's personal CSR with all the up-to-date information requested.

Benefits

The following benefits have been achieved:

- Using the universal queue and dynamic enterprise routing strategies, HSN can immediately decide which of the three contact centers will receive the call.

- Overflow calls can be routed to the third party only when agents at both HSN sites are operating at full capacity, keeping HSN's costs at a minimum.

- Customers can now contact CSRs familiar with their profiles and purchasing requirements.

5.8   Technology

Company: 3COM

Profile

3Com Corporation, headquartered in Santa Clara, California, provides easy-to-use connectivity products and solutions for consumers and commercial organizations. 3Com enriches people's networking experience in the areas of home networks and gateways, Internet appliances, broadband Internet access, local area network (LAN) and mobile access, business LAN telephony, wireless mobility, high-speed LANs, and carrier-class platforms delivering IP telephony, wireless, and broadband services.

Challenge

3Com receives millions of calls each year at its help desk support center. The company needed a solution that would allow agents to quickly and efficiently manage the high volume of customer interactions received daily. The solution needed to map agent skillsets and provide premium levels of service through personalization. The existing system provided minimal statistics and limited on-line data. A solution was required that would improve this situation and result in increased customer and CSR satisfaction.

Solution

After a thorough review and evaluation, 3COM selected Apropos Multimedia Interaction Management, a product providing immediate identification and intelligent routing that automatically distributes calls to the appropriate CSR for personalized handling. In addition, the system enables CSRs to manage call flow and high call volume, even in peak times. The multimedia visual queue feature displays each interaction and its status. Pertinent information is captured and viewed to produce key statistics and historical reporting.

Benefits

Among the benefits achieved by the Apropos solution were the following:

- Automatic dispatching and routing quickly routed the calls to the appropriate agent and enabled the agent to handle each interaction in a more personalized and efficient manner.

- Statistics and reporting produced key information and business metrics that enabled management to make well-informed business decisions.

- Powerful interaction management instantly displayed all interactions and pertinent information, allowing agents to deliver a more efficient response and increasing customer satisfaction.

Company: SGI (Silicon Graphics, Inc.)

Profile

SGI, also known as Silicon Graphics, Inc., is a technology solutions provider with a broad range of high-performance computing, advanced graphics, and consulting services that enable its technical and creative customers to maintain a competitive advantage in their core businesses.

Challenge

To improve customer service while reducing costs, SGI decided to overhaul its contact center strategy. SGI created a virtual contact center by installing a new switch that connected its four facilities located throughout the country. Previously, the company developed schedules manually, relying on local critical needs assessment to develop a plan. However, a more efficient and accurate method for accommodating the complexities of a workforce physically located in four time zones was required.

Solution

Blue Pumpkin multiskilled workforce optimization software was selected to optimize workforce utilization and improve customer service.

Benefits

The following benefits were achieved:

- New volumes were handled with only an 8% increase in staffing.

- The optimized staff plan resulted in a 37% increase in agent productivity.

- Customer service levels were improved by 40%

- Millions of dollars were saved in additional employee-related expenses.

- Monitoring and managing schedule compliance was accomplished more efficiently, resulting in a 40% improvement in adherence.

- Better matching of head count to the response-time commitment was achieved.

- Customer satisfaction ratings improved by 47%.

- Service revenues in the Americas grew as a result of customer satisfaction with contact centers and on-site field support.

Company: Crystal Decisions

Profile

Crystal Decisions, of Vancouver, BC, a Seagate Company, is a leading software developer of solutions that enable organizations to analyze, manage, and protect the hidden value of critical corporate information. With over 20 offices worldwide, Crystal Decisions' Vancouver contact center provides technical support to customers all over the world.

Challenge

Because Crystal Decisions supports everything from shrink-wrapped customer products that sell for less than $200 to multimillion-dollar corporate installations, the company needed to find a way to support customers across this broad spectrum consistently. A key requirement was to identify customers who had basic 60-day free support and high-end customers who were paying for premium customer service.

Supervisors were especially challenged. The closest thing the company had to real-time information was a periodic recycling of the message reader board. Crystal Decisions had 14 queues, so 14 message boards were downloaded to the network and flashed every minute. With contact center offices operating from Vancouver, Florida, Texas, Australia, and the United

Kingdom, an enterprisewide interaction management solution became a critical requirement for a seamless information flow regardless of media type or physical location.

Solution

After careful evaluation of a half-dozen vendors, Crystal Decisions chose LGS Group and its Interaction Management Solutions (IMS) system to deliver the Apropos Multimedia Interaction Management Solution. The IMS solution emphasized "agent empowerment." The capability of Apropos to display all interactions and allow agents to select those calls that took priority, had been waiting longest, or fell into a specialty area helped them be prepared and proactive when answering a call. A caller preview function allowed agents to see caller information while calls are still in the queue. In addition, integration with the corporate customer relationship management (CRM) database provided a screen pop of the customer's data on the legacy system. Agents had immediate access to customers' detailed records, providing consistent and effective support to every customer.

When customers call, they are asked to enter their product registration number and/or call incident number. Calls are routed based on these numbers. If customers have a valid support contract or are entitled to 60-day free support, they are identified and, based on their support contract, placed in the appropriate queue. This important functions allows Crystal Decisions to recover lost revenue by segmenting clients into those who have 60-day free software support or those whose contract has expired.

Benefits

The following benefits have been achieved with this vendor solution:

- Customers can check telephone wait times on Crystal Decisions' technical support Website.

- The scalability and flexibility of the system made it easy for the company to grow to its present 250 agents in over 100 different workgroups (skill-based and product-based) in five contact centers around the world.

- Cradle-to-grave reporting capabilities and resource management tools enable supervisors to monitor CSR activities easily and conveniently, to move agents from one queue to another quickly, and to make agents with various skills available to more callers.

- An alarm notification feature enables supervisors to control the contact.

- Supervisors can switch agents from one queue to another immediately or place agents in multiple queues.

- All interactions received by the system can be tracked and reported.

- Supervisors can set up various alarms to notify them and/or agents of any unusual activities that could disrupt operations.

- Managers are provided with accurate data on the total number and type of interactions received, how many have been serviced, by whom, for how long, and at which location.

- Supervisors can monitor the center from their desktop—real-time information about activities are graphically displayed.

- Supervisors can choose from a variety of canned reports on interaction, agent, and queue activity—real-time and historical.

- Dozens of custom reports are created that merge Apropos data and other enterprisewide data in a format that specifically addresses senior management issues.

- Allowing certain agents to specialize in "trouble" calls has cut the duration of these calls in half.

- E-mail management capability has resulted in $1.20 per minute savings for interactions in the Asia Pacific region.

- The ability to check telephone wait times on the Web has encouraged customers to purchase premium technical support where the wait times are always very low, thus adding greatly to company revenues.

- A more complete database of customers is available, because every client needs to register the product before obtaining support.

- IVR functionality, shorter wait times, choice of music or silence while on hold, and ability to check call wait times on the Web have all contributed to a significantly higher level of customer satisfaction.

Company: Primavera Systems

Profile

Founded in 1983, Primavera Systems, Inc. is the leading provider of enterprise and Web-based project management, control, and execution software. Headquartered in Bala Cynwyd, Pennsylvania, Primavera has offices in New York, San Francisco, Chicago, Concord (New Hampshire), London, and Hong Kong. Primavera's products include project management, planning, and scheduling; methodology management; risk analysis; resource planning;

issue tracking; and team communication for integrated project execution. Primavera software is also designed to easily integrate with other systems in the enterprise, including leading enterprise resource planning (ERP) software for a total business solution. Primavera's customer base spans a broad range of industries, including information technology, financial services, telecommunications, chemical processing, energy, engineering, construction, utilities, aerospace, and defense.

Challenge

Primavera was looking for a solution to support its customer service. It needed a robust solution for both of its contact centers in Concord, New Hampshire, and Bala Cynwyd, Pennsylvania, to manage roughly 5000 phone calls and 100 Web requests from customers on a monthly basis. The solution had to meet the following requirements:

- Enable agents to derive value from every customer interaction

- Empower agents to view and manage all communications within a fully integrated solution

- Provide comprehensive reporting and monitoring to enable changes to be made instantly based on report findings

- Instill a sense of confidence that all customers are receiving the attention and responses they deserve

- Keep costs down

- Integrate with an existing Onyx software customer database

Solution

Taking into consideration the requirements they were looking for in a contact center solution, Primavera chose Apropos Technology's Multi-Channel Interaction Management Suite to manage phone and Web customer interactions. The Apropos Intelligent Call Distribution (ICD) system gave Primavera more control over call routing, distributing customer calls to the most appropriate agent in a quicker and more efficient fashion. Primavera also gained improved real-time visibility and more in-depth historical reporting functionality to better manage both of the company's contact centers with the Apropos solution.

Primavera uses the Apropos solution to manage inbound customer interactions within the contact center and to integrate with its existing Onyx customer database through Touch-Tone inputs into the interactive voice response (IVR) unit, without changing any hardware or software configurations. The flexibility and customization of the solution allows Primavera to service its customers based on individual needs. It allows CSRs to provide a high degree of relationship-based service through the ability to view incoming and outgoing customer interaction requests based on the interactions's priority or Primavera's specific business rules. Using these business rules also allows calls to be routed to the most appropriate agent and interactions to be managed on a priority basis.

In addition to handling interaction workflow, Apropos provides Primavera's contact center with a single point of management for systemwide agent, supervisor, and server configurations. The Apropos solution also enables Primavera to seamlessly manage all voice and Web customer interactions. Primavera's on-line customers have the flexibility to conduct interactions over the Internet through e-mail or Web collaboration and access to personal "live" assistance through either an interactive Web chat or voice interaction to help complete sales or service transactions.

Primavera also takes advantage of customizable voice features available in the Apropos product. These features includes automatic call distribution, programmable interactive voice response, voice mail management, voice recording, abandoned-call management, call blending, and text-to-speech automation.

Primavera's agents can monitor both of the firm's contact centers, which service all of its North American customers. This monitoring capability allows interactions received by the system to be tracked, alarmed, and reported on, which ultimately gives contact center managers accurate data on the performance of the center, allowing them to react in real time to any changing business conditions while monitoring quality assurance.

Primavera uses the Apropos Interaction Vault™ (iValult™) application to keep a record of interactions and gain instant access to interaction histories through archived records of all customer interactions. Apropos' iVault is a browser-based application. Its search capabilities allow Primavera's contact center agents and supervisors to immediately view the entire history of any interaction based on date, time, or business data. From a single source, agents and supervisors can review all previous customer communications from a variety of sources.

Benefits

The following benefits were achieved:

- Reduced research time from three hours to less than 15 minutes a week

- Improved real-time visibility and in-depth historical reporting functionality

- Improved data quality, allowing management to compare agent-recorded interaction metrics and notes found in their CRM application to reality

- Increased customer service with intelligent call distribution, providing more control over call routing and distributing customer calls to the most appropriate agent in a quicker and more efficient manner

5.9   Travel

Company: Thomas Cook Direct

Profile

Thomas Cook Direct has a mission to become a major travel service for holiday and flight bookings. To succeed in this goal, customer care must be second to none. The company is pursuing a reputation as a world-class contact center; it has four separate centers in the United Kingdom and employs more than 1000 CSRs, operates seven days a week, from 8 A.M. to midnight, and handles more than 80,000 calls each week.

Challenge

The company needed a technology that could support and simplify the process of managing and optimizing a complex and busy workforce, but the solution also had to make financial sense and show quantifiable returns.

Solution

The company selected Blue Pumpkin's solution for several reasons. The key differentiators from other products were the capability to schedule staff according to skillsets and the easy-to-use graphical user interface. Contact center managers could now monitor all four centers from their desktop, enabling them to instantly compare resource levels and overlap and identify where staffing and skill levels could be improved for the next day.

Benefits

The benefits provided by the vendor solution selected included

- Enabling agents to manage their own schedules through a self-service, browser-based interface—Web-Enabled Self-Service (WESS)

- Improved morale and satisfaction as a result of empowering agents with the freedom and flexibility to make their own decisions
- Quick return on investment (ROI)
- A 25% drop in call-abandon rates
- Overall 49% productivity improvement and first-year ROI of 3000%
- 37% increase in agent productivity
- 40% improvement in service levels
- 10% reduction in management workload for workforce management functions
- 47% increase in customer satisfaction ratings
- 40% improvement in schedule adherence

6

Building Customer Relationships with Call Centers

Customer relationship management (CRM) has been defined as a corporate wide approach to understanding customer behavior, influencing it through continuous relevant communication, and developing long-term relationships to enhance customer loyalty, acquisition, retention, and profitability. This chapter describes the importance of the interrelationships between call/contact centers and the stages of developing and implementing a CRM strategy. The center is the first point of customer contact and is therefore the first entrée to establishing and maintaining long-term customer relationships.

CRM is often perceived by senior management with mixed feelings—on the one hand, it is a great opportunity to enhance customer relationships and to increase revenues and profitability at the same time, and on the other hand, it is a costly and time-consuming process that will alter fundamentally the corporate culture. CRM is also fraught with the numerous potential pitfalls that confront any major corporate project involving people, processes, and technologies. Aligning the vagaries of operating a call center with CRM poses some serious challenges for corporate executives. CRM is not a technology or even a group of technologies; it is a continually evolving process that requires a shift in attitude away from the traditional internal focus of a business and defines the approach a company takes toward its customers, backed up by a thoughtful investment in people, technology, and business processes.

CRM is a logical step in the series of major commercial and IT initiatives that have been implemented since the 1980s, beginning with downsizing. Most of these early initiatives had a cost-cutting focus on the internal workings of the business, concentrating on employees, working methods, or technology. Increased profitability was the desired result, which was to be engineered through cost savings. All of these initiatives were based on decreasing costs through increasing efficiency, which is one of the key benefits of a successful CRM strategy in addition to its significant impact on the customer.

6.1   A rationale and methodology for CRM

Corporations large and small, from Old Economy to New, have been confronted with the dire predictions of software companies and consultants pointing out that if their organizations did not jump on the CRM bandwagon, they would be ground into the dust by competitors who were more aggressive and open to new corporate practices. CRM, although a powerful tool in both the business-to-business and business-to-consumer environments, has been, however, both oversold and underutilized. In many cases, more has been promised from CRM than it could possibly deliver; and in other cases, companies have not properly planned or implemented CRM strategies and consequently have failed to achieve its benefits.

Some CRM vendors and consultants focus on CRM as a transorganizational strategy, one that must be rapidly implemented and that required immediate commitment throughout the organization. However, the CRM process is more readily accepted by organizations if the process is a gradual one that evolves from a series of data marts to an enterprisewide data warehouse and CRM solution. This type of CRM development process has proven much easier for organizations to manage and accept, and in the long run, it will pay dividends in enhanced customer relationships. When CRM is seen only as a corporate strategy that must permeate all aspects of an organization's activities immediately to be effective, there is a natural tendency to want to roll it out all at once in what has been called the "big bang" approach. Too often, the big bang turns out to be a big bust! Organizations confronted with more corporate changes than they can handle all at once may find the challenges faced by employees exceed the challenges faced by the software. Because of the complex nature of even a modest CRM program, successful CRM implementation requires above-average consulting services. Vendors tend to want to solve all the problems at once, and, although consultants can assist in analyzing a business and its processes, there are more issues to be considered, addressed, and resolved. It is important to devise a plan, implement it, and make it stick.

Planning

Companies should not be expending precious financial and human resources on particular communications channels and customer segments out of all proportion to their profitability and practicality. The key is to define a customer service strategy by determining investment priorities and then to select the best supportive technology. Making the proper choice of technologies is critical, but this can only be accomplished with a coherent, executable plan. Often, companies are expected to "go live" with salesforce automation, customer service, and marketing all at once. As noted, this approach has resulted in the failure of CRM strategies and, more importantly, a loss of confidence in CRM itself.

Rather than going with the "big bang," knowledgeable consultants advise going deep, not broad. Using a gradual approach, a company identifies the most important application of CRM and ensures that this implementation is successful before moving on to the next one. It is better to identify specific customer segments and communications channels for the initial execution and focus on doing this aspect well before tackling the next segments and channels. CRM tends to overwhelm organizations with its expanding variety of communication channels. Just because one lone customer wants to send a company a wireless e-mail from a data-equipped cell phone to order a replacement burner for a barbecue is no reason for an organization to be prepared to accommodate the order. This could be viewed as carrying customer relations to their illogical conclusion!

Making it work

The business processes must be mapped into the underlying technology. Customers are supported by the way organizations work; the technology provides that support. Technology itself should not be in the driver's seat. Companies frequently buy CRM technology in the name of customer service and then forget about the customer—implementing the application becomes an internal issue in which the main reason for the implementation in the first place gets lost in the process. The focus must be on the customer at all times.

Making it stick

For CRM to have long-term practicality and benefits, an organization has to believe in its underlying proposition of improving customer relations. It is more than software and digital switching systems, in the same way that these elements alone do not make a successful call center. A customer-focused mindset must take root in the organization, and this takes time. Ideally, the change in focus should begin well before the CRM technology is rolled out. Employees need to develop the skillsets to serve customers better; senior executives need to show the type of leadership that encourages a customer-centric culture. People need incentives to believe in CRM.

Customer service has to be more than a slogan; tangible benefits, whether from data mining that allows sales and marketing to hone their efforts or from measurable successes in repeat customers and overall satisfaction, have to be seen and appreciated. Advances in technology do tend to move at breakneck speed—it's often said that an Internet "year" lasts about four months—but the frantic pace of these advances doesn't mean that the development and implementation of CRM systems solutions should also be frantic. Just as CRM is about cultivating a long-term relationship with the customer by enhancing the value of a company's service, implementing CRM should be approached as a long-term strategy, based on a step-by-step progression.

Integration

Software-driven CRM systems integrate front-office activities such as sales, customer service, and technical support with back-office resources such as accounting and inventory management. Only a few years ago, many organizations considered CRM to be a call center with rows full of customer service representatives working telephones in front of computer monitors. An explosion in communication channels, particularly through the Internet, means that call centers have become multichannel components of CRM strategy with the capability to address and integrate telephones, Web presence, e-mail, real-time text chat, and wireless data. As product offerings for this new capability became more complex, they became more difficult to implement. In fact, CRM's scope has become so ambitious that there are serious doubts any one vendor can deliver a product that performs as promised. A single-vendor product may soon be within reach, but the most important factor in CRM success is not what is installed, but *how*.

Some organizations have invested millions of dollars and thousands of hours over long periods of time to deploy and integrate corporate applications—salesforce automation (SFA), help desk, enterprise resource planning (ERP), marketing automation, e-commerce, call/contact centers, and Web platforms—to implement and support CRM strategies that build customer loyalty through intelligent and trusted communication. Using innovative technologies to achieve this goal while containing costs is a fundamental challenge for every company that embraces CRM. For many organizations that adhered to the old ways of doing business, the move to a CRM strategy began with the realization that the customer, the market, and the competition had changed and would continue to change. Treating customers as "mass markets" is no longer a viable business strategy, and success in business in the 21st century requires a new vision, a vision that demands changes in the processes, people, and practices with which the customer is involved. The reason is that as businesses merged and grew, customer bases grew and the customer changed along the way. Armed with their newfound understanding of the levels of service that suppliers can and should provide, customers expect much more. And the power they wield in the marketplace can only increase with time. Organizations following the old ways of doing business have a greater challenge and will require a few years and major changes in corporate culture to evolve a successful CRM strategy. (see Figure 6.1) Other organizations that have continually examined and revised their methods of relating to customers, as well as adopted appropriate technologies along the way, have a relatively short route to follow in evolving a formal CRM strategy. Only a fine-tuning of existing processes, a refinement of

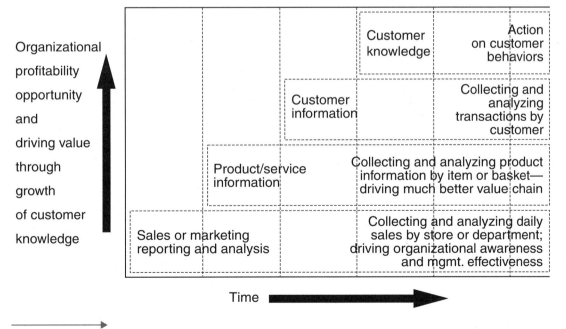

Figure 6.1   *Sources of customer information.*

current technologies, and additional training of staff may be required to ensure the transition to a complete CRM solution.

6.2   Strategies for managing customer information

Large organizations routinely collect vast amounts of personal information about their customers through the transactions they conduct. Organizations such as financial institutions, health care providers, travel agencies, retailers, automotive manufacturers, and communication companies, among others, use this data in a variety of ways and for several reasons:

- For targeted marketing based on individual preferences

- To analyze customers for profitability

- To evaluate their own service levels

Simply gathering information and storing it will not produce measurable business results; many CRM strategies have failed to achieve objectives because of difficulties in developing a strong understanding of *who customers are and what they really want* and applying this knowledge to customer relationship strategies and processes. (see Figure 6.2) Some companies build

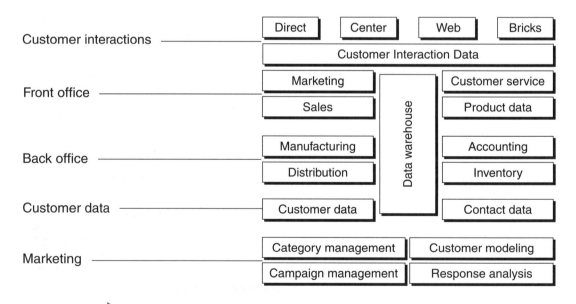

Figure 6.2   *Corporate functions and customer interactions.*

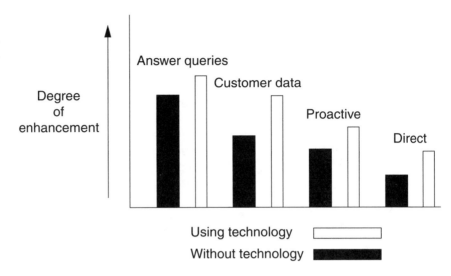

Figure 6.3
Enhancing customer service with technology.

large multiterabyte (1000 gigabytes equals 1 terabyte) data warehouses to crunch information about their customers in an effort to determine their buying habits or product preferences. Oftentimes, correlating customer purchasing habits is not properly done—just because data can be correlated doesn't mean the relationship between one set of data and another is significant from a business viewpoint. Obviously, technology and business processes must be applied in a logical context to ensure that customer data are applied in a way to meet CRM objectives. (see Figure 6.3)

CRM brings technology to bear on business processes to enable organizations to use historical customer transaction data to manage customer relationships better. CRM is based on a set of technology tools that allows organizations to capture, analyze, and apply large volumes of detailed customer data to achieve a fuller understanding of their customers and to make more informed business decisions. Informed business decisions are the ultimate beneficial result of successful corporate CRM strategies. Those companies that adopted formalized CRM strategies early in their corporate histories have been achieving measurable business results through CRM initiatives, but, as noted previously, others may have to totally revise their corporate cultures, even completely do away with their traditional ways of dealing with customers in their sales and marketing programs. Organizations that do not have a formal process for managing customers by monitoring and gathering historical transaction data and then analyzing this data to determine how to respond to each customer's needs will have to put major efforts and budgets into developing CRM strategies. (see Figure 6.4)

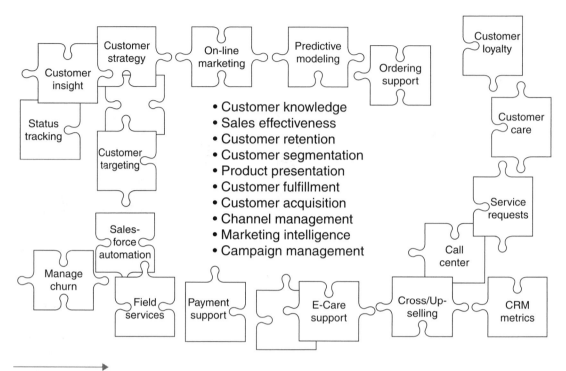

Figure 6.4   *Integrating customer knowledge with corporate functions.*

6.3   Technology and business tools to support CRM

It is important to choose the right technology tools to support CRM. Direct and indirect supporting technologies include:

- Data warehousing

- Data mining

- Database systems

- Wireless communication

- Voice-over IP

- E-mail-based Internet communications

These tools have evolved to the point that they have made available many more channels for customer interaction and sources of data, all of which impact the call/contact center. Business tools that support CRM include:

- Customer contact software

- Marketing campaign programs

- Channel integration
- Product literature

Where legacy systems exist, the acquisition of "middleware" may be required in order to interface the legacy systems with the CRM solutions. The key challenge for the CRM project team is to select a series of tools that fit the needs of the business, to evaluate these tools, and to select the best ones. The IT department plays a very prominent role in this selection process and in the development, implementation, and support of a CRM solution and its integration with the call/contact center. The various technology tools involved should be seamlessly integrated into the IT environment. This aspect of a CRM strategy requires a formal plan to manage the selection of the tools—from data warehouse and database software to the business applications and processes.

CRM and the new marketing paradigm

CRM has several definitions within the industry, but one short definition best describes the process and the objectives: "*the capability of an organization to evolve from a mass marketing model of millions to a market of one,*" that is, dealing with customers as *if they were the only customer.* This is a new way of thinking for many companies in virtually every business sector where customers often number in the thousands or millions. Managing customer relationships successfully in these large customer environments means learning about their habits and needs, anticipating future buying patterns, and finding new marketing opportunities that add value to the relationship. It also means using technologies that enable the data gathered to be useful in making better business decisions that will attract, retain, or motivate customers.

Successful companies make their customer relationships something the customer values more than anything else they could receive from the competition. How do companies do this? By examining their experiences with customers, including transactions and demographics, and every form of interaction—including a Website visit, a phone call to a call center, and a response from a direct mail campaign. Building the data and information technology architecture around customers—a *customer-centric* approach—ensures that they enjoy a seamless and rewarding experience when doing business with a company. This new marketing paradigm places the customer at the focal point of an organization's marketing programs.

Key elements

The two following key elements will ensure the success of a CRM strategy and meet the objectives of the organization to develop long-term customer relationships:

- Build a system that allows *tracking, capturing, and analyzing* the millions of customer activities, both interactions and transactions, over a long period of time.

- Create *promotions, develop new products and services, and design communication programs* that attract, reward, and retain customers. (see Figure 6.5)

CRM strategies are designed to manage all of an organization's interactions with its customers and to use information to maintain a single, long-term view of each customer across multiple channels—face-to-face or via phone, kiosk, or Website. These points of interaction, often referred to as *customer touch points*, may involve many types of transactions. And, of course, CRM includes customer billing, marketing, and other support functions that directly or indirectly interact with the customer. In fact,

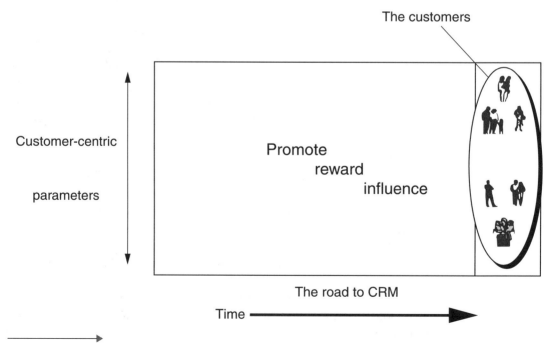

Figure 6.5   *Enhancing customer service.*

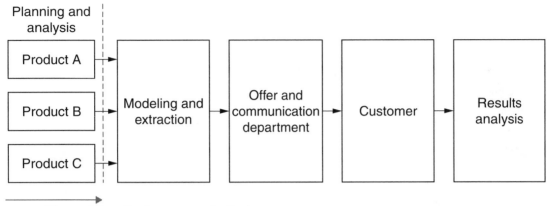

Figure 6.6   *Getting customer feedback.*

every department, division, and employee in an organization has a role to play in CRM. (see Figure 6.6)

Managing customer relations using proven processes and technologies can maximize the revenue opportunity from each customer and create a foundation for satisfaction that will ultimately drive loyalty independent of the channel used. CRM can enable companies to maximize profitability by using "measurements" that quantify and qualify customers, differentiating between high- and low-value customers, with the objective of managing the lifetime value of a customer.

Customer knowledge through CRM

A successful CRM strategy can provide answers to many questions that every organization typically has about its customers: (see Figure 6.7)

- Who are my best customers?

- How do I attract them?

- How do I ensure that I'm selling them the products and services that meet their specific needs and still make a profit?

- How do I keep them coming back?

- How do I manage relationships with unhappy customers?

CRM places the customer at the center of the organization and involves every function and department in serving the customer. Sales, service, and support functions as well as relationships with business partners form a continuum, because *this is how these corporate functions are viewed by customers.*

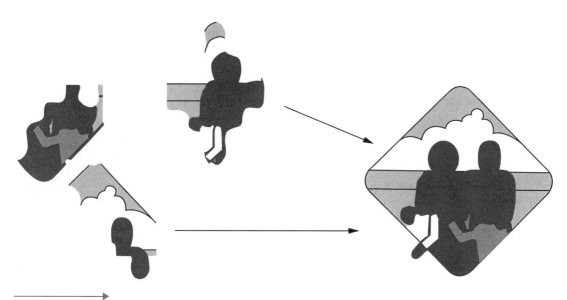

Figure 6.7   *Integrating customer information.*

When customers make purchases from a supplier, they believe they have a relationship with the whole organization, from sales to shipping and even to the CEO.

Companies that believed technology alone would solve customer relationship problems learned the hard way that technology is only an *enabler*. CRM implementations based on this premise failed because they did not change the corporate culture to permit the technology to perform its primary function: *developing and retaining loyal and profitable customers.* Technology's role as an enabler is to support the strategies, tactics, and processes that result from a defined, enterprisewide CRM solution. The creation and execution of a successful CRM strategy depend on close examination and rationalization of the relationship between an organization's vision and business strategy. If the customer is not at the center of this vision, the vision must be reexamined and altered to be *customer-centric*.

Customer data

One of the common problems many organizations share is integrating customer information. When information is disparate and fragmented, it is difficult to know who the customers are and the nature of their associations or relationships. This also makes it difficult to capitalize on opportunities to increase customer service, loyalty, and profitability. For example, knowing that other family members are also customers provides an opportunity to upsell or cross sell products or services, or knowing that a customer uses several sources of interaction with a supplier may also provide opportunities to enhance the relationship.

In building toward a CRM solution, the organization must analyze how well it is aligned to deliver the following core capabilities:

- Customer value management

- Prospecting

- Selling

- Collection and use of customer intelligence

- Customer development (upselling and cross selling)

- Customer service and retention

Ultimately, the success or failure of CRM depends on the capability of the organization and its employees to integrate human resources, business processes, and technology to create differentiation and excellence in service to customers, and to perform all of these functions better than its competitors. The customer is in control! (see Figure 6.8)

Shifting from a product focus to a customer-centric focus

In the e-commerce business world, a customer can switch to a competitor's product with a click or two on a Web page. A customer-centric focus—the best means of building lasting customer relationships in both the traditional and new ways of doing business—has become absolutely imperative in the new business economy, but shifting to a customer-centric approach is not a straightforward process, nor is it a natural one. The reason for this is that, in general, businesses are launched on the basis of a unique product or service. Initially, the focus is on building that product or developing that service and informing the marketplace of its availability and desirability. When another company eventually begins producing and marketing a similar product, the original company loses its competitive edge.

At this point, companies adopt other strategies to regain the competitive edge they had when they had a unique product or service. They begin streamlining operations to produce the product better, faster, and cheaper. But improved performance is a short-lived advantage because the competition inevitably applies the same strategy, resulting in a leap-frogging process common to many business sectors. Customer relationships then become

Figure 6.8
*Customer in
control.*

more important than simply building a good product or delivering good service. Building good products is often easier than building good customer relationships, and although product quality is still important, it is no longer the key to *sustainable competitive advantage* when the competition's products are just as good. In the long term, the organization with the best customer relationship strategy will win out. And the call/contact center has to be a primary conduit for this strategy. (see Figure 6.9)

Becoming customer-centric—that is, shifting from marketing products to building lasting customer relationships—is, as we have said, an evolutionary process. It cannot be done overnight and usually requires a major change in corporate culture. A fully customer-centric organization has the ability to *successfully manage customer knowledge*. Product-focused organizations use sales

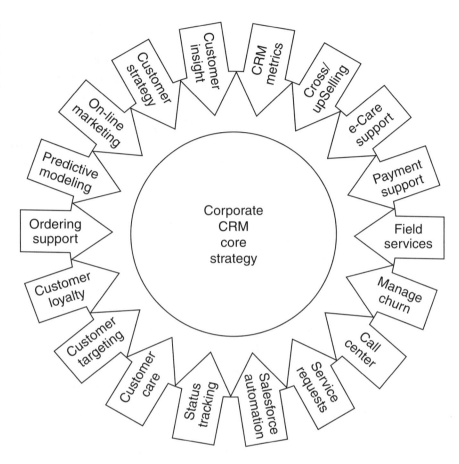

Figure 6.9
Maximizing the value of each customer interaction.

data primarily to report on progress in reaching financial targets. A customer-centric organization, on the other hand, stores, analyzes, and uses sales, billing, service, support, and other data in an ongoing relationship with customers to accomplish the following objectives:

- *Forge* personal relationships

- *Increase* staff awareness of customer importance

- *Improve* the product development process

- *Deliver* value-added service better than competitors

Customer value

Transforming *customer knowledge* into *customer value* can create a significant competitive advantage. For example, when high-value customers are identified and their needs anticipated, new value is created for them where it did not exist before. Ultimately, customer-centric organizations build customer loyalty, a customer response characteristic that leads to higher profitability. There are several ways organizations can categorize customers by their "value." Tracking revenues, cost, and profitability is not the only way to assess customer value. Another, more advanced method of evaluating customer value is by assessing their *value potential*, which has been defined as the willingness of customers to participate in the creation of products and services, sharing with them information and other resources and sharing control over the design and production of products and services.

6.4   The CRM planning phase

As noted previously, CRM is not an event, but a process that is evolutionary in nature and that requires a road map to guide organizations through the many alternative routes that could be taken. Following that road map involves a concerted effort from several organizational components: people, processes, culture, and technology.

An overview of the CRM planning phase will assist call center personnel to understand the complexity of developing a corporate CRM strategy, and give them some insight into the call center role.

There are four key elements in the development of a CRM road map, and they need to be approached in the following order:

- Analyzing the current state of customer interactions

- Predicting the future course of customer interactions

- Developing the Plan of Action to meet the predicted future course

- Building and presenting the business case to secure CRM project funding

Analyzing the current state of customer interactions and associated historical customer data will determine where the enterprise is along the path to its CRM objectives. Examples of questions about current customer relations that need to be answered are: Does the organization *track and manage* each customer as a single entity or do individual sales offices maintain their own set of customer records? Is customer database information *accurate* and *up-to-date*? An early assessment of these elements of the business operation will highlight customer administration procedures that may need to be changed to take advantage of the new CRM strategy. (see Figure 6.10)

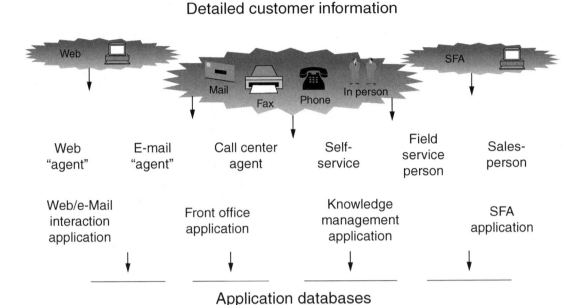

Figure 6.10   *Accessing detailed customer information.*

The CRM plan of action

One of the first requirements for the CRM Plan of Action is establishing priorities of functionality, which breaks the CRM development process down into two phases: establishing a list of essential features and developing a list of optional features. This approach to planning—adding functionality in a modular way—is consistent with the modular approach adopted by many CRM hardware and software vendors. Taking a building-block approach to incorporating functionality will also assist in developing the CRM Plan of Action and in the subsequent design and deployment of the CRM solution.

The following organizational elements must be included in the CRM Plan of Action:

■ Call/contact center management

■ The IT department

■ Other departments and resources that will be impacted by the CRM strategy

All corporate departments must participate in the planning, including the user community, executive sponsors, and others. Participation may involve providing design inputs, taking part in pilot tests of the system, or helping to train others to use it during the system rollout.

Also included in the Plan of Action will be target time frames and expected project milestones in the form of reporting dates to meet management expectations. The plan should mesh with the business case so that requests for resources—people, time, and money—are linked to anticipated business benefits. The business case should describe a rationale for investing in CRM. It should include information about what competitors are doing, how such a system supports the company's strategy, and the expected qualitative and quantitative benefits, including return on investment (ROI). Although ROI is a significant benefit of CRM over the long term, financial or quantitative benefits do not represent the complete picture. Among the other, more or less tangible, but not easily tracked benefits of a well-executed CRM strategy are the following:

- More sales per customer
- Lower cost of sales
- More referral sales
- Higher profitability

Selecting the technology solutions

As noted previously, many enterprises believe that a large-scale CRM technology deployment is the only solution to their problems. However, the right technological enablers for an organization are those that *solve the organization's business problems* as they are identified during the CRM planning stage. Some of the solutions may be

- Improving call center telephony infrastructure
- Enabling customer/contact center calls over the Web
- Deploying or enhancing data warehouse or data mart information to collect and analyze customer and market data
- Improving customer relationships through customer-facing e-business

During the evolution of CRM over the past several years, a number of CRM projects failed to deliver projected results because companies seized on technology as an immediate solution to enhanced customer relations rather than modify their corporate culture. In those organizations that took the "technology is the key" route to CRM and were unable to devise a successful CRM strategy, the people, the support systems, and the processes—including the corporate culture—were not ready to manage the new technology and to apply proven principles of CRM to their day-to-day operations.

Technology is a significant element in the CRM mix; however, selecting the best enabling technologies for CRM solutions must be based on solid business practices and readiness to implement. Selection of both tools and vendors, is a critical process, but goals and metrics must be established to measure the effect of the tools.

Changing the focus

In the past, large and small organizations have not needed to formalize their customer relationships by means of a definable customer strategy to achieve successful relations with their customers. In the new era, in which the customer reigns supreme, businesses must change their focus to ensure that customer relationship practices *maximize* customer benefit.

When a business knows its customers and targets its communications to their specific interests and shopping behaviors, the result is increased revenues and loyal, long-term customers. This is the power of *one-to-one CRM*. If the CRM strategy does not focus on individual customer's transactions, both in the process of segmentation and in the contact strategy, it will not be successful. Tracking the transactional details of a customer's purchase allows the most effective communication possible. With CRM, the benefit of the commercial relationship with each individual customer can be maximized. Today, based on practices that evolved in the retail industry, every business can, for example, effectively define a customer's needs without incremental cost or complexity. Following these practices accomplishes the following objectives:

- Achieve more effective merchandise buying and planning and faster inventory turnover

- Maximize return on marketing dollars by targeting customers with selected promotions

- Minimize the number of transactions at sale prices by creating customized triggers that stimulate buying at full price

- Easily attract new customers whose tastes and preferences relate to those of selected current customers

- Design more efficient stores, with designs based on customer cross-shopping behavior

- Ensure each customer buys more and remains a customer for life

6.5   A 12-stage CRM strategy

In the experience of many organizations, CRM is a powerful growth strategy capable of producing significant benefits and transforming both organizations and industries. However, for every company that has achieved dramatic success, there are many others that are still struggling to realize the full potential of their customer-driven growth strategies. For these latter organizations, the path of implementation has been filled with obstacles and the pace of implementation has been far slower and more frustrating than anticipated.

The lessons learned by others and the methodologies and technologies available can be used by any organization to make the change from a product or service orientation to a customer-focused orientation that provides strong returns on the CRM investment in a matter of months rather than years. The *12-stage CRM strategy* outlined in this section is a proven methodology for resolving many issues in a logical, efficient manner. Although no two companies can follow precisely the same implementation path, the stages defined here need to be a part of the process, and most of them can be carried out simultaneously. Some organizations will already have moved through some of these stages; others will need to start at the beginning. The following paragraphs describe in detail the activities involved in each stage and the significance of each of the 12 stages.

12-Stage CRM Strategy

1. Develop a clear set of business objectives.

2. Formulate a detailed Plan of Action.

3. Provide strong leadership.

4. Institute changes in corporate culture.

5. Obtain support of a senior management member.

6. Build in stages, starting with the most crucial area.

7. Create an integrated business design.

8. Concentrate on activities that create economic value.

9. Develop a customer-driven product and service development process.

10. Encourage the development of organizational capabilities in team members.

11. Generate early "wins" to create a self-funding process.

12. Include customers in a two-way flow of communication.

Develop a clear set of business objectives

Defining clear business objectives is an obvious first step in any project, major or minor. However, because of the evolutionary nature of a CRM strategy and the involvement of so many areas of an organization, it is extremely important to establish business objectives that will create a competitive advantage and guide the overall implementation process. These objectives should relate to the fundamental concept behind a CRM solution.

The business case prepared to convince senior management of the benefits of CRM should be firmly and logically based on overall corporate objectives—perhaps the corporate mission statement, if one exists. It should include information about direct competitors and how the system supports corporate strategies, plus the expected qualitative and quantitative benefits. As mentioned earlier, improving customer satisfaction and creating a base of more loyal customers will have both qualitative and quantitative benefits—more sales per customer, lower cost of sales, incremental sales via referrals, and ultimately more profits. Some of these benefits may be intangible, but collectively, they are powerful reasons to support CRM.

Formulate a detailed plan of action

Four to eight weeks will be required to develop a comprehensive plan defining the type of customer-focused initiatives that will establish the new way of doing business, the organizational operational changes, and enabling technologies that will be the driving forces behind implementation.

Technology planning and implementation should be closely integrated with the business planning phases to create a self-correcting process. With an integrated process, the planned business objectives and the organizational and operational changes define the requirements for the enabling technologies. The process of selecting the enabling technologies may identify feasibility issues that require adjustment to the original business plans.

To structure the planning process, it is very useful to develop a framework that describes the role and interrelationship of each of the operational areas required. A staged approach, in which operating capabilities are developed only to the point needed to realize near-term objectives, is far more viable than one designed to meet every conceivable need for the next 20 years. Five guidelines for a staged project are

- Build for the near term
- Make it scalable
- Use it

- Determine the changes required to increase productivity
- Build on this knowledge

Provide strong leadership

For any major project, sound leadership is a prerequisite; therefore, the people selected as team or project leaders need to have leadership attributes that will keep the project and the project staff on track. A balance between business and technology backgrounds is preferable for leadership candidates—knowledge in both areas will assist at all stages of the process.

Institute changes in corporate culture

At the heart of CRM strategies is changing fundamentally the decision-making process within the company. Rigorous data analysis is replacing business instinct as a basis for both day-to-day decision making and strategic planning. Other changes in the corporate culture may also be required.

Obtain support of a senior management member

The success of every CRM project will depend on several factors and the effective integration of all stages; however, the support the project receives internally is of particular value. The support of a senior management member—for example, the vice president of marketing or sales, vice president of finance, or other member of the senior management team—is crucial to the success of the CRM strategy. The importance of this stage of the process cannot be overemphasized. The designated senior management person must be an integral part of the CRM team and committed to attending and actively participating in all project meetings and workshops.

Build in stages, starting with the most crucial areas

The first stage of development should focus on the operations and technology needed to implement a top-priority set of CRM business objectives, as identified in Stage 1. Typically, the first stage of development can become operational in two to four months, and at a small fraction of the costs that have traditionally been incurred for new systems. Many companies use the first stage to establish a "*proof of concept,*" to demonstrate to management that CRM really works, and then follow up with subsequent stages to scale up the operations and technology as well as to expand the scope of the overall program.

Create an integrated business design

Many companies have realized significant returns from CRM strategies simply by building systems and launching programs. Yet, to realize the full potential, CRM strategies must become a way of doing business managed through an integrated business design involving the entire organization, all elements pulling in the same direction.

Develop a customer-driven product and service development process

Product-driven companies have a tradition of building products based on instincts and engineering requirements rather than on customer requirements. Even when these companies agree that an "outside-in," customer-driven process could remove much of the risk of product development, they may not make the transition easily. A significant step forward in becoming customer driven is establishing a process for monitoring customer purchase rates and then using the value proposition to quickly identify the changes in customer behavior that signal a need for revitalization and new development. It is not necessary to dismantle or even radically change the product development component of an organization. The strengths of that component need to be preserved while integrating a stream of customer input. The objective is to establish a dynamic product and service development process that can adapt as quickly as the marketplace can change.

Concentrate on activities that create economic value

Often, the transition to CRM strategies requires new skills and organizational processes. An ideal way to learn is to *learn through action*, that is, by applying new practices and processes guided by experienced leaders. This "rapid deployment" methodology enables companies to immediately launch a range of sophisticated customer programs by relying on the resourcefulness of their own staff and, to the extent needed, guidance from experienced consultants. To optimize results, the work should be carried out by cross-functional teams that are unified under a shared set of objectives. In addition, the teams should be focused on using innovative methodologies and, most importantly, should be committed to producing *tangible, measurable results.*

A "test and learn" process is becoming a basic requirement for CRM success. This process is much more than a measurement system. It is a way of doing business. Its foundation should be a rigorous test- and control-based measurement system that is integrated with customer initiatives and other areas of investment to measure business outcomes in a systematic way. A key metric should be *impact on customer value*. In addition, the process should include regular review sessions that bring together senior management, analysts, and key operating staff to plan refinements and steer the business based on both internal and external (customer) feedback.

Encourage the development of organizational abilities in team members

It is no longer necessary for companies to spend millions of dollars and years of effort before producing measurable returns from CRM. Compelling returns can be generated within months of the launch, which in turn helps to build valuable momentum. Companies in many industries have consistently realized dramatic gains that provide a proof of concept in the early stages of CRM development. These gains also become the basis for developing economic projections, and in some cases, they provide a self-funding, self-sustaining mechanism for the CRM strategy. The examples in the sidebar illustrate the magnitude of gains realized from the first CRM programs launched by companies in various business sectors under their new CRM strategies.

CRM Gains for Different Business Sectors

- **Automobile manufacturer:** 60% increase in the repurchase rate based on improved targeting and communication

- **B2B communications company:** 50% gain in cross selling effectiveness among small business customers

- **Pharmaceutical manufacturer:** Sharply reduced product introduction and marketing costs based on channel optimization

- **Software manufacturer:** 50% reduction in marketing costs associated with upgrade sales

- **Credit card issuer:** 15% reduction in attrition of high-value customers based on proactive intervention

- **Communications company:** 15 to 1 return on investment in improved customer acquisition

- **Property and casualty insurer:** 400% increase in campaign response rate over forecasts

---

Generate early wins to create a self-funding process

For most companies, adopting a formal CRM strategy results in a fundamental shift in goals. Priorities are established based on their potential to drive profitable growth, and the primary means for driving the growth is to *grow customer value.* Successful organizations in this era of the customer are placing top priority on measuring and tracking customer value in clear economic terms.

Customer valuation has become a core capability that companies need to develop. Customer value can be measured on an individual customer level. The results typically prove the rule that a large majority of the value is coming from a small proportion of the customer base—often referred to as the 80/20 rule. They may also reveal that the company has been allocating for too many resources to the least valuable customer segment. With this vital information in hand, a wide range of strategic and operating decisions can be made based on the projected impact on customer value.

Include customers in a two-way flow of communication

Customer information has become a major strategic asset for businesses, creating requirements for information management and control that are just as important as those for managing an organization's finances. An advanced information control capability requires the significant involvement of the call/contact center and should integrate two major components of CRM:

- *Managing customer contacts*—an active control process for information exchange with customers

- *Managing customer knowledge*—a control process for the retention of information and accessibility

Radical changes in the marketplace, as emphasized throughout this book, mean that it is no longer sufficient to conduct periodic surveys to monitor changes in the marketplace. The marketplace changes daily and customer expectations can change significantly and quickly, often because of aggressive competition. The continuous and systematic capture, retention, and analysis of customer information, from virtually every point of customer contact, is an essential activity in a successful CRM strategy.

Major advances in contact management software are being made to support ongoing information exchange between a company and its customers and for seamless integration of multichannel communications with customers. There are several important sources of customer information:

- *Customer contact channels*, including call centers, retail outlets, and e-commerce Websites

- *Transaction systems* for detailed customer behavioral data

- *Outbound marketing programs* to measure results of promotional campaigns

- *Secondary data sources* such as credit data and compiled demographic and lifestyle data

- *Market research* for insights beyond those revealed by actual customer behavior and dialogue

When properly integrated into the CRM framework, these information sources provide a continuing stream of updates from customers that enables companies to respond quickly to their evolving needs and priorities. (see Figure 6.11)

Core components of a CRM infrastructure

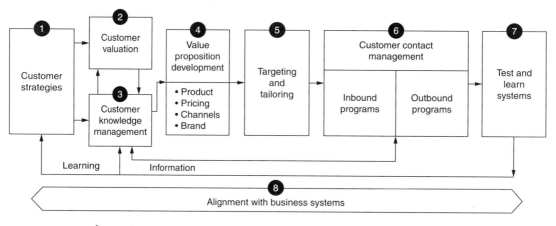

Figure 6.11   *Eight areas of operational and customer-oriented capabilities in CRM.*

6.6   Applying the CRM strategy

The goal of CRM is to evolve from a marketing model that was based on a product-centric marketing structure to one based on dealing with each customer as if that customer were the only customer. Managing customer relationships successfully means learning about the habits and needs of customers, anticipating future buying patterns, and finding new opportunities to add value to the relationship.

Customer behavior patterns

In the financial sector, for example, banks—early beneficiaries of successful CRM strategies—are using data warehousing and data mining technologies to learn to anticipate their customers' needs from the millions of transactions and interactions they have with their customers. The patterns of customer behavior and attitude derived from this information enable the banks to effectively segment customers by predetermined criteria. Such detailed customer data can provide answers to the following questions:

- Which communication channel do customers prefer?
- What would be the risk of their leaving the bank to go to the competition?
- What is the probability the customer will buy a service or product?

With this knowledge, the financial institution can develop marketing programs that relate logically and psychologically to each customer segment, provide valuable customer information to the call/contact center, support cross selling and customer-retention programs, and assist the staff to maximize the value of each customer's interaction.

Maximizing individual customer experiences

How does an organization manage each customer relationship individually? Several fundamental changes in business functions can be made on the way to a complete CRM solution. Marketing departments need systems that allow employees to track, capture, and analyze millions of customer activities, both interactions and transactions, over a long period of time. This knowledge helps the organization to create promotions, develop new products and services, and design communication programs that attract, reward, and retain customers. Two other fundamental concepts behind a successful

CRM strategy are operational and technological excellence. Attaining leadership in these areas enables an organization to predict and maximize the value of each customer relationship.

6.7   CRM issues and tactics

Companies assessing a CRM strategy or in the process of implementation have many issues to consider. For example:

- Deciding how and where to start

- Minimizing costs

- Reducing risks

- Generating tangible returns quickly

- Accelerating implementation and maintaining momentum

- Minimizing disruption to the organization

- Establishing a foundation for continuing gains

Although there is no one "right" CRM framework for every business sector, eight areas of capabilities and operations are the core components of the required infrastructure for most companies. More details about these specific areas are given in the paragraphs that follow.

CRM workshops

Holding CRM workshops can be extremely valuable in bringing together management groups to establish an in-depth understanding of the concepts, methods, and implications of the new strategies as well as conveying a common viewpoint. Senior management should play a prominent leadership role in this process by providing a supporting member to the CRM project team, as noted earlier in Stage 5. It is also very important for senior management to meet separately in the initial planning and objective-setting stages with key managers and groups to establish an understanding of why the transition to CRM is needed as well as to examine the implications and opportunities for each group's area of responsibility. The leadership role remains critical throughout the implementation process, both to provide a compelling vision, driven by senior management, of where the company is going and to instill a sense of urgency and commitment to the changes that are needed.

Exact transaction analysis

The next step in developing a CRM program retraces the retail sector's original roots, when neighborhood store owners knew their customers and took special care to serve their interests and needs. The megastore and a reduction in customer service came next. But now CRM technology is allowing retailers to rebuild customer relationships and keep customers coming back, the same way the neighborhood store did in a bygone era. Over the past decade, CRM has evolved from being a relatively small part of marketing operations at a few forward-thinking retailers to becoming a core corporate strategy of many retail businesses as well as of businesses in other major sectors. Customer purchase history and demographic information are now used not just in marketing programs, but in every facet of a retail business, including real estate sales and acquisitions, store locations, e-commerce, and merchandise selection. Despite its detractors and the failure of poorly designed and/or poorly implemented CRM projects, there are numerous testimonials to the success of the effective application of CRM strategies in organizations from every major business sector.

As the term *exact transaction analysis* implies, it is a process of analyzing every customer transaction exactly. It is the ultimate method of deriving the full benefit of CRM, because CRM can only be successful if an organization has the capability to interact with *each and every* customer on an individual level. Only when a complete, one-on-one relationship is achieved can an organization realize the goal of lifelong, profitable customer relationships. Access to extremely detailed customer information, down to the level of individual transactions, is the key to the full realization of CRM's potential.

Relationship technologies

Four factors are key elements in the application of relationship technology to managing customer relationships:

- Selecting the technologies that will meet customer needs

- Teaming up with the right partners to implement them

- Applying relationship technologies to customer transactions

- Implementing a CRM strategy in stages

Relationship technologies make customer transactions more personal, more individual, and more exact. More than ever, they have become important elements in the way an organization manages its customer relations. A well-defined customer relationship management (CRM) solution, based on a data warehousing system, enables businesses to capture and analyze customer interactions and transactions and reduce customer churn, which may be defined as the constant and continual movement of customers from one organization to another.

Properly aligned with customer needs, CRM can also help companies better understand customer requirements and changes in buying patterns and lifestyle and build long-term relationships of value to them. Various customer surveys have shown that people want businesses to keep in touch with them, to be responsive to their purchasing needs, even to anticipate these needs. In short, they expect a relationship that has *value*. This relationship may well begin with the call/contact center, and it is important that every customer contact point—a phone call, a click on a Website, a response to a direct mail campaign—be used to establish and maintain this relationship. Organizations that achieve high ratings for customer relationships are those that make the relationship *of value to the customer*. This factor has become a significant differentiator among organizations.

Privacy

Another element of customer relationships that has become a significant issue in the consumer marketplace is *privacy of personal information*. As organizations build large data warehouses of customer demographic and transactional information, protecting the privacy of this information becomes very important in developing and retaining customers and in fostering customer-centric relationships. In short, customers expect organizations to respect their privacy. If they do not, customers can use their purchasing power to register their dissatisfaction, or in some jurisdictions where there are legal statutes in place to protect privacy, they can resort to the law.

A rationale for CRM

Clearly, transforming customer information into customer value can create a significant competitive advantage. High-value customers are identified, their needs anticipated, and new value created for them where it did not exist before. The end result for a customer-centric organization is customer loyalty, which translates into higher profitability. Product-centric values—delivering functionality and quality on time and on budget—should be augmented, not replaced, by a CRM solution. In a customer-centric organization, the traditional product-centric values become more meaningful when supported by effective CRM strategies.

The importance of assessing the company's current capabilities and plotting the many dimensions of the business along the continuum from product-centricity to customer-centricity cannot be overstressed. Comparing corporate attributes with what is happening in the marketplace should also be a part of this assessment. This process will enable the organization to benefit from the potential of CRM processes and technologies by building on an objective assessment of the company's customer-oriented capabilities, based on a defined set of projects, including investment estimates and business cases.

6.8   Customer input to CRM

Businesses can maximize the effectiveness of CRM systems in creating more intimate, intelligent, and profitable customer relationships by using a new approach: giving customers control over a subset of the information stored in CRM systems. A customer-directed layer in an existing CRM system allows the customer access to important, account-specific information when, where, and for whatever reason the customer specifies. This further reinforces the development of one-to-one relationships with customers, a major objective of CRM, as noted previously. By incorporating a one-to-one approach, the CRM system can deliver actionable response options tuned precisely to a customer profile and related specifically to a company's call/contact center infrastructure.

An additional benefit in extending CRM systems to provide proactive outbound customer service from its call/contact center and relevant inbound response options is that unnecessary inbound calls will be reduced and customer satisfaction and revenue increased—without increasing staff. When customers are forced to place a call or e-mail to a company about their account, they most likely have a problem with a product or service or require information. Providing an outbound CRM resource helps save customers' time and effort, eliminating or reducing the voice mail syndrome that has become a fact of everyday life. (see Figure 6.12) When a company proactively or preemptively provides information that is relevant to and frequently requested by an individual customer—monthly account balance, shipping status, itinerary changes, and so on—the company solidifies a positive, helpful image in the customer's psyche. Customer surveys reflect the

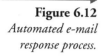

Figure 6.12
Automated e-mail response process.

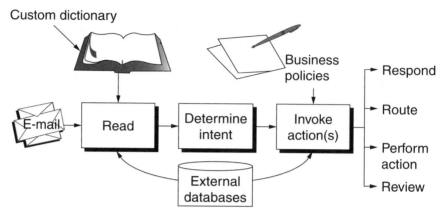

fact that consumers appreciate doing business with companies that provide personalized attention and service.

The alert platform

An *alert platform* provides, as the name implies, an alerting mechanism that enables customers to communicate with supplier companies about their products or services, for example, to place or change an order or to advise of problems, defects, or other aspects of the supplier's product or service. To provide adequate coverage of alert/response applications to the widest market, an alert platform must support a broad range of communication media, including

- High-quality voice via land-line telephone and cell phone

- Properly formatted text and interactive applications for e-mail, pager, Internet, fax, and wireless devices

Proactive communications from companies to customers need to be through their existing preferred communication devices. Offering only one contact mode is not adequate for the media-diverse and mobile customer base that is characteristic of today's marketplace. This is not to say, however, that the land-line telephone should be neglected. Voice alerts governed by detailed customer preferences are mandatory in every system. Although the use of wireless text devices and e-mail is rapidly accelerating, voice is and will be the dominant communications channel for delivering timely alerts that require immediate response and interaction. An alert formatted for voice delivery reaches the broadest audience and enables the business message to rise above the flood of e-mail. Voice formatting adds a human quality and time-sensitive value to a message. Voice alerts are also the most conducive to eliciting a customer response because of their familiarity and simplicity ("press 1 to speak with a customer service agent" or "press 2 to buy"). Given the option, customers will select voice delivery for many of their alerts, and the responses associated with these alerts will be higher than any other media.

Although voice will serve the broadest customer base, some customers will insist on other media formats. With a call/contact center platform that supports mixed-media alert/response applications, a business may decide to include chat or call-me-now functionality as a feature of an outbound e-mail alert. The business could decide that certain outbound voice alerts will offer the customer options linked to a variety of services, for example, two-way messaging or wireless text messaging. An alert/response platform should continue to evolve to support the latest consumer devices when the volume of customer requests justifies it.

Implementing alert/response applications

A sophisticated alert/response platform is the perfect companion to a company's existing call/contact center systems to augment and integrate with the CRM system. The recent evolution of CRM to supporting outbound customer contacts may mean that traditional CRM hardware and software cannot support the new applications, however. The typical CRM system does not have the built-in capability to enable companies to anticipate customer calls and to reach out to customers with information tailored specifically to them before they call.

If a CRM system is capable of being integrated with alert technology, the alerts typically do not contain the customized, deep-enterprise data that customers want. For example, they may offer only limited syndicated content that is individually addressed and broadcast, making the alerts more like generic spam messages. Or, if the information is deep and customer-specific, these systems typically support delivery via a single medium only, usually e-mail. Moreover, those companies that have already made the initial foray into alert systems rarely table an integrated approach to managing responses to alerts. There is a critical void when it comes to delivering customer-specific information in a variety of mediums, enabling intelligent two-way interaction, or making the most of a company's existing data to serve customers better and successfully involve them in one-to-one outbound interactions.

Integrating with existing systems

Armed with their existing customer systems and the right outbound alert/response platform, companies can learn from their customer interactions how to offer a continuously higher level of successful customer service, adding customer input to enhance their CRM system. Existing customer contact systems need to be integrated with an alert/response program. With a touch of the keypad or a click of the mouse, customers must be able to connect easily to the business, talk to a live agent, transfer to an automated transaction system for purchasing, or add personal comments and forward the alert to others who may be interested in the information.

For customers to find alerts useful and to respond to them in a positive way, the alerts must be triggered on detailed, account-specific information and governed by the preferences of each customer. The data that trigger these alerts could be stored in a variety of different databases or even in multiple databases within the same organization. XML, one of the newer computer languages and one that is rapidly becoming a developer preference, can handle this problem. XML-based technology seamlessly integrates many disparate back-office, call/contact center, and database systems, including computer telephony integration (CTI), voice processing, collaboration, legacy, CRM, and Web-oriented systems. An XML-based extraction platform is a powerful, flexible way to trigger alerts.

Configuring the alert/response content

Alert content must be dynamic, easy to create, easy to manage, and appealing to the alert recipient. To maximize the application and create the highest value for the customer, administrators must be able to change alert content and create new alerts as business conditions change—via a packaged management solution, not via customer development. Contact center management and nontechnical administrators need to be able to "tune" alert/response systems on an application-by-application basis. The administration components should include the following:

- Prerecorded voice content

- Rules for conditional use of text-to-speech, retry frequency, and logic

- Links between alert behavior and call center hours and real-time load

Given these requirements, companies strapped for IT resources will look to vendors to provide graphical user interfaces that incorporate easy-to-use, drag-and-drop alert development and maintenance.

Preemptive alerting has both operational and strategic benefits for the business. It eliminates unnecessary, costly, non-revenue-generating inbound customer contact, resulting in increased customer satisfaction, dramatic cost-per-call savings, call elimination, and better service levels, as well as a reduction in the number of agents required in call centers. On a strategic level, proactively giving customers the information they want increases customer satisfaction and gives companies a competitive advantage. In addition, offering alerts with intelligent response options enables companies to combine sales and service initiatives that increase revenue, generate highly qualified inbound traffic, and make the most efficient use of both customer and company time. Companies are recognizing that their call/contact centers are a vitally important part of their overall business strategies and operations and are particularly critical to CRM strategies. As noted elsewhere in this book, customer service has become a major competitive differentiator in many business sectors. By using an enterprise alert/response platform to leverage existing legacy systems, CRM systems, and Web investments, large businesses with many thousands or millions of customers, can now engage customers in an intimate, trusted, two-way dialogue that creates measurable improvements in customer loyalty and profitability.

6.9   Managing the CRM program

Management may be loosely defined as the art and science of getting from here to there. Most large organizations have more than one CRM project touching many parts of the enterprise. And these projects are managed by many different players, some in call centers, on Websites, or run by salesforces or different business groups. Pulling all this activity together into an enterprisewide program is a major challenge. CRM program management guidelines offer a sound approach to program and project management. Developing CRM program guidelines brings managers back inside the enterprise to the starting point.

Program manager guidelines

The following guidelines provide an overview of the practical steps that can be taken to ensure that the CRM program (or programs) will work at all levels, from strategy articulation to software installation and training. The goal of these eight guidelines is to improve the success rate of CRM programs and to enable an organization to measure success through clear linkages between program initiatives and desired business results. Each of the following eight steps matches a phase of CRM program design and implementation:

1. Program diagnosis

2. Strategy review

3. Enterprise architecture

4. Enterprise application integration services

5. Package selection and implementation

6. Application outsourcing assessment

7. Implementation review

8. Program and project management

Each step and its associated activities have been proven effective in previous large-scale change and improvement programs, such as business process reengineering and enterprise resource planning (ERP). The hard lessons learned in implementing these projects also apply to CRM programs.

The eight steps recommended in the program management guidelines are described next in more detail.

Program diagnosis

An organization needs to assess its business objectives against current CRM programs to highlight the areas of needed improvement and to identify where it can get the biggest bang for its investment. The diagnosis can examine CRM approaches, conversation design, relationship styles, organizational structure, and IT infrastructure. Understanding how these compare with other organizations and with best practices and how they fit into the enterprise's business strategy will help identify areas for improvement.

Strategy review

An organization needs to review and assess its CRM strategies. The aim of this review is to develop an understanding of the conversation designs and spaces that make its customer relationships profitable. This forms the basis for a CRM game plan that is right for the organization and for the joint development of business and IT strategies.

Enterprise architecture

The program diagnosis and strategy review steps will highlight the benefits of pulling all the CRM-related initiatives that may be scattered across the company into a comprehensive, enterprisewide strategy. A CRM enterprise architecture will help create new conversation spaces; transform customer information into a strategic tool to profile, segment, target, and retain valuable customers; organize sales, marketing, and customer care in a consistent way; and integrate back-office and front-office processes. The architecture should integrate all elements of a CRM solution—people, processes, technologies, and organization.

Enterprise application integration services

One key to success in enterprise architecture development, and in CRM overall, is the seamless integration of channels, people, and technologies into conversation spaces that deliver value to customers. Seamless customer experiences, in turn, depend on the seamless integration of enterprisewide CRM application packages, legacy applications, and Web-enabled systems. Meeting this challenge is the purpose of an enterprise application integration (EAI) game plan.

Package selection and implementation

An organization needs a system for navigating through the crowded marketplace of CRM packages and assessing the effect of changes on its business. Expert assistance is often required both for package assessment and for implementation. Packages must be integrated into the IT environment and attention paid to process design and change management. The aim is to develop a game plan for managing package selection, implementation, and testing through multiyear life cycles. Beyond technical installation, the transformation of business processes must be managed so that new software packages deliver maximum value.

Application outsourcing assessment

Like other software packages, CRM applications require support, maintenance, and enhancement over a period of years. An organization needs to assess whether it would benefit by outsourcing responsibility for this technology-intensive side of the CRM program. Outsourcing may help it evolve and maintain its CRM application portfolio—call centers, e-commerce, and so on—in a logically phased, cost-effective manner. All such contracts need to define clearly the service-level agreements. The aim of this activity is to allow the enterprise to focus on customer relationships, not the supporting technology.

Implementation review

An organization may need to get an overview of all CRM implementation activities to help it focus on the game plan for building the complete set of business and technical solutions, whether in one area of the company or across the enterprise. The aim is to ensure a coordinated approach to the design, redesign, or consolidation of CRM programs—e-commerce initiatives, call center operations, integrated customer information systems, and campaign management.

Program and project management

CRM involves a multiplicity of initiatives. Each initiative needs to be well managed. Just as importantly, all need to fit into coherent CRM programs. Often advanced program and project management methods are required to accomplish this. Program or project management offices (PMOs) can be created to ensure that CRM-related projects deliver value and fully support strategic business initiatives.

6.10   CRM solution: the value to the business

A CRM solution that bridges service, sales, and marketing initiatives enables businesses to resolve problems quicker, increase sales, achieve customer acquisition more effectively, and greatly enhance customer loyalty.

Referrals

It is an axiom of the marketplace that satisfied customers tell their friends about a supplier who maintains good customer relations. One of the most powerful ways to acquire customers is word-of-mouth referral from a friend, colleague, or family member. Businesses can harness these referrals when one of their customers adds personal comments to an alert and forwards it to others who may be interested in the information and/or opportunities the alert presents.

Analytics

The CRM analytics model has evolved to meet modern-day requirements. Although the concept hasn't changed much from its early days, the process certainly has become far more scientific. Analytical CRM is the mining of data and the application of mathematical, and sometimes common-sense, models in order to understand the consumer better. By extrapolating useful insights into market and customer behaviors, companies can adjust business rules and react to customers in a relevant, personalized manner.

Because business is conducted with fewer face-to-face exchanges, getting to know and understand the customer has become more complicated. The rise of e-business has driven the demand for more comprehensive tool sets for data mining and knowledge interpretation. For an effective CRM initiative to accomplish its goals, CRM analytics need to be incorporated into the process. CRM analytics provide the comprehensive insight necessary for pinpointing revenue opportunities, enhancing sales channels, and mitigating cost risks. By providing meaningful insight into data as well as transactional predictions, CRM analytics enable businesses to ensure that rules and workflow are in step with customer demands. Analytics can be derived through several different channels, including

■ The Internet

■ Retail point of purchase

■ Direct marketing activities

The challenge is to make sense out of the data gathered from customers from the multitude of customer touchpoints into the organization.

Analytical data mining solutions are a significant component of most CRM system packages, and call center personnel should have some understanding of the relationship of data mining to their own call/contact center roles. Data mining provides insight into corporate data stored in the data warehouse by using a variety of analytical techniques to isolate causes and correlations within the customer interaction model. Data mining analytics can perform predictive modeling of customer behavior, customer segmentation grouping, profitability analysis, what-if scenarios, and campaign management, as well as personalization and event monitoring. These functions take advantage of a customer's interactions with a business in real time. (see Figure 6.13) Strong analytics are necessary to give a functional view of data relationships in today's extremely complex business processes. By means of analytics, CRM can model future transactions, predict the interests and behavior of individual customers, and translate data into more traditional channels within the enterprise, such as the supply chain.

CRM is a highly iterative process. When data from any source are harvested and fed back into the system, the personalization capability of every customer transaction or e-mail campaign is improved. More traditional marketing techniques such as direct marketing often have months of lag time between a campaign's execution and its results. With each loop of the

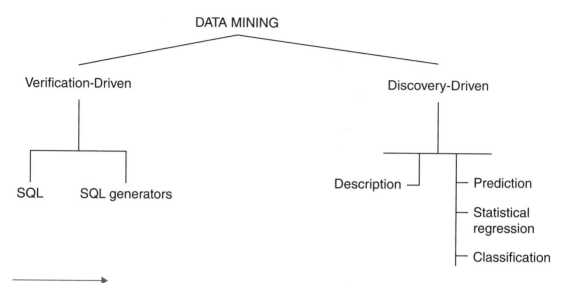

Figure 6.13   *Elements and processes of data mining.*

cycle, Internet-based CRM analytics are updating, tweaking, and improving delivery of personalized, relevant sales opportunities, all in real time. They also help build a more finely tuned relationship between a business and its customers.

In addition to the personalization that benefits a customer's purchasing decisions, CRM analytics can provide useful data to benefit enterprisewide processes and can also be integrated into the general operational workflow of noncustomer systems, including financial systems and manufacturing, to provide a more focused, single and collective view of customer-centric data than do the traditional, departmentally segmented views offered by a legacy CRM.

When all of this data is applied to a variety of systems, transactional decision making and enterprise planning—from cross-selling opportunities to supply-chain and just-in-time inventory control—become more effective. But it is good to keep in mind that CRM analytics is more of a process than a technology and so it demands a degree of human interpretation for the data to yield the most beneficial results.

CRM and the customer experience

Automation streamlines internal processes, but technology can also quickly depersonalize the customer's experience. CRM analytics offer insight and personalization that can go a long way toward improving that experience and building customer loyalty.

When they first start, all businesses have to focus on the needs of their customers. As businesses get larger and more complex, however, they become more inward-looking as they try to cope with their internal issues. Often, the customer gets treated as an afterthought. One goal of CRM is to make the individual customer become important once again at an acceptable cost to the company. Until relatively recently, it was impossible for large companies to form relationships with customers. With a customer base of millions, how can a company know their preferences or dislikes? This is where technology can help businesses. Realistically, businesses do not implement CRM because they have had a change of heart and decided to be nice to the long-suffering customer. Loyalty equals profit, and both customers and businesses can gain from it. The "management" part of CRM demonstrates that it is the business which ultimately controls the relationship with the customer. It provides the right information at the right time, it offers the right price to keep the customer happy enough to stay, it anticipates what else the customer would like to buy, and understands why. Thus, the business objective of CRM is to maximize profit from customers as a result of knowing them, treating them well, and fulfilling their needs.

Salesforce automation, customer contact solutions, multimedia routing, and data management tools—all have been claimed as the key to a CRM solution. All are useful and reliable aids to a business, but none of them on their own is a CRM solutions. They do, however, contribute to meeting CRM objectives.

A CRM checklist

Answers to the following questions can provide an organization with insight into its current customer-related practices:

- Is there a single view of the customer across the enterprise?

- Do employees fulfill customer needs regardless of where in the company they are working?

- Do customers receive a high level of service no matter which channel they decide to use?

- Does the organization proactively and intelligently inform customers about products and services they will be interested in and yet keep marketing costs under control?

- Does the organization know who the most profitable customers are?

- Are the strategy and tactics in place to keep them?

6.11   Call/Contact center: driving force behind CRM

The call/contact center plays a crucial role in developing and fulfilling corporate CRM strategies. Companies whose main channel to their customers is through the telephone or e-mail, cannot become truly CRM-focused without putting the center at the heart of any operational enhancements to their CRM strategy. It is both the recipient and disseminator of information, relating to customers and to the business. CRM is about increasing revenues and growing the business aggressively. Industry sectors such as retail, banking, and communications were among the first to implement CRM, and their profit-focused approach toward their call or contact center operations is a model for other sectors.

When incorporated into a CRM strategy, the multimedia "customer contact center" brings both opportunities and problems. Customers still need to be served, no matter what the communication medium is; however, managers may initially encounter problems running a multimedia center in a CRM-focused business. There are a number of channels to manage, training is more complex and diverse, and new CSR skills are required. Chapter 3 described the key issues involved in moving from a telephony-only call center to a multimedia contact center as part of a larger, enterprisewide CRM process. As this shift takes place, the call/contact center becomes less of a cost center and more of an integrated, strategic, and profitable part of the enterprise and a key component of a CRM strategy.

CRM support mechanisms

CRM is not a technology, but few companies can reengineer themselves to be truly customer facing without providing their business and staff with the necessary tools. As for any major corporate project, there should be a defined business need for the technology first, along with a measurable goal. Almost any technology can legitimately be said to provide support for CRM implementations if the wider aim is to provide a superior level of customer contact based on knowledge of that specific customer.

Successful CRM depends as much upon attitude as it does upon technology, however. CRM is primarily an enabler of growth for optimistic, aggressive companies wishing to expand. Business trends bear this out. Consider these two approaches to CRM:

IT-focused CRM

Many first-wave CRM implementations focused very much on putting in technology solutions and improving efficiency. Business processes and employees may not even be affected by IT-focused CRM, and in many cases, the solution is CRM in name only—it may in fact be only a series of point solutions rather than a true CRM implementation.

Business-focused CRM

Business-focused CRM involves a fresh look at how customers and prospects are actually dealt with by the enterprise and focuses on discovering and solving commercial problems, changing the culture of the enterprise as a whole to serve customers more effectively and profitably. Business-focused CRM encourages enterprises to understand the value of an individual customer and to customize interactions to build loyalty and profit.

Much of the difference between these approaches concerns attitude. The solution may end up being the same, but the problem needs to be understood before it can be addressed.

The impact of each of these CRM approaches is quite different on the call/contact center. In the IT-focused CRM approach, a nontechnical customer who contacts the call center and who is likely to be amenable to upselling might be pushed to a Website, which would be counterproductive. In this case, simply employing more sales agents or increasing training would increase profitability. On the other hand, business-focused CRM may use a low-tech solution for the customer—it does not simply look for ways to squeeze new technologies into the existing structure of the enterprise. When considering the impact of each approach on the call/contact center, the following should be taken into account:

- Two-thirds of a contact center's running costs are CSR salaries.

- Customers do not care about the IT department or business workflow—they decide whether the company is a good one by the quality of its staff and the services they provide.

- The common perception of the contact center is that it is a necessary evil.

This latter point is at least as big an issue as anything related to technology. It is possible to run an adequate contact center with a large proportion of semiskilled, inexperienced staff, and this is happening in many organizations. However, the message for those organizations is that it is not possible to provide outstanding customer service across all channels, increase profit per customer, and grow the company's market share—some of the key goals of CRM—without having an experienced and empowered call/contact center team.

Technology and business processes can provide powerful solutions that enhance a center's productivity; however, it should be remembered that one of the most important reasons customers call a center rather than use a Website is that they prefer talking to real people. One of the primary objectives of CRM is to provide customers with what they want. If customers decide they want to talk to real people, then that is what the customer-oriented company has to provide.

CRM plays no favorites

Every company that wants to increase profitability, reduce customer churn, gain market share, provide an outstanding level of customer care, and foster customer loyalty needs to have a CRM strategy. True CRM implementations are complex by nature and also require significant investment. However, because CRM is a long-term strategic goal, a gradual rollout of supporting technologies is possible, as long as the company is aware of where it is heading overall. Otherwise, the organization is just implementing a series of point solutions, which do not have the value of an integrated solution.

At first glance, CRM implementations seem to follow a pattern similar to most projects: analysis of requirements followed by detailed design. After actual implementation comes postproject review. CRM is different not only in the details but in the important role taken by the review stage. For many projects, a successful review is the end of the story. Not for CRM—it is just another stage. CRM is an ongoing process, and so the review stage is fundamental to the success of the project as a whole. For this reason, it should never be undervalued.

Feedback should be given both in the analysis stage (for example, target metrics have been achieved, the overall target is still viable) and also in the design stage, especially on any unforeseen technical issues that may require changes in dependent subprojects. And while the expertise of external suppliers and consultants can be relied on in the actual design and implementation of solutions, reviewing the business analysis stage in more detail can be beneficial, because this is where complex CRM projects can fail through lack of planning or even through failure to set specific targets.

CRM success factors

To sum up, when planning and implementing a CRM strategy, such as the 12-stage strategy described previously in this chapter, the following key CRM success factors need to be considered:

- Complete the business analysis stage before the design phase begins.

- Pass on experience from the design and implementation stages in order to integrate it into major changes in company direction and operation.

- Choose at least one senior company member to drive the CRM initiative both from a commercial and cultural perspective.

- Get buy-in from senior members of all departments in the organization and establish a steering committee.

- Benchmark operations before implementing any technology.

- Consult customers on how they would like to see the business change.

- Specify quantifiable improvements to the aspects of the business that are most important.

- Work only with suppliers who have a proven track record and who will be reliable partners for the foreseeable future.

- Measure the impact of each subproject and feed the results back into the overall analysis and dependent design phases of the CRM project.

- Consult, inform, and train employees at every stage of the process to move the business culture more toward a customer-focused organization.

APPENDIX A

Call Center Vendor Resources—Product and Service Offerings

The following is a guide to a number of selected vendors of call center products and services. The list provides vendor name, Website or telephone number, and a brief description of the products or services offered. It is not a complete or definitive list of vendors, but it does represent an extensive cross section of proven vendor products and services. The list was current at time of publication; however, the nature of the call center environment is dynamic and changes rapidly. There will always be new vendors in the market.

The products and services provided by these vendor organizations include call center communications systems, CTI, ACD products, outsourcing services, as well as workforce measurements systems, consulting services, and a variety of PBX systems designed for call center operations.

Accelerated Payment Systems www.ncms.com   Automated check-debiting system for call center transaction processing

ACI Telecentrics (612)928-4700   Call center outsourcing for telephone-based sales and marketing services, primarily to publishing, financial, insurance and telecommunications service industries

Active Voice www.activevoice.com   Repartee voice processing and unified messaging applications

Aculab www.aculab.com   Computer telephony hardware, particularly boards

Acuvoice www.acuvoice.com   Speech synthesis system and text-to-speech system

Adante www.adante.com   ACD e-mail

Adaptiv Software Corporation www.adaptiv.com   Workforce management software

Adaptive Innovations www.adaptiveinno.com   Software that converts statistics and data normally sent to a CSR via a LCD reader board to a desktop monitor for blind CSRs

Aditi Corporation www.aditi.com   Software for transacting customer service over the Internet

Advanced Access www.advaccess.com   Electronic commerce, call center, and fulfillment solutions

Advanced Recognition Technology www.artcomp.com   Voice recognition software

Advantage kbs www.akbs.com   Problem resolution software and customer support applications

Aegis Communications Group (214) 361-9870   Outsourced telecommunications-based marketing, customer service, and call center management services

Affinitec Call Center Systems/AAC www.aaccorp.com   Call center management software, reader board drivers, and call accounting systems

Ahern Communications www.aherncorp.com   Headset distributor

Alert Communications www.alertcom.com   Service bureau and outsourcer of call center services

Alltel www.alltel.com   Call center solution including consulting, implementation, and dedicated or shared outsourcing

Alpha Technologies (800) 322-5742   Power protection, CFR Series UPS, and ALCI industrial line conditioners

AltiGen Communications www.altigen.com   Computer telephony and Internet solutions for small to mid-sized businesses

Amcom Software www.amcomsoft.com   A suite of call center applications including auto-attendant, voice response, and various messaging features

Amend Group www.amend.com   Site selection assistance as well as commercial real estate services for call centers

American Power Conversion www.apcc.com   UPS, power protection, and surge protectors

American Productivity & Quality Center www.aqpc.org   Benchmarking and other research related to call centers

Ameritech www.ameritech.com   Turnkey, end-to-end, call center systems

Amtelco www.amtelcom.com   Call center systems with modular ACD functions, directory systems, departmental registry, and e-mail

Analogic www.analogic.com   Speech recognition and text-to-speech systems

AnswerSoft www.answersoft.com   Telephony automation software

Apex Voice Communications www.apexvoice.com   High-density, scalable systems for call centers

Applied Innovation Management www.aim-helpdesk.com   Web-based software for managing external product support

Apropos Technology www.apropos.com   Integrated suite of switch-independent call center applications

Ariel Corporation www.ariel.com   Design, manufacture, and marketing of DSP-based data communications hardware and software products

Aspect Telecommunications www.aspect./com   ACD voice processing system and software for linkage between applications

Artisoft www.artisoft.com   Telephony systems with call center features

Astea www.astea.com   Field service and internal help desk environment

Atio Corporation www.atio.com   A modular call center solution

AT&T www.att.com/business/global   Long-distance, toll-free, and call center consulting

AuBeta Telecom www.aubeta.com   An out-of-the-box family of call center systems

Aurora Systems www.fastcall.com   Computer telephony software (middleware)

Aurum Software www.aurum.com   Integrated applications for field sales, channel sales, telesales, telemarketing, corporate marketing, and customer service

Automatic Answer www.taa.com   Automated attendants and voice processing systems based on industry-standard PC platforms

AVT www.avtc.com   Open systems based on advanced computer telephony products

Balisoft www.balisoft.com   A Web/call center integration suite with collaborative tools

Banksoft www.banksoft.net   Small call center system that provides call processing and backend data processing

Bard Technologies www.bardtech.com   ACD simulator system for call centers

Barnhill Associates www.barnhill.com   Systems integrators and consultants on process reengineering

BCS Technologies www.bestechnoliges.com   PBX/ACD for small call centers

Bell Contact Centre Solutions   Contact center consulting, organization, and training

Bigby, Havis & Associates www.bigby.com/callcenters.htm   Human resource consulting for call centers

Blue Pumpkin Software www.blue.pumpkin.com   Workforce management software

Bogen Communications (201) 934-8500   Messages on hold, digital announcers, voice loggers, and recorder

Boston Communications Group www.bgci.net   Call center outsourcing services

Brady Group www.thebradygroup.com   Planning, design, and implementation of customer service strategies, work processes, and technologies

Bramic Creative Business Products (905) 649-2734   Ergonomic furniture for call centers

Brigade Solutions www.brigadesolutions.com   Internet customer support outsourcing

Brightware www.brightware.com   Web-based customer interaction systems

Bristol Group www.bg.com   Large-scale faxing systems

Brite Voice Systems www.brite.com   Voice processing and IVR systems that integrate voice, fax, CTI, and Internet capabilities

Broadbase Information Systems www.broadbase.com   Enterprise performance management systems

Brooktrout Technology www.brooktrout.com   Fax, voice, and telephony products, mainly at the component level

Buffalo International www.opencti.com   Object telephony server, a high-performance, flexible telephony platform

Business Telecom Products www.btpi.com   Professional-quality headsets

CACI Products Company www.caciasl.com   Call center tool to set up a model of staffing and volume

Call Center Network Group www.ccng.com   Membership   organization for call center professionals

Call Center Solutions www.callcenters.com   Predictive dialers and call-blending equipment

Call Center Technology www.callcentertechnology.com   Supervisor and call center knowledge management tool

Call Center University www.callcenteru.com   Professional organization that promotes certification programs and call center management standards

Call Interactive www.callit.com   IVR and call center outsourcing

Call One www.call-1.com   Headset and conferencing equipment distribution

Callscan Australia www.callscan.com.au   Call center products and services for the Australian and New Zealand markets

Calonge & Associates www.ca.script.com   Scripting and script consulting for business-to-business and business-to-consumer marketing campaigns

Carnegie Group www.cgi.com   Consulting, application development, and systems integration for call centers

Cascade Technologies www.cascadetechnologies.com   Software for employee benefits and human resources

CCl-Hansen Limited www.hancorp.com.au   Workforce management systems

CCS TrexCom www.ccstrexcom.com   Hardware and software platforms for IVR

CCT Group www.cctgroup.com   Call center support tools and full-service call center consulting

CellIT www.cellit.com   Call center system with blended multimedia support, inbound (ACD), outbound predictive dialing, IVR call logging, messaging, and unified SQL reporting

CenterCore www.centercore.com   Cubicles and agent workstations

CenterForce Technologies www.cforcetech.com/   Call center optimization system for outbound campaigns

Centerpoint Technologies www.ctrpoint.com   Computer telephony systems

Centigram www.centigram.com   Voice processing equipment

Century Telecommunications www.cticallcenter.com   Call center outsourcer

Chordiant Software www.chordiant.com   Software for managing customer data, including transaction data, customer histories, and business processes

Cicat Networks www.cicat.com   ISDN specialists

Cincom Systems www.cincom.com   CTI-enabled call center application

Cintech www.cintech-cti.com   ACD for small and mid-size call centers

Cisco Systems www.cisco.com   Networking products and systems

ClearVox Communications www.clearvox.com   Hands-free headsets for PCs, cordless phones, the Internet, and other applications

Clientele Software www.clientele.com   Customer service software

Com2001 Technologies www.com2001.com   Provider of a telephone system service and a range of communication services

CoMatrix (800) 888-7822   Supplier of used telecom equipment

Comdial www.comdial.com   LAN-based ACD software product

Comdisco Disaster Recovery www.comdisco.com   Disaster recovery and service assurance programs

CommercePath www.commercepath.com   EDI to fax system

Commetrex www.commetrex.com   Computer telephony boards

CommuniTech www.communitech.com   Distributor of headsets

ComputerTalk Technology www.icescape.com   Server-based ACD with digital switching and built-in CTI

Comverse Information Systems www.cominfosys.com   Digital recorders, voice loggers, and monitoring systems

Contact Dynamics www.contactdynamics.com   Software and services for interactive Internet communications

Convergys Corporation www.convergys.com   Conversational voice technologies

ConServIT www.cvtc.com   Inbound service bureau

Copia International www.copia.com   Business fax/voice software

CoreSoft Technologies www.coresoft.com   Multifunction telephony equipment

Cortelco www.cortelco.com   Switching systems, ISDN equipment, and software

CosmoCom www.cosmocom.com   Integrated multimedia customer service for Internet and telephone callers

Crystal Group www.crystalpc.com   Fault-resilient computer systems

CSI-Data Collection Resources www.csiworld.com/dcr   Automated voice and data products for call centers

CT Solutions www.solutions4ct.com   Computer telephony VAR equipment for a variety of manufacturers

CTL www.ctline.com   Voice processing system for the low end of the market

Dakotah Direct www.dakotahdirect.com   Outsourcing call center service bureau

Daktronics www.daktronics.com   Multiline readerboards with custom and standard interfaces

Data Processing Resources Corporation www.dprc.com   Applications and technologies for call centers, network, and telecommunication organizations

Datapoint www.datapoint.com/   Computer-based communications solutions, including client-server, video communications, and integrated telephony applications

Davox www.davox.com   Predictive dialers as well as a CTI/blend system

Dialogic www.dialogic.com   Voice cards, SCSA hardware, fax boards, and CTI software

Digisoft Computers www.digisoft.com   Call center software for PC-based networks

Digital Software International www.digisoftware.com   Scripts for use by CSRs in outbound or inbound call centers

Digital Techniques www.digitaltechniques.com   Design and manufacture of telephony products for the call centers

Distributed Bits www.dbits.com   E-mail tracker and response automator for call centers

DP Solutions www.dpsol.com   Help desk and customer support software

Drextec www.drextec.com   PC-LAN-based open predictive dial and telemarketing software system for centers of 12 to 144 agents

DSP Group www.dspg.com   Speech compression technology

Dytel www.dytel.com   Automated attendants

E-Speech Corporation www.espeech.com   Speech recognition

E-Voice Communications www.evoicecomm.com   Voice mail systems that incorporate unified messaging technology

Easyphone SA www.easyphone.com   Call center management software

EasyRun www.easyrun.com   Desktop computer telephony systems

Edify www.edify.com   IVR and workflow software

EFusion www.efusion.com   A platform for application creation using combined voice and data networks

eGain Communications www.egain.com   Customer service solutions for electronic commerce

EIS International www.eisi.com   Predictive dialers, outbound, and integrated inbound/outbound applications for call centers

Energy Enterprises www.energyenterprises.com   Call center training and consulting services

Enterprise Integration Group www.eiginc.com   Services geared to CTI

Entertainment Technology 416-598-2223   Call center display board system

Envision Telephony www.envisiontelephony.com   Monitoring and quality assurance software for call centers

Envox www.envox.com   Script editor for developing multimedia call center applications

Epigraphx www.epigraphx.com   Fax on demand and Internet-enabled fax/ Web combos

eShare Technologies www.eshare.com   Web-based customer service and support

Estech (972) 422-9700   Telephone/voice mail product

Evolving Systems www.evolving.com   Operational support systems for IP

Exacom www.exacomusa.com   Automated messaging system

Executone Information Systems www.executone.com   Integrated digital system platform, ACDs, and predictive dialers

Expert Systems www.easey.com   IVR development product

Eyretel www.eyretel.com   Quality monitoring and multimedia recording systems

FaceTime Communications www.facetime.net   Internet/call center systems

Far Systems www.farsystems.com   Interactive voice response application generation software and systems

FaxNet www.faxnet.com   Enhanced fax services

FaxSav www.faxsav.com   Internet fax systems

FaxStar (800) 327-9859   Enterprisewide fax server systems

Figment Technologies www.unimessage.com   Unified messaging product

Flashpoint Solutions www.flashpointsolutions.com   Custom and generic music and messages on-hold CDs and service

Franklin Telecom www.ftel.com   Systems for voice over Internet communications

Fujitsu Business Communication Systems www.fbes.fujitsu.com   A variety of call center tools—core switches, CTI links, and specific applications and services

Funk Software www.funk.com   Remote control technology that incorporates screen monitoring and screen record and playback

Fuseworks www.fuseworks.com   A live Internet marketing solution

GBH Distributing www.gbhinc.com   Headsets for a variety of applications, including call centers

Genesys Telecommunications www.genesyslab.com   Combined inbound/outbound call processor

GM Productions www.gmpvoices.com Professional recording of voice prompts and other kinds of announcements

GN Netcom www.gnnetcom.com Wireless and corded headsets

Graybar www.graybar.com Distributor of telecom and call center products

Hammer Technologies www.hammer.com Testing for call center telecommunications systems, CTI, and voice over IP applications

Harris www.harris.com Switching systems and PBX

Hello Direct www.hello-direct.com Catalog distributor of headsets and other consumer telephony devices

HTL Telemanagement www.htlt.com Calculator for simulating call center conditions

IBM/Early Cloud www.earlycloud.com Distributed software for large-scale call center automation that allows companies to automate customer contact applications

IEX www.iex.com Call center management and workforce management software

Inference www.inference.com Case-based problem resolution engine for help desks

Infinet www.infinet1.com LANS and WANS, CTI, remote office connectivity, network management

Infinite Technologies www.ihub.com E-mail, Internet, and remote access products

Info Group www.infogrp.com Telemanagement and call center information systems

Info Systems www.talkie.com Voice processing application generator

InfoActiv www.infoactiv.com Call center consulting and systems integration, computer telephony, interactive voice response, voice messaging, enterprise and operations management

Infobase Services Inc. (ISI) www.ctiguys.com CTI systems, CTI-Link integration systems, monitoring and routing systems, systems integration services

Information Gateways (703-760-0000) Switchless call center platforms that incorporate ACD, PBX, IVR, dialing, scripting, and campaign management functions

Information Management Associates (IMA) www.imaedge.com Enterprise customer interaction software for call centers

InfoServ USA www.infoservusa.com Specialist in the design of IVR systems and applications for vertical markets

Intecom www.intecom.com ACD and PBX functions on a single communications platform

IntegreTel www.integretel.com Billing and collection services for the telephone industry and call center outsourcing

Intek Information www.intekinfo.com High-end outsourcing services and technology consulting

Intellisystems www.intellisystems.com Interactive expert system that provides self-support on the phone and on the Web

Interactive Communication Systems www.icstelephony.com Customer services for computer telephony deployment

Interactive Digital www.easytalksoftware.com Add-on software for reducing call duration on interactive voice response systems

Interactive Intelligence www.inter-intelli.com Computer telephony product for enterprises and call centers

Interactive Quality Services www.iq.services.com Quality assurance consulting and testing services

Interalia Communications www.interalia-inc.com Announcement and messaging systems

Interfax www.interfax.uk.com International network services via the Internet

Interior Concepts www.interiorconcepts.com Furniture systems for call centers

Interprise www.ntrpriz.com Architectural interior design for call center design and development

InterVoice www.intervoice.com Advanced call and business process automation systems

ISC Consultants www.isc.com Call center consulting and optimization

Jabra www.jabra.com Headsets for call centers

Kaset International www.kaset.com Customer service training programs

Key Voice Technologies www.keyvoice.com Small office and corporate voice systems

KnowDev www.knowdev.com Systems for agent training and evaluation

Knowlix www.knowlix.com Knowledge tools for seamless integration into existing internal help desks and customer support centers

KSBA Architects www.ksba.com Architecture, planning, interior design, and project management of call centers

Lernout & Hauspie www.lhs.com Speech recognition, text-to-speech, speech-to-text systems

Line 4 www.line-4.com CTI middleware software

Linkon www.linkon.com A variety of call center products, including voice boards that support a wide range of advanced voice processing applications

Locus Dialogue www.locus.ca Speech recognition systems

Lucent Technologies www.lucent.com ACDs, voice processing system, and other devices

MarkeTel Systems www.predictivedialers.com Predictive dialing systems

MasterMind Technologies www.mastermindtechnologies.com Telephony application development platform

MasterX Corporation www.masterx.com Tool suites that facilitate the real-time transport of data

MATRAnet www.matranet.com Internet software for e-commerce applications

Maxxar www.maxxar.com Platform for running call center and computer telephony applications

MCI Call Center Solutions www.mci.com A full spectrum of services for the call center industry

MCK Communications www.mck.com Remote voice systems

MediaPhonics www.mediaphonics.com Hardware, firmware, software, and CTI architectures and products

Mediasoft Telecom www.mediasoft.com Computer telephony and Web systems as a strategic technology partner to OEM

Melita International www.melita.com   Predictive dialing systems

Mercom www.mercom.com   Audiolog voice logging server system

Merlin Systems Oy www.merlin.fi/   Value-added services for call centers including PBXs, Lan PBXs, and VoIP services

Metasound www.metasound.com/   Messaging on hold systems

Micro Computer Systems www.mesdallas.com   A product to route inbound e-mail to reps in support environments

MicroAutomation www.microaut.com   Call management software

Microlog www.mlog.com   IVR systems for UNIX and DOS

Mitel www.mitel.com   PBXs to manage ACD groups for small call centers

Molloy Group www.molloy.com   Enterprise knowledge management software solution for customer support

Multi-Channel Systems www.mesmk8.com   PC-based predictive dialers

Mustang Software www.mustang.com   E-mail management solutions

N-Soft www.n-softna.com   A family of CTI modules and a CTI development environment

National TechTeam www.techteam.com   Computer and customer service solutions

Natural Microsystems www.nmss.com   Major supplier of voice boards and voice processing platforms

Netaccess www.netacc.com   ISDN and modem technology

NetDialog www.netdialog.com   Web-based customer interaction front end for call centers

NetManage www.netmanage.com   Visual connectivity solutions

NetPhone www.netphone.com   CTI servers, boards, and applications for NT

Netphonic www.netphonic.com   Call voice browser to integrate the Internet with an IVR system

Netrics.com www.netrics.com   Analyzes and measures Website traffic and log analysis software for Web servers

Network Associates www.nai.com   Software for help desk, data security

Neuron Data www.elements.com   Call center automation systems

NewMetrics Corporation www.newmetrics.com   Workforce management solutions

NexCen Technologies www.nexcen.net   Customer care products to integrate billing, network management, trouble ticketing, and order management systems

NICE Systems www.nice.com   Digital call-logging system to integrate with all major switches and CTI servers

Noble Systems www.noblesys.com   Customized call center automation with inbound, predictive dialing, and blended call management

Norrell Corporation www.norrell.com   Call center outsourcing services

Nortel www.nortel.com   Switches, ACDs, software, fiber cable

North Highland Company www.north-highland.com   Management and technology consulting including call center consulting services

Nuance Communications www.nuance.com   Speech recognition system

Nuera www.nuera.com   Digital circuit multiplication equipment

Octane Software www.octanesoftware.com   Internet/call center front-end products

Omtool www.omtool.com   Internet/intranet fax server system

OnQueue Call Center Consulting (215) 491-4636   Workforce management services

Ontario Systems www.ontario.com   PC-based predictive dialers

Oracle www.oracle.com   Database software

Outreach Technologies www.outreachtech.com   Conferencing technology

Ovum www.ovum.com   Consulting and market research

Paknetx www.paknetx.com   Internet-based ACD systems

Panamax www.panamax.com   Surge protectors and power-related systems for protecting phone systems, networks, and PCs

Para Systems www.minuteman.com   Power protection devices

Parity Software Development www.Parity.com   Software tools and hardware components for developing computer telephony applications

PaylinX Corporation www.paylinx.com   Real-time credit card authorization software for call centers, IVR, Internet, and POS applications

Pegasystems www.pegasystems.com   Customer interaction solutions

Perimeter Technology www.perimetertechnology.com   Centrex and SL-1 ACD product

Periphonics www.peri.com   Voice processing

Phonetic Systems www.phoneticsystems.com   Speech-enabled, telephony-based directory search solutions

Picazo Communications www.picazo.com   PC-based phone system that includes ACD

Pipkins www.pipkins.com   Call center management software, workforce management

Plantronics www.plantronics.com   Headsets

Platinum Software Corporation www.clientele.com   Developer of client/server enterprise resource planning software

Portage Communications www.portagecommunications.com   Call center designer, Windows-based software tools

PrairieFyre Software www.prairiefyre.com   ACD management information system

Prestige International www.prestigein.com   Multilingual and international call center company

PRIMA www.prima.ca   System integration professional services for the IVR and CTI markets

Primus www.primus.com   Problem resolution and knowledge management software

Priority Fulfillment Service (888) 330-5504   Inbound telemarketing, order entry and fulfillment, credit card authorization, customized reporting, and outbound telemarketing service offerings

ProAmerica www.proam.com   Service call management help desk software

Product Line (800) 343-4717   Live-agent inbound and outbound call handing and help desk services

Professional Help Desk (PHD) www.phd.com   Help desk software

Promodel Corporation www.promodel.com   Simulation product and systems

Pronexus www.pronexus.com   Fax server and interactive voice application generator

PTT Telecom Netherlands US (212) 246-2130   National telecom carrier of the Netherlands

PureSpeech www.speech.com   Speech recognition product suite

Q.Sys www.qsys.com   Telephony servers

Qronus Interactive www.qronus.com   Testing systems for CTI products

Quality Call Solutions www.quality.com   Turnkey system integrator of IVR and CTI for call centers

Quintus Corporation www.quintus.com   Broad-based suite of front-end software for call centers

Racal Recorders www.racalrecord.com   Voice loggers, with up to 96 channel capacity

Remedy www.remedy.com   Help desk and customer service software

Response Interactive www.responseinc.com   Software to provide a live link between visitors to a Website and call center CSRs

RightFax www.rightfax.com   Enterprise fax servers

Rockwell www.ec.rockwell.com   Integrated call center platform technologies, including ACD, CTI, and information management tools

ScheduleSoft Corporation www.schedulesoft.com   Scalable personnel scheduling solutions

Sento Corporation www.sento.com   Phoneless phone centers, all IP-based

ServiceWare www.serviceware.com   Software for knowledge management

Shark Multimedia www.sharkrmm.com   Voice messaging and data/fax communications systems

Siebel Systems www.siebel.com   SFA and enterprisewide customer management systems

Siemens www.siemenscom.com   Switches; large, high-end ACDs; software for call routing

Silknet Software www.silknet.com   Internet-based customer service application

Sitel Corporation www.sitel.com   Outsourced telephone-based customer service and sales

Skywave www.skywave.net   IP telephony gateway for service providers

Softbase Systems www.netlert.com   Nonintrusive desktop messaging system for intranets

Soundlogic www.soundlogic.net   Help desk systems

Spanlink www.spanlink.com   Internet call center products and services

Specialized Resources www.sritelecom.com   Telecom consulting, systems integration, and systems maintenance

Spectrum Corp. www.specorp.com   Wallboards used to communicate ACD information to agents in a call center

SpeechSoft www.speechsoft.com   IVR and application generation systems

SpeechWorks www.speechworks.com   Interactive speech systems for automating telephone transactions

Sprint www.spring.com   Long-distance and consulting services for call centers

SPS Payment Systems www.spspay.com   Call center outsourcing services

Square D EPE Technologies (714) 557-1636   Power protection systems

StarVox www.starvox.com   A business-to-business VoIP system for enterprisewide deployment

StepUp Software www.stepupsoftware.com   Simple help desk for small centers

Steve Sibulsky Productions www.onhold6.com   Message-on-hold production services

Sungard Data Systems www.sungard.com   Disaster recovery and service assurance programs

Swisscom www.swisscom-na.com   Swiss national telecom carrier

Symon Communications www.symon.com   Readerboards and middleware for call center client/server applications

Syntellect www.syntellect.com   Voice processing, IVR, predictive dialing, and Web-related call center products

Systems Modeling www.sm.com   Simulation tool for modeling call center performance

Sytel Limited www.sytelco.com   Predictive dialers, high-speed campaign simulation, and workforce management tools

TAB Products www.tabproducts.com   Call center facilities and design systems

Tandem Computers www.tandem.com   High-reliability servers and platforms for call center applications

TargetVision www.targetvision.com   Employee communication systems (readerboards), services and software

Taske Technology www.taske.com   Call center management software for telephone systems

TCS Management Group www.tcsmgmt.com   Workforce management systems

Technology Solutions Company www.techsol.com   Consulting and systems integration

Teknekron Infoswitch www.teknekron.com   Call center software for job applicant screening and agent monitoring and evaluation

Tekno Industries (708) 766-6960   Call center network management systems

Tekton www.tekton.com   Digital voice logging systems for recording and archiving telephone transactions

Telecorp Products www.telecorpproducts.com   ACD management system with readerboard

Telegenisys www.telegenisys.com   Call processing systems that include CTI applications, predictive dialing, and IVR

Telegra Corp. www.telegra.com   Fax test equipment to analyze Internet fax, fax servers, and networks

Tele-Serve Call Center www.tele-serve-1.com   Call center applications, answering services, telemarketing, and other telemessaging functions

TCT House www.tctc.co.uk   Consultancy, training, recruitment, and performance auditing

Telephonetics www.telephonetics.com   Algorithms for music and message-on-hold service, and audio production and programming

Telequest Teleservices www.telequest.com   Inbound and outbound telemarketing and teleservices

Telespectrum Worldwide www.telespectrum.com   Inbound and outbound telemarketing, customer service, interactive voice response, customer care consulting, call center management, training, and consulting services

Telesynergy Research (USA) www.telesynergy.com   PBX/voice/fax boards, application generator, and CT solutions for small to medium-sized business

Teloquent www.teloquent.com   Distributed call center (DCC), ISDN-based remote agent ACD

Teltone Corporation www.officelink2000.com   Telecom/call center products, including telecommuting and agent-at-home systems

Telus Marketing Services www.tms.telus.com   Call center services to businesses, specializing in inbound and outbound sales and customer service marketing programs

Teubner & Associates www.teubner.com   Advanced fax processing systems

Texas Digital Systems www.txdigital.com   Visual message alert system (readerboard)

TMSI www.tsb.ca   CTI suite for call center applications

TNG TeleSales and Service www.worldshowcase.com   Outbound and inbound telephone and Web-based marketing services

Tripp Lite www.tripplite.com   Power protection products, including UPS systems, surge suppressors, line conditioners, power inverters, and network management accessories

Trivida Corporation www.trivida.com   Data mining products

Trustech www.truster.com   Voice analysis software with call center monitoring applications

TSB International www.tsb.ca   PBX data and networking products, including CTI middleware, call accounting and service bureau systems, and PBX data and network management

Unica Technologies www.unica-usa.com   Services and software for customer management in and through call centers

Uniden (817) 858-3300   Products that interface with PBX and desk set telephones to provide wireless headsets

Unimax Systems www.unimax.com Database and "information control" systems for PBXs and voice mail systems

Unitrac Software www.unitrac.com Software applications including customer service, inbound/outbound telemarketing, campaigns, mass mail management, salesforce automation, and fulfillment processing

Utopia Technology Partners www.utosoft.com Help desk software

V*Channel www.vchannel.com Interactive voice and fax servers

Vantive www.vantive.com Help desk software

Venturian Software www.venturian.com IVR and call center integration systems

Viking Electronics www.vikingelectronics.com Fax/data switches, auto attendants, digital announcers, toll restrictors, auto dialers

VIP Calling www.vipcalling.com Wholesale international telecom servers over the Internet

VIPswitch www.VIPswitch.com High-performance Ethernet/intranet switches and communications platforms

Visionyze.com www.visionyze.com Packaged analytical application solution software for customer service centers

Visual Electronics www.digital-fax.com Readerboard systems

Vitrix www.vitrix.com Time and attendance software for call centers

VocalTec Communications www.vocaltec.com IP telephony systems and gateways

Vodavi www.vodavi.com Key telephone systems, Web-based unified messaging, ACD, CTI, Internet telephony, voice processing, and IVR

Voice Control Systems www.voicecontrol.com Speech recognition tool kit and call control/CTI/IVR systems for call centers

Voice Print International (VPI) www.voiceprintonline.com Digital multimedia voice data recording and storage

Voice Processing Corporation www.vpro.com Speech recognition

Voice Technologies Group www.vtg.com PBX integration products, unified messaging, and other CTI systems

Voiceware Systems www.voiceware.net Call processing systems integrator

Voysys www.voysys.com   Computer telephony products for small centers, especially IVR

VXI www.vxicorp.com   Headsets and microphones for CTI applications

WebDialogs www.webdialogs.com/   Internet-initiated telephony, IP telephony, chat, computer-to-computer collaboration

WebLine Communications www.webline.com   A Web-based call center adjunct that combines telephone connectivity with the Web

Witness Systems www.witsys.com   Develops and supplies client/server quality monitoring software for call centers

Wygant Scientific www.wygant.com   Voice processing applications

Xircom www.xircom.com   Networking products

XL Associates www.xla.com   Call center consulting services

xPect Technologies www.xpecttech.com   Processes and systems to maximize performance

Xtend www.xtend.com   Develops PC-based CTI and telemanagement systems

Ziehl Associates www.ziehl.com   Headsets and other small-scale telecom equipment

APPENDIX B

Glossary of Call Center and CRM Acronyms and Definitions

Call center definitions and acronyms

ACD   See Automatic Call Distribution.

ACD Overflow   A system feature wherein a call waiting in queue for an answer resource is offered to other centers operated by the enterprise. In better implementations, the caller becomes queued at all sites waiting for the first appropriately skilled CSR in any of the locations to become available.

Advisory Tones   The dial tone, busy signal, and dialing signal heard when using a phone system.

Agent   A generic term applied to all people working within call centers. The term became associated with call centers because airlines were among the first large ACD users; the people on the phones were reservation agents.

Analog   A term applied to telephone transmissions wherein the voice signal is converted into an electrical signal nearly identical to the sound waves produced by the human voice. Signals in the telephone network are either analog or digital.

ANI   Automatic number identification. A sequence of digits at the beginning of a phone call that identifies the calling phone number. Central to CTI applications, ANI can be deciphered and used to link the call to information on the call or caller that is available in host or workgroup databases. Called ANI by long-distance carriers, it is CLID—calling line identification to local phone companies.

Answering Supervision   A signal returned from the Central Office (CO) to indicate the call has been answered at the distant end.

Applications Programming Interface (API)   The software interface between application programs and the interface to network services or program-to-program communications. Standardized APIs are critical for developing or writing applications, allowing developers to focus on the front end as opposed to protocols.

Application Service Provider (ASP)   An organization that provides software suites to companies on a usage fee basis, usually via VPNs or the Internet. The economic justification for this approach is that the using company does not have to develop or maintain an IT organization or the expertise requisite to support the complex software suite. The ASP business model is usually directed toward providing enterprise resource planning (ERP) software and customer relationship management (CRM) applications.

Area Code Allocation   A process associated with routing 800 calls among multiple contact centers where the area code of the caller is used to determine which center will receive the call attempt.

Automated Attendant   A device that answers and processes incoming calls, directing callers to options such as extension directories or allowing access to live operators or attendants.

Automatic Call Distribution   Also commonly referred to as ACD, it is a functionality available in some PBX systems designed to handle and manage large volumes of incoming calls. Typical applications include customer service desks, telemarketing operations, reservation systems, and so on. An ACD allows efficient distribution of calls to available operators or voice processing options such as voice mail.

Average Speed of Answer (ASA)   One of the earliest metrics associated with handling telephone calls. ASA has slowly lost favor as the top metric for service level because averages tend to disguise the queue times that a significant, usually a minority, of callers actually experience.

Basic Rate Interface   A circuit that provides the user with two bearer (B) channels and one data (D) channel and is referred to as 2B+D. The bandwidth allocation is two 64,000-bits-per-second channels and one 16,000-bits-per-second data channel for signaling.

Call Accounting   Used to gather and monitor information about all telephone calling patterns, particularly long distance. Also monitors incoming calls. Usually a computer-based system linked to a telephone system.

Call Center   The location for centralized calling (inbound or outbound) or call reception activity. Staffed by CSRs, the call center usually involves an ACD linked to customer databases for order entry and so forth.

Call Control   Signals used to start or set up a phone call as well as to monitor and terminate (tear down) phone calls.

Call Processing   Activities related to starting, connecting, monitoring, or disconnecting phone calls. Pre-CTI, these functions were normally provided by the PBX and central office equipment.

Caller ID   A telephone service that provides the telephone number of the party placing a call to the called party.

Central Office or CO   The name given to the local telephone company's servicing exchange or "office"; usually where the big switches are located.

Centrex   A telephone system usually supplied by the local telephone company. The switching equipment is located in the telephone company central office. The only equipment at the customer premises is the telephones. One of the attractions of Centrex systems is that the system is rented rather than owned.

Circuit Switching   A methodology for moving digital and analog information wherein computer-controlled switching equipment is instructed to set up a continuous connection from the sender to the receiver. This connection remains in place even when no bits are being transmitted. Circuit switching is the technology upon which the existing telephone system is built. It is the opposite of packet switching.

CLID   Calling line identification.

Client/Server Architecture   Information technology in which the client (PC or workstation) requests information from a server. Servers may provide the user interface and perform some or all of the application processing. The server maintains databases and processes requests from the various clients to extract data from or to update the database.

CODEC   A word derived from the words *code* and *decode* referring to a solid-state device that digitizes human analog voice waveforms into bit streams and then back into analog voice waveforms.

Conditional Transaction Routing   A functionality in transaction routing whereby the system can access a set of real-time variables concerning the system, application, and CSR conditions. These variables are tested, and depending on the outcome of the test, different actions are taken.

Contact Center   A term increasingly being applied to multimedia-enabled call centers, which are evolved call centers that integrate the Internet into their operations. Typically, contact centers include text chat, e-mail handling, Website support technologies, and self-help devices that operate in the voice and Web environments.

Contention   A situation in which several phones or devices are attempting to access the same line. Telephone systems establish protocols (first-in, first-off, etc.) to establish connection and inform other callers of call status (busy signal).

CPE   Customer premise equipment; sometimes referred to as "customer provided equipment" to identify equipment on the premises owned by the customer.

CSR   Customer service representative; also referred to as an agent.

CTI   Computer telephony integration. The process, by which a telephone switch passes certain call information to a computer, allowing the computer to manage the call based on commands from a software application. Also refers to the process of using an adjunct computer to provide number crunching or database-intensive activities for the host PBX.

Custom Local Area Signaling Service (CLASS)   Services received from a local telephone company such as CLID (see ANI). Other CLASS services could include distinctive ringing, call waiting, selective call forwarding, and selective call screening.

Data-Directed Routing   The process of routing a caller based on information that exists about that caller within enterprise databases. For example, a contact center might wish to route calls from its best customers to selected CSRs ahead of other callers.

Dense Wavelength Division Multiplexing (DWDM)   A fiber-optic technology in which each fiber strand is actually divided into the individual wavelengths of light that make up white light. In this way, each wavelength of light on each strand can carry its own data stream.

Dialed Number Identification Service (DNIS)   An interexchange carrier service offering in which typically the last four numbers dialed by the calling party are transmitted to the ACD to help identify what kind of transaction the caller requires. DNIS is fundamentally similar to direct inward dialing (DID), a feature commonly found in private branch exchanges (PBX).

Digital   A device that uses binary code to represent information. In the world of telephony, this term refers to the encoding of an analog voice waveform into digital values represented by bits. The advantage of digital transmission over analog transmission is greater fidelity and resistance to noise.

Direct Inward Dialing (DID)   Calls to a DID number are routed directly to that number without the use of an operator and extension numbers.

DS-0   Digital service, level 0. The global standard for digitizing one voice conversation (64,000 bpd or 64kb/s).

DS-1/T-1   Digital service, level 1. There are 24 DS-0 channels in a DS-1, also known as a T1 (1.544 megabits) in North America.

DSP   Digital signal processor. A specialized microprocessor used extensively in telecommunications and multimedia applications.

DTMF   Dual-tone multifrequency. The low and high frequency tones that comprise Touch-Tone signals.

Dumb Switch   A switching mechanism that has no call control capability. It responds to call control instructions from a connected computer.

E1 Line   The European version of a digital circuit that provides 32 voice channels and a signaling channel. The U.S. version is called a T1 line.

E-mail   An electronic message usually sent from one person to another. The message contains the recipient's address, subject line, message, attachments, and signature. Attachments to e-mail messages might consist of data files, programs, audio or video files, and links to other Websites.

E-mail Auto Response   This function involves receiving a customer's e-mail message and providing responses, usually prewritten, based on a software routine's analysis of the message content.

Erlang   A Danish engineer who more than 100 years ago created several statistical tables that are still used today to calculate the number of trunks needed to handle calling demand, expressed in hours and the number of agents required to meet a particular service-level goal. The two tables most frequently used are Erlang B (used for trunk calculation) and Erlang C (used for CSR staffing and scheduling).

Ethernet   A local area network transmission protocol wherein devices with information to transmit "listen" to the traffic on the network and insert their packets when possible. Devices are sensitive to packet collision and will retransmit packets so affected.

Event Code   Also sometimes called a "wrap-up code," this term refers to digits entered by the CSR at the conclusion of a telephone call that represents call disposition information.

Facsimile (Fax)   The communication of anything printed on a page between distant locations. Fax machines are able to scan a page and transmit a coded image over telephone lines. The receiving fax machine prints a replica of the original page.

Fax-Back   PC-based IVR (see IVR) application that faxes callers' requested information

Fax-on-Demand   This is a technology enhancement to an existing system whereby callers can automatically request that information be transmitted to them via fax machines.

Fax-Server   A LAN-based interactive voice response application used to send and receive faxes.

Fiber-Optic Cable   A cable made up of thousands of individual glass fibers arranged in a bundle. These bundles are laid along railroad rights-of-way or inside pipelines and serve as backbones for high-speed and high-capacity networks. Fiber networks typically utilize packet-switching technologies. Each fiber strand is capable of handling high-speed data streams.

First-Party CTI   Computer telephony integration application performed entirely upon the agent's desktop. No CTI server is involved. Caller identification information is conveyed to the softphone application running on the agent's PC and is automatically pasted into the data access application.

Freephone Service   Telephone service offering that does not charge the caller for the call; rather, the receiving party pays for the call. In the United States, this offering is called "800" or In-Wats service.

Graphical User Interface (GUI)   Referred to as "gooey", a graphics-based user interface that employs icons, pull-down menus, and mouse clicks on the part of the user to cause the system to function in desired ways. This technique has largely replaced the text-based command-line approach used in earlier generations of software.

Ground Start/Loop Start   A way of signaling on subscriber trunks in which the tip (plus side of circuit) and ring (minus) are bridged (grounded) to get a dial tone.

Hypertext Mark-Up Language (HTML)   A high-level language used to create the look and feel of the content found on Web pages.

Integrated Services Digital Network (ISDN)   Digital service from local or long-distance telephone companies. The implementation varies greatly from country to country. In ISDN, the signaling channel is coined the D channel. Channels carrying the content of the information are called B channels (other channels carry link setup information but are not involved in user-to-user signaling).

Integrated Software Vendors (ISVs)   Telecoms and computer experts that have the capability to integrate system and software from multiple vendors.

Interactive Protocol (IP)   The protocol responsible for ensuring that packets are sent to the right destination.

Interactive Voice Response (IVR)   A software application residing on a powerful PC that permits a caller to retrieve information from computer databases by listening to voice prompts and responding with telephone key-pad depressions. This technology has been enhanced with natural language, speaker-independent voice recognition.

InterExchange Carrier (IXC)   The term applied to telephone companies that provide long-distance service.

Jitter   This term refers to the frequent occurrence of packets arriving out of order in a packet-switching environment, where individual packets can traverse multiple different routes to their destination. This situation imposes either greater delays on the assembly of the entire message or causes the message to have small missing pieces. In Voice over IP, jitter accounts for lower fidelity.

Latency   This term refers to another type of delay in packet-switching networks. It refers to the delay imposed by the distance (minimal) and the number of routers (potentially many) the packet traverses to arrive at its destination.

Local Area Network (LAN)   A communication network that provides service to users in a defined area, such as a building. A LAN consists of servers, workstations, a network operating system, and a communications link. The two most prevalent LAN technologies are Ethernet and Token Ring.

Local Loop   The traditional view of a physical wiring network (hard wired) between a telephone company central office and a subscriber. In a PBX environment, the local loop (trunk) is between phone company equipment and equipment on the customer premises.

Management Information System (MIS)   Software designed to provide real-time and historical reporting of information of interest to management and staff about contact center performance.

M-Commerce   Coined by William Safire, this term defines the world of mobile commerce.

Multi-Vendor Integration Protocol (MVIP)   Consists of standard bus, switching, and operating systems and enables application developers to integrate different PC board telecommunications/voice technologies.

Network Interface   The point at which telephone company network resources connect with equipment on the premises.

Network Interface Module   The electronic component providing the network interface for a PC or workstation, from simple connections such as loop start lines to T1 or ISDN services.

NLM   NetWare loadable module (Novell).

NPA/North American Numbering Plan   Refers to the assignment and management of the area code system for North America.

Occupancy   A measure expressed as a percentage of the total sign-in time spent by an agent handling transactions and doing any necessary work related to that transaction.

On-Hook/Off-Hook   When a telephone handset is in the cradle, it is idle or "on hook" (the term dates from phones that had hooks for hanging up the earpiece). When a handset is "off hook," it is ready to be used (this is the "original" I/O process).

Open System   A term used to describe a manufacturer-independent system. In contact centers, products from other vendors can be easily integrated. In a larger sense, it means that the hardware required to run the application can be purchased from any of a variety of sources, which helps ensure lower acquisition costs.

Packet Switching   A methodology for moving digital information wherein small containers carry a discrete number of bits of information. Each package contains an address representing the packet's destination. Implicit in packet networks is the notion of no central intelligence.

PCM Expansion Bus (PEB)   Provides an interface between the telephone network and processing resources.

Percent Allocation   A term used to describe the allocation of "800" calls among multiple contact centers by percentage points. In practice, the service control point would be instructed to send 30% of the calls to Center A, 50% to Center B, and 20% to Center C, for example.

Plain Old Telephone Service (POTS)   Basic telephone service, a single line with dial tone and no call processing or applications.

Port   Point of access into a telephone system (an analog line).

Portal   The term applied to a "gateway" to information on the Internet.

Power Dialer   A system that automatically dials numbers from a list, differentiates between system-intercept tones, busy signals, answering machines, ring-no-answer, and actual human voice to present agents with live contacts.

Predictive Dialer   An application that has a computer dial numbers from specified databases. If the call is answered, it is passed to an agent/operator. If the call is not completed, the dialer moves on to a new number.

Preview Dialing   Part of an automatic dialing application. Allows on-screen preview of the number being dialed prior to the actual dialing process.

Primary Rate Interface (PRI)   An ISDN circuit, equivalent to T1, running at 1.544 megabits per second.

Private Branch Exchange (PBX)   A business telephone switch residing on the customer's premises used to aggregate trunks and feed calls from the telephone company central office to the destination telephone.

Protocol   The rules governing the transmission of data.

PSTN   Public switched telephone network.

Queue   A waiting list. Callers are frequently placed into a queue awaiting an available agent.

RJ-11   The "common" telephone jack, which is usually wired with four wires with the red and green wires signifying the tip and ring circuits.

Router   A highly specialized, high-power computer that accepts packets, reads their destination addresses, and sends them to the router next closest to their final destination at incredibly fast rates.

Sampling Rate   Number of times per second an analog signal is sampled in order to convert to binary code, with the objective of producing a digital signal.

Screen Pop   The capability of an ACD system to communicate with a firm's database through CTI software so that information about the caller appears on the agent's screen at the same moment the caller is connected to that agent.

Script   Agents sometimes use an on-screen script to handle a call. A well-written script that considers all potential branches that a conversation might take can dramatically reduce training time for new agents in the contact center

Server   A computer in a client/server environment that processes requests from clients.

Service Control Point (SCP)   A high-speed, high-power computer database used by interexchange carriers (IXCs) in conjunction with signaling system 7 to decode the physical telephone number behind 800 numbers.

Service Level   The contact center metric that specifies what percentage of calls is answered in a given time frame. Typically, call/contact center service levels may be expressed as 80% in 20 seconds or less.

Signal Computing System Architecture (SCSA)   An open standard architecture for specifying the interfaces for PC-based CTI applications.

Signaling System 7 (SS7)   A telephone company network for providing signaling information regarding calls on the network.

Spam   A derogatory term applied to unwanted e-mail or e-mail messages mass-mailed to groups or lists of people.

Station   Another name for a place where a call can be answered. It may be a telephone, an attendant console, a PC, or any other device.

T1 Line   A digital circuit with a bandwidth of 1.544 million bits per second capable of handling 24 voice paths and a signaling channel.

Telephony Services Application Programming Interface (from Novell/ AT&T) or TSAPI   An interface developed to allow computer telephony integration of Novell LANs with AT&T switches.

Text Chat   A Website support technology enabling a Website visitor to click on a "contact us" button to obtain needed real-time support. The browser window opens a secondary window in which the visitor and a Web-enabled agent can conduct a real-time text-chat session.

Third-Party CTI   A computer telephony integration that is facilitated by a server with access to the ACD system and to enterprise databases. The ACD system sends caller identification information together with the position number of the agent who will get the call. The server can then fetch the caller's data and paint it on the screen simultaneously with the connection of the caller to the agent.

Tip & Ring   The traditional telephony indication of "plus/ground" and "minus/positive" in electrical circuits.

Token Ring   A local area network transmission protocol wherein each device receives a software "token" sequentially permitting that device to transmit a packet of information. The device then passes the token to the next device.

Transmission Control Protocol (TCP)   This software breaks down data files into packets of about 1,500 characters at the origination point and reassembles those packets at the receiving end.

Virtual Contact Centers   Multiple contact centers, located in different geographical areas, function as a single center by using links between the sites or by performing call routing within the network before the calls arrive at the sites.

Virtual Private Network (VPN)   This product offering from carriers gives user organizations more control and security over communications than the public network. As the name implies, control and security issues are easier to deal with if an organization does not share the facilities. This service provides the user with the benefits of having a private network without the cost of building one.

Voice mail   A specialized software application that digitizes incoming human voice messages and stores them on disk. The application segregates the disk into discrete mailboxes and gives the owner the ability to restore and delete voice messages.

Voice over IP (VoIP)   The capability of engaging in a voice conversation over the Internet, typically through a multimedia-equipped personal computer (e.g., a PC equipped with microphone and speakers). The advantage of the technology lies in the capability to provide real-time support to Website visits on a single phone line. VoIP is also very attractive to contact center users because it could potentially replace the need for freephone service like 800 calling.

Voice Recognition Unit (VRU)   A product used in IVR systems.

Web Call-Back   A Website support technology wherein the Web visitor fills out a brief form on the Website requesting a telephone call-back at a specific number and specific time to receive needed information.

Web Page Push/Collaboration   This technology allows a contact center agent to interact with a Website visitor in real time by synching the two browsers. This permits the agent to cause new Web pages to appear in the visitor's Web browser while they engage in text chat or VoIP conversations. This is critical functionality for organizations wishing to cross sell and upsell on the Web.

Wide Area Network (WAN)   A communications network that spans a larger geographical area than a local area network, such as campus remote facilities. Wide area networks require facilities from interexchange or local exchange carriers.

Windows Telephony   A Microsoft/Intel collaboration, including a telephony interface standard for applications developers, hardware OEMs, and service providers.

Windows Telephony Application Programming Interface (WTAPI)   A programming interface and architecture operating under Microsoft's Windows operating system designed to stimulate third-party development of shrinkwrapped telephony applications for Windows-based PCs and LANs.

Wireless Application Protocol (WAP)   A subset of Hypertext Mark-Up Language used to translate Web pages to a format more compatible to the small screens found in mobile phones.

Workflow   A term that refers to how a task is performed. Typically, a call is analyzed and broken down into discrete steps. Information needed at each step is identified to keep screen clutter at a minimum. Information not germane to the current task is not provided.

Workforce Management   In the contact center, this term refers to software systems that accept transaction-handling history, generate forecasts for transaction demand, permit acceptable workshifts to be defined, allow agents to establish workshift preferences, and create individual agent schedules that attempt to meet service-level goals with a minimum expenditure of agent time and effort.

CRM definitions and acronyms

Active Loyalty   Customers who repeatedly purchase products and services from the same company are described as being "actively loyal." (See also Passive Loyalty.)

Analytical CRM   Analytical CRM (*analytics*) refers to the analysis of data created on the operational side of the CRM equation for the purpose of business performance management. Analytical CRM is directly related to data warehouse architecture.

Association   This term refers to rules that enable the presence of one set of items to be correlated with the presence of another set of items.

Attrition   A term used in the banking industry to describe customers leaving to use the services of another bank. The more commoditized products become, the more frequently this process takes place. In the telecommunications industry, the same process is called *churn.*

Business Drivers   External influences that affect a business and cause a shift in focus and/or change in course; for example, increased competition may force an increased investment in R&D to maintain a competitive position.

Campaign Management   Management of single and multichannel marketing campaigns based on the customer intelligence gleaned from mining a data warehouse.

Channel Management   Monitoring the effectiveness of sales and distribution channels (e.g., Web, ATM, face-to-face, call center, and so on) to ensure maximum return on investment and increased client satisfaction.

Chief Customer Officer (CCO)   Many organizations that implement a CRM strategy have a Chief Customer Officer (CCO), whose role is to oversee the continued implementation of the CRM strategy, ensuring that the cultural and customer interaction changes necessary for successful CRM are in place.

Churn   A term used primarily by telecommunications companies to describe the loss of customers to competitors. (See Attrition.)

Clustering   A data mining approach that attempts to identify distinguishing characteristics between sets of records and then place them into groups or segments.

Collaborative CRM   Collaborative CRM refers to the application of collaborative services (e.g., e-mail, conferencing, real time) to facilitate interactions between customers and organizations and between members of the organization around customer information (e.g., customers to sales, sales to marketing, and community building).

Conditioning   Preparing data for input to the data warehouse or data mart.

Corporate Culture   Refers to the operating parameters of an organization—the way it conducts business and manages customer relationships.

CRM   CRM is a companywide, ongoing process whereby customer information is intelligently used to serve customers more effectively and efficiently, fostering customer loyalty and retention by optimizing customer satisfaction and improving corporate profitability.

CRM Architecture   The infrastructure of a CRM system, including the data warehouse architectural model that supports analysis of customer relationship management systems through the use of technology, tools, and applications for the purpose of business performance management.

Customer Interface/Point of Interaction (POI)   The point of interaction (or contact) between a customer and an organization. This can include the Web, telesales operator, call center, and sales counter.

Customer Retention   The strategy of keeping existing customers.

Data Cleansing   The process of removing inaccurate and historical data from operational systems to use in a data warehouse. Data must be accurate and consistent in order to increase the accuracy of the data mining process.

Data Mart   A departmental data warehouse, or summary data store, usually storing only one specific element of a corporation's customer data at a summary level.

Data Mining   Data mining refers to the sorting and exploration of data with a view to discovering and analyzing meaningful patterns and rules. A variety of tools and techniques is used—some of which have been developed explicitly for this purpose, others of which have been borrowed from statistics, computer science, and other, similar disciplines. These include clustering, classification, time series analysis, and OLAP (online analytical processing).

Data Model   To analyze data it is often necessary to build a "data model." In its most simple form, a data model takes a given number of inputs and produces a given number of outputs. For example, a churn data model might take in information on customer transaction history, demographics, and product information and provide an indication on how likely a customer is to leave the company.

Data Warehouse   A data warehouse is a database of information explicitly designed for decision support purposes. Unlike a database, which is just a means of recording and storing transactional data, a data warehouse is designed to make the right information available at the right time.

Delta Updating   A learning algorithm that uses a linear approximation to an error function to compute and apply a correction factor.

E-CRM   Electronic CRM is the use of Web channels as part of the overall CRM strategy and may include other electronic business elements, such as e-sales, e-marketing, e-banking, e-retailing, e-service, and multimedia customer contact centers.

Event-Driven Campaigns   Campaigns whose genesis comes from customer intelligence, for example, banks conducting a marketing campaign for car loans based on the knowledge that a target group X will be graduating soon and is likely to start work, have a disposable income, and therefore be prospective new car buyers.

Operational CRM   Operational CRM refers to the automation of horizontally integrated business processes involving customer touch points—sales, marketing and customer service, call center, field service—via multiple, interconnected delivery channels and integration between front office and back office.

Pareto's Law   Also know colloquially as the "80/20 law" and meaning that 80% of profits are derived from the top 20% of customers. Some analysts increase this to 140/20 when dealing with financial institutions.

Passive Loyalty   Customers may appear to be loyal on examining the database; however, they may not have transacted business with an organization in years. (See also Active Loyalty.)

Pilot Test   A pilot test is the small-scale implementation of a new CRM system within a small section of a company to help employees familiarize themselves with it. This process provides feedback, helps solve any unforeseen problems prior to full implementation, and evaluates different approaches to achieving CRM objectives. .

Points of Interaction (POI)   The point of interaction (or contact) between a customer and an organization, including the Web, telesales operator, call center, and sales counter. (See Customer Interface.)

Recency and Frequency   Both recency and frequency are used to measure customer loyalty. *Recency* refers to the last time that a customer contacted an organization, and *frequency* refers to the regularity of their contact. Both definitions exclude contact initiated by the company to the customer, for example, direct marketing campaigns, telemarketing, and so on.

ROI   Return on investment—the return, in terms of increased revenue, that can be achieved from an investment in a CRM strategy or other major corporate project.

Segmentation   Dividing target markets into segments with homogenous characteristics such as lifestyle, demographics, or even consumer behavior.

Touch point   See Points of Interaction.

Transaction History   The data recorded after every customer transaction, which is often used in data mining to gain valuable insights about customer segments and behavior.

Visualization   This process takes large amounts of data and reduces them into more easily interpreted pictures.

APPENDIX C

References and Bibliography

References

Anton, Jon, and Laurent Philonenko. *20/20 CRM*. The Anton Press, 2002.

Bodin, Madeline, and Keith Dawson. *The Call Center Dictionary*. Telecom Books, 1999.

Cleveland, Brad, and Julia Mayben. *Call Center Management on Fast Forward*. Call Center Press, 1999.

Curry, Jay. *The Customer Marketing Method: How to Implement and Profit from Customer Relationship Management.* New York: Free Press, 2000.

D'Ausilio, Rosanne. *Wake Up Your Call Center.* Ichor Books, 1998.

Dawson, Keith. *The Call Center Handbook: The Complete Guide to Starting, Running, and Improving Your Customer Contact Center,* 4th ed. CMP Books, 2002.

Durr, William. *Navigating the Customer Contact Center in the 21st Century.* Cleveland, OH: Advanstar Communications, 2001.

Waite, Andrew J. *A Practical Guide to Call Center Technology*. CMP Books, 2001.

Bibliography

Adelman, S. *Project Management for Data Warehousing*. In Proceedings of The DCI Data Warehouse Conferences and The Data Warehouse Institute's Implementation Conferences. DCI, 1995–1999.

Anahory, Sam, and Dennis Murray. *Data Warehousing in the Real World*. Reading, MA: Addison-Wesley, 1997.

Anderson, Paul, and Art Rosenberg. *The Executive's Guide to Customer Relationship Management*. Houston, TX: Doyle Publishing Company, 2000.

Anton, John. *Customer Relationship Management*. Upper Saddle River, NJ: Prentice Hall, 1999.

Berry, Michael, and Gordon Linoff. *Mastering Data Mining: The Art and Science of Customer Relationship Management*. New York: Wiley, 1999.

Berson, Alex, and Stephen J. Smith. *Data Warehousing, Data Mining and OLAP*. New York: McGraw-Hill, 1998.

Bischoff, Joyce, and Ted Alexander. *Data Warehouse: Practical Advice From the Experts*. Upper Saddle River, NJ: Prentice Hall, 1997.

Brobst, Stephen, and NCR Corporation. *Integrating Your Data Warehouse into the World of E-Business*. In Proceedings of "The Power of One" CRM Conference, Nice, France, May 2000.

Brown, Carol V., ed. *IS Management Handbook,* 7th ed. New York: Auerbach, 2000.

Burrows, Cathy. *The Royal Bank of Canada (Canada), Client Relationship Management—A Journey Not a Destination*. In Proceedings of "The Power of One" CRM Conference, Nice, France, May 2000.

CGI Group Inc. White Paper, *Building Competitive Advantages Through Customer Relationship Management*, CGI, January, 2001.

Charles, Cheryl. *Security, Privacy, and Trust in Financial Services*. BITS Financial Services Roundtable. In Proceedings of the NCR Partners Conference, Orlando, FL, October 1999.

Church, Nancy W. *Customer Relationship Management: Solutions for the Insurance Industry*. In Proceedings of the Insurance Industry Roundtable Seminars, New York, Boston, Hartford, and San Diego, 1999.

Deviney, David E., and Karen Massetti Miller, eds. *Outstanding Customer Service: The Key to Customer Loyalty*. New York: American Media, 1998.

Direct Marketing Association. *Customer Relationship Management: A Senior Management Guide to Technology for Creating a Customer-Centric Business*. New York: DMA Publishers, 1999.

Eckerson, Wayne W. *How to Architect a Customer Relationship Management Solution*. Boston, MA: Patricia Seybold and Company Publishers, 1997.

Hackney, Douglas. *Architecture and Approaches for Successful Data Warehouses*. Reading, MA: Enterprise Group, 1998.

Inmon, Bill. "Creating a Healthy Centralized Data Warehouse," *Teradata Review,* NCR Corporation, Spring 1999.

Inmon, Bill. *Building the Data Warehouse*. New York: John Wiley, 1993.

Mackenzie, Ray. *The Relationship-Based Enterprise*. Toronto, ON: McGraw-Hill Ryerson, 2001.

Meltzer, Michael. *Data Mining—Dispelling the Myths*. NCR Corporation, 1998.

Meltzer, Michael. *Using Data Mining Successfully*. NCR Corporation, 1998.

NCR Corporation. "The Race to Real-time: Operationalizing the Data Warehouse," *Teradata Review,* Fall 1999.

NCR Corporation. White Paper, *Scalable Data Warehouse Solutions: Overview*. 1997.

Newell, Frederick. *Loyalty.com: Customer Relationship Management in the New Era of Internet Marketing*. New York: McGraw-Hill, 2000.

Shapiro, Andrew L. *The Control Revolution, How the Internet Is Putting Individuals in Charge and Changing the World We Know*. New York: A Century Foundation Book, 1999.

Swift, Ronald S. *Accelerating Customer Relationships: Using CRM and Relationship Technologies*. Upper Saddle River, NJ: Prentice Hall, 2001.

Index